ALSO BY ROBERT J. SAMUELSON

*The Good Life and Its Discontents: The American
Dream in the Age of Entitlement, 1945–1995*

*Untruth: Why the Conventional Wisdom
Is (Almost Always) Wrong*

THE

GREAT INFLATION

AND ITS

AFTERMATH

RANDOM HOUSE

TRADE PAPERBACKS

NEW YORK

ROBERT J. SAMUELSON

THE

GREAT INFLATION

AND ITS

AFTERMATH

———

THE PAST AND FUTURE OF

AMERICAN AFFLUENCE

2010 Random House Trade Paperback Edition

Copyright © 2008, 2010 by Robert J. Samuelson

All rights reserved.

Published in the United States by Random House Trade Paperbacks,
an imprint of The Random House Publishing Group,
a division of Random House, Inc., New York.

RANDOM HOUSE TRADE PAPERBACKS and colophon are registered
trademarks of Random House, Inc.

Originally published in hardcover by Random House, an imprint of The Random House
Publishing Group, a division of Random House, Inc. in 2008.

LIBRARY OF CONGRESS CATALOGING-IN-PUBLICATION DATA

Samuelson, Robert J.
The great inflation and its aftermath : the past and
future of American affluence /
Robert J. Samuelson.
p.   cm.
Includes bibliographical references and index.
ISBN 978-0-8129-8004-2
1. Inflation (Finance)—United States.   2. United States—Economic policy.
3. United States—Economic conditions.   I. Title.
HG540.S26 2008
332.4'10973—dc22   2008023468

Printed in the United States of America

www.atrandom.com

2 4 6 8 9 7 5 3 1

Book design by Jessica Shatan Heslin / Studio Shatan, Inc.

To Judy,
without whom this book
would not have been finished;
and without whom
it would not have been worth finishing

CONTENTS

A NOTE TO READERS

Telling this story inevitably involves using some economic and financial terms that may not be familiar to all readers. I have tried to keep them to a minimum. On first usage, I have defined the terms. Later references are usually freestanding. For those who want a reminder or further clarification, a glossary at the end of the book provides detail. For the numerically inclined, two appendixes give overviews of the American economy since World War II. The first shows basic annual statistics—economic growth, unemployment, inflation, interest rates, stock prices. The second describes business expansions and recessions.

ACKNOWLEDGMENTS

A book is ultimately the responsibility of its author, but in the process of becoming a book, it imposes burdens on many others. This book is dedicated to my wife, Judy, on whom the burden was greatest. Even in the best of times, I am not the easiest person to live with, and as I struggled to make this book say what I wanted it to say, I became even moodier than usual. The book evolved into an all-purpose excuse not to do things I should have wanted to do and that she wanted to do. "Oh no, we can't do that, because I've got to work on the book" became a constant refrain. Judy responded with routine encouragement, patient self-restraint and only infrequent exasperation. Thanks, Jude.

Next on the list of people who helped bring this project to conclusion is my longtime *Newsweek* colleague Richard Thomas, who for many years was the magazine's chief economics correspondent. He has forgotten more about the economy and its connections with politics and the everyday lives of Americans than I will ever know.

Rich has that rare combination among journalists of superb reporting skills (which are common) and an unconventional mind (which is rare) that allows him to see the larger significance of events even as they are unfolding, and well before most others. Rich read countless drafts of the manuscript and made many valuable substantive and editing suggestions. He also strove to be an amateur therapist, repeatedly declaring that the manuscript was "brilliant" even as he advised me to abandon entire sections of the "brilliant" draft or amend it to increase its "brilliance." Rich deserves much credit for the book's strong sections and warned me against some of the remaining weaknesses. Thanks to him for improving the manuscript and toiling so hard to lift my spirits.

David Lindsey, a former top staff economist at the Federal Reserve, also read multiple drafts of the book and worked diligently to ensure that I got the sequence of events correct and explained technical issues in terms that were clear and accurate. I may have failed, but if so, it's not Dave's fault.

At a crucial point in the process of revising and rewriting, I asked my old friend Jon Rauch—a writer for *The Atlantic* and *National Journal* and a 2005 winner of the National Magazine Award, the magazine equivalent of the Pulitzer Prize—to give me his impression. He read the whole thing, and by highlighting the book's strengths and weaknesses—often echoing what Rich and my editor, Jonathan Jao, had said—convinced me to do a fair amount of cutting and rearranging. Jon's candor and clarity in identifying unnecessary parts of the manuscript improved it significantly.

A number of other people read the manuscript and made helpful suggestions, not all of which I was smart enough to include: Joel

Havemann, the longtime editor for my column in *The Washington Post;* my brother Richard and my cousin Richard (we Samuelsons are not too original on names); Prakash Loungani, a friend and economist at the International Monetary Fund; and John McCusker, an economic historian at Trinity University in San Antonio. Thanks also to Mark Zandi of Moody's Economy.com, who provided me with much of the statistical information found in the two appendixes and, aside from that, has consistently helped me understand the economy. Malcolm Gillis, the ex-president of Rice University, invited me to give a lecture at the university (where my daughter was then a student) that helped convince me to write the book. Pat Jackman at the Bureau of Labor Statistics has, over the years, helped me better understand the Consumer Price Index.

At the Federal Reserve, Dave Skidmore and Michelle Smith have responded quicky and cheerfully to my many requests for information, both in the course of my regular reporting and in the reporting for this book. Athanasios Orphanides, a former economist at the Fed who has studied extensively the period from the late 1960s to the early 1980s, gave me a very useful interview and provided some helpful background material. (Orphanides has since left the Fed to become the head of the Central Bank of Cyprus.) Allan Meltzer of Carnegie Mellon University, author of a two-volume history of the Fed, was kind enough to give me an advance copy of one chapter from his forthcoming second volume. In an interview for this book and over many years, he has also improved my understanding of the economy and the making of economic policy.

Paul Volcker, former chairman of the Federal Reserve Board, submitted to two interviews for the book and also reviewed parts of the manuscript for accuracy. I am indebted to him for his cooperation. An interview with Alan Greenspan, Volcker's successor, was also helpful in confirming the importance that he attached to achieving a crude price stability.

At Random House, this book went through four editors—the number had little to do with the book and mostly reflected changes in the editors' personal lives (two of whom left Random House). But in Jonathan Jao, I found an editor who skillfully maneuvered the project to completion. His comments and suggestions were always thoughtful and often confirmed what I had been hearing from others. Where I was disorganized, he was organized. When he said he would do something, he did it—and did it when he said he would. He was open-minded—he listened to all my suggestions and preferences—but also strong-willed when he thought I was wrong. And he was always pleasant. My agent and neighbor, Rafe Sagalyn, remained optimistic about the project even when there were ample grounds for pessimism. As we walk our dogs, it will be easier now to have relaxed conversations.

Finally, there are my children: Ruth, Michael and John. They didn't have anything to do with the book. But they are everything that life is about. They help me keep things in perspective, and they are now old enough to have views of their own. After watching his dad wrestle with this book, Michael made one of his affectionately caustic suggestions: Don't do it again. It seems like good advice, though it remains to be seen whether I will take it.

Inevitably, this book will contain errors of fact and interpretation. For these, I claim exclusive responsibility.

INTRODUCTION TO THE
PAPERBACK EDITION

Just as the hardcover edition of this book reached stores in mid-November 2008—and many months after its last words had been written—the United States was plunging into its worst financial crisis since the Great Depression. The trust and confidence that constitute the invisible glue that enables financial markets to function, creating the presumption that transactions entered into will be honored and that prices will mainly reflect underlying values and not panic, all but dissolved. Headlines announced the bankruptcy or merger of once-proud investment houses: Bear Stearns, Lehman Brothers, Merrill Lynch. The hysteria and fear prompted a hoarding of cash and a stampede for safety, conspicuously symbolized by a flight of money into U.S. Treasury bonds and securities, then deemed the world's least risky investments. Values collapsed on almost all markets: for stocks, corporate bonds and commodities (oil, wheat, copper). The panic, though it began in the United States, soon spread to countries around the world. From Brazil to Germany to China, the loss of optimism and the escalation of anxiety were virtually universal. Turmoil in the markets deepened the fright, and vice versa.

Nor was the chaos confined to finance. Fear and uncertainty quickly spread to the "real economy" of consumption, production and employment. The American economy, which had been weak all year (in December 2008, a panel of economists retrospectively concluded that a recession had begun exactly a year earlier), deteriorated rapidly. Shoppers retreated from malls and auto dealerships in a desperate attempt to replenish their savings in the face of the ravages of falling home and stock values. Companies quickly followed suit, announcing huge layoffs and canceling new investment projects for computers, machinery, office buildings, stores and factories. A bunker mentality took hold. Workers prepared themselves for possible joblessness; companies reacted to vanishing profits. Here, too, the fallout was global. Trade contracted at a terrifying rate, and the world economy was projected to shrink—overall output declining—for the first time since World War II.

These momentous events seemed to suggest that the subjects of this book, double-digit inflation and its aftermath, had been overtaken. They were no longer of much relevance to our economic condition; indeed, many commentators worried about global deflation, a downward spiral in prices that would trigger more bankruptcies and unemployment. But regarding inflation, just the opposite is true. The economic cataclysm that struck would not have occurred the way it did—and, quite probably, would not have occurred at all—but for the preceding inflationary episode. It was in these events that the seeds of catastrophe were sown. What happened affirmed the book's central thesis that the rise and fall of high inflation was the most significant economic event of the past half century. All that is necessary is to explain why.

For all its ferocity, what happened was simply an old-fashioned "boom and bust." Things got good in the boom—too good, as it turned out. Loans were made to borrowers who couldn't repay them; people spent beyond their means; businesses expanded based on demand that could not last; stock and commodity prices rose on the (false) presumption that it would. Once these illusions shattered, the bust followed with its own manic destructiveness. Loans went into delinquency and default, lenders failed, demand declined, "bubbles" in home prices burst, stocks dropped, confidence fell and unemployment rose. Though demoralizing, these destructive events seem historically unoriginal.

It is easy enough to blame the debacle on the intrinsic flaws of capitalism and the frailties of human nature—and that has been done. Capitalism is inherently unstable; so goes the argument. Unless it is tightly regulated, it comes to grief. In this case, greed and ambition ran amok. People and firms overreached. Once the scale of the economic collapse became apparent, narratives of this sort multiplied. They presumed to explain what happened and why. There was often a political dimension. The crisis was blamed on the deferred consequences of the free-market policies of Ronald Reagan. But most of these explanations, though containing some obvious truths, ultimately miss the mark and are unsatisfying.

On inspection, the deficiencies are obvious. Greed and self-interest have never vanished; they're enduring human characteristics. So what suddenly made them so ruinous? The same can be said of post–World War II American capitalism. It has always been a mix of private power and government regulation, and it did not fundamentally change in the 1980s or 1990s. Reagan's policies tilted it slightly more toward market power and away from governmental power, but the change was at the margins. Major regulatory agencies (the Securities and Exchange Commission, the Environmental Protection Agency, the Federal Deposit Insurance Corporation) all remained. Banks, at the center of the crisis, were regulated. The size of federal spending and the resulting tax burden did not shift dramatically. There was more continuity than change. Why then did the economy become so unstable? Since World War II, nothing comparable to the recent financial breakdown had occurred. Something must have caused all concerned (consumers, investors, business managers, government regulators and legislators) to act in ways that brought about the financial and economic collapse.

That "something" was the inflationary experience. When thinking about the consequences inflation, both experts (economists, bankers, corporate executives) and laypersons have an overwhelming tendency to consider only inflation's *rise*—and, as the following pages demonstrate, these were enormously disruptive and significant. But a major argument of this book is that the consequences of *falling* inflation were as important and as powerful but that they are routinely overlooked or minimized by almost everyone, including the "experts." Recall the contour of the inflationary and disinflationary cycle: from 1961 to 1979, inflation climbed from about 1 percent to 13 percent; by 2001, it had fallen to a bit more than 1 percent. It was the second half of this period that led to the present crisis.

For roughly a quarter century, from, say, 1983 to 2007, the United States enjoyed a prolonged prosperity that was probably the greatest in its history (and, if not, was certainly on a par with any earlier period). To be sure, there were periodic setbacks and many complaints, from too much inequality to a loss of manufacturing jobs. But on the whole, the picture was favorable. There were only two recessions, those of 1990–91 and 2001, and they were brief and mild by comparison with the past. Stock and bond prices rose spectacularly; so did home values. Household incomes increased, and Americans enjoyed a plethora of new technologies, from personal computers to cell phones. Global trade expanded, and the increases in cross-border money flows were phenomenal. These were the basic building blocks of the American and global booms.

They did not arrive by accident. To a large extent, they emerged from the benefits of disinflation. Had the suppression of double-digit inflation not occurred in the early 1980s, the subsequent history would have been much different. Lower and falling inflation stabilized the economy, whereas high and rising inflation had destabilized it. From 1969 to 1982, there were four recessions. In an almost mechanical way, falling inflation led to higher stock, bond and housing prices, whereas high and rising inflation had depressed stocks and bonds (though not home values). Reversing high inflation restored worldwide confidence in the dollar as the major international currency—its purchasing power could again be trusted—and thereby encouraged the growth in trade and cross-country money movements. Low inflation was a powerful precondition for the high economic performance of these decades.

But in time, it exacted a terrible toll; the second-order effects were punishing and perverse. The very fact of so much continuous prosperity and wealth accumulation conditioned people—ordinary households, corporate executives, money managers, government officials—to begin to take them for granted. There might be, almost certainly would be, temporary pauses and reverses. But the general trend lines were auspicious and preordained. They were up. The downs were annoying aberrations. The economic world seemed less risky. Given these convictions, which were only rarely articulated but became deeply embedded in mass psychology, Americans began to act in ways that subverted their good fortune and made the world more risky. Lax lending standards, casual borrowing, complacent regulation, permissive government policies, all proceeded from a climate that fostered false confidence.

The boom and bust were not freestanding events, caused only by the inevitable undulations of capitalism or the failings of human nature. Those failings are permanent, but their effects are shaped by events, beliefs and institutions. The bust took root in a historical context, which was, paradoxically, the aftermath of falling inflation. For many years, the chief consequence was to bolster the American economy and promote broad-based prosperity. The hard-won triumph over the double-digit inflation of the early 1980s undoubtedly qualifies as one of the great achievements—perhaps the greatest—of economic policy since World War II. But the irony is that its very success ultimately sowed the seeds of failure by creating misleading and self-defeating expectations.

The implications are sobering. In reconstructing the story of inflation's rise and fall, the temptation is to create a pleasing morality tale. The economic theories and practices that led to higher inflation were bad; the theories and practices that subdued higher inflation were good. Superior ideas displaced inferior ones. Virtue was its own reward, measured by the restoration of economic stability and prosperity in the 1980s and later. But the actual history confounds the satisfying morality tale, because good policies ultimately inspired bad behavior. Prosperity seems to be self-limiting. Too much of it for too long may undo itself by luring people, government officials and firms into risky, sloppy or speculative practices. There seems to be no ideal economic policy that can overcome this contradiction. Business cycles, gentle or otherwise, seem destined to recur.

The careful reader of the hardcover edition, though perhaps not the less-careful reader, would have detected all these themes. The possibility of a major financial and economic crisis was anticipated—but not predicted. Certainly I didn't outline anything like the actual course of events that began in the fall of 2008 and carried over into 2009. In revising and updating the manuscript for the paperback edition, I have sketched what happened and sought to demonstrate how the crisis originated in the larger inflationary experience. This puts events, I think, in a larger, more accurate and understandable historic setting. Most of the revisions occur in the first and last chapters; the intermediate chapters contain a few modest clarifications and elaborations.

Depending on your point of view, my explanation either contradicts or complements the conventional wisdom. One of the inevitable rituals of any crisis is the retrospective search for scapegoats and villains. That process has been under way for many months now, with a large gallery of accused having already been assembled: mortgage brokers for making many dubious home loans; investment bankers for packaging them in opaque mortgage-backed bonds and securities; bond rating agencies for giving these securities undeservedly high ratings; politicians of both parties for excessively promoting homeownership; the Federal Reserve, then under the leadership of Alan Greenspan, for easing credit too much; China and other Asian countries for amassing huge trade surpluses that, invested in U.S. Treasury securities, depressed American interest rates.

In some cases, the accused are guilty as charged. But the political and media indictments and the ensuing convictions more often than not beg a fundamental question: Why did they do what they did? It is too glib simply to assert that they were stupid, selfish or even criminal. Although that was certainly true in some cases, it was not true in all cases, and it does not explain why the selfishness or stupidity appeared—at the time—to be reasonable and justifiable, as often happened. Nor does it explain why so many people who were smart, conscientious or both made what we now know were grievous blunders. The larger explanation for these puzzles is that all these people lived through an economic era in which they were slowly and subconsciously conditioned to believe that the trend lines would move irresistibly upward, justifying optimism and providing shelter against mistakes. That was the much-delayed and unanticipated legacy of falling inflation.

In a sense, the present crisis is a bookend for an era, the half century beginning in 1960 when inflation's rise and fall was a powerful driver of events in the American economy and society. The crisis and the response to it create new conditions and pose new choices. Hardly anyone imagined two or three years ago that an economic collapse would bankrupt some of the most fabled U.S. corporations (Chrysler, General Motors) or weaken the entire banking system. The aggressive reaction by the Federal Reserve aimed to prevent a severe recession from turning into a worldwide depression, as too much supply chased too little demand. Vast amounts of money and credit were pumped into the American and global economies to counteract the tendency by consumers and businesses to hoard cash and cut spending. In theory, at least, the huge quantities of cheap money and credit might threaten a subsequent inflation if the economy recovers and they are not withdrawn in a timely fashion. The outcome will help define the next economic era.

Meanwhile, a new president, Barack Obama, proposed a sweeping agenda of greater financial regulation, health-care spending and control of energy use that, if enacted, would redefine the relationship between government and business. The government's role would be enlarged, and private enterprise's reduced. How all these issues are resolved may well constitute the first bookend of a new economic era. In the last chapter, I offer my own suggestions as to how we might best enhance our prospects in this new era.

ROBERT J. SAMUELSON
JUNE 9, 2009
BETHESDA, MARYLAND

PREFACE TO THE
HARDCOVER EDITION

I decided to write this book because no one else had and, it appeared, no one else would. It seemed obvious to me, as a journalist covering the economy for the past half century, that the rise and fall of double-digit inflation had exerted an enormous influence during the entire period—and the effects were not confined to the economy. Because Americans place so much stock in their economy's performance, inflation's roller coaster deeply influenced the nation's psychology and politics. It also changed the way in which major corporations managed their businesses and their workers. All these relationships seemed fairly plain, and I waited for someone to make the connections. Because I am a slow writer and my previous book (*The Good Life and Its Discontents: The American Dream in the Age of Entitlement, 1945–1995*) had exacted a huge toll in time and spirit, I was not eager to begin a project that someone else was just finishing. But no one else did, and so I set out to do it myself lest the entire episode slip from our collective consciousness.

As with much of my journalism, the main aim here is to explain what happened, why and with what consequences. The basic outlines of the story are straightforward. Ambitious economic doctrines, embraced and promoted by some of the nation's leading academic economists, promised to control the business cycle by minimizing or eliminating recessions, but these ideas came to grief. The unintended side effects were not only higher inflation but also more frequent and harsher recessions, stretching from the late 1960s to the early 1980s. At the time, the resulting inflationary psychology was so deeply embedded that almost everyone despaired of purging it. Only the unexpectedly savage recession of 1981–82, when unemployment peaked at nearly 11 percent, succeeded in doing so. The aftermath of inflation's decline—and, to a significant extent, a consequence of it—was a prolonged period of national prosperity, marked by fewer and milder recessions. But simultaneously and paradoxically, the aftermath also led to greater insecurity for individual firms and their workers. There is (and was) a connection. The insecurity and competitive pressures felt by individual firms and workers were consequences of a less inflationary economy and, to some extent, helped keep inflation in check.

In many ways, the book's publication—about two years later than I originally expected—is more timely now than if I had written faster and made my initial schedule. Until recently, the danger of higher inflation seemed fairly remote; but as I write, in the early summer of 2008, consumer prices are rising at about 5 percent a year in the United States and, spurred by costlier oil and food, are rising even faster in some other countries. It is now an open question whether this modest rise of U.S. inflation is a prelude to something much worse or simply an unfortunate aberration that will soon give way to a return of price increases to an unthreatening range of less than 2 percent a year.★ The book does have an unambiguous message about inflation: If we fail to contain it, we are courting serious economic trouble, although we can't be entirely certain what form that trouble will take. High inflation is an enormously disruptive force.

Even if inflation subsides, there is another reason for the book's timeliness. I argue that the roughly half century from 1960 until now represents one long economic cycle dominated by inflation's rise and fall—and that, in particular, the engines of economic expansion of the past quarter century are now largely spent. These included strong increases in consumer spending based on rapidly rising stock and home values, which in turn were heavily driven by the falling interest rates that accompanied declining inflation. Ultimately, the increases in stock and home prices inspired speculative excesses that ended badly for many investors and home owners. What started as realistic increases evolved into "bubbles." But even when these excesses are purged from the economy, as has already occurred for stocks, there will be no resumption of the outsized gains that many Americans once mistakenly took for granted. Americans' economic confidence and the economy's expansion will need other sources, and if they are not forthcoming, growth will slow. It is important to recognize this change and understand why it is happening. The fact that this coincides with a presidential election

★ As the paperback edition goes to press, the deep 2008–2009 recession has virtually eliminated increases in consumer prices.

is also fortuitous. At the end of the book, I offer some suggestions as to how we might improve our economic prospects.

As readers will discover, I view "the economy" as much more than the amalgam of different markets for goods, services, labor, savings, investment, work and leisure. To me, "the economy" is also a social, political and psychological process. It is the convergence of ideas, institutions (private and public), values, beliefs, habits, technologies that intersect with one another to create our system of production and distribution. What this means is that changes in ideas, institutions, values and beliefs can alter the way the economy works just as much as—and sometimes more than—changes in prices, wages or in interest rates. The story I tell here traces the evolution of the economy in this larger sense. It recounts how one set of ideas and values gave way to another, because the first did not live up to its promises, and how these changes affected politics, popular attitudes and corporate management. The outward expression of these shifting ideas was rising and falling inflation; but the price movements were consequences, not causes.

My book aims to serve a popular audience in the best sense of the word. It's written for people who are reasonably curious and intelligent. It does not presuppose specialized knowledge about the economy. I have tried to provide enough explanation and background to make the story accessible to the specialist and the generalist, the young and the old. Someone need not have lived through all these events to grasp their significance. Although the book is intended mainly for a general audience, I hope that its different perspective on America's recent history will also prove illuminating for scholars—economists, historians and political scientists. My aim is for readers to come away with a better appreciation of how America got where it is now and to understand why the story of inflation holds essential lessons for the future. These include not just the importance of maintaining stable prices but also the desirability of judging proposed public policies not by their advertised intentions (which are always good) but by their likely long-run consequences (which are often perverse).

Economic commentary tends to veer to one of two extremes. Either we are going to paradise—some fabulous, unending boom, created by a wondrous new technology, entrepreneurial genius or flexible markets—or we're headed to hell, in the form of some calamitous collapse or prolonged stagnation, brought on by foolish speculation, uncompetitive companies, unskilled workers or dumb government policies. Sensationalism, whether for good or ill, sells. I have tried to avoid either extreme, believing that neither is usually realistic. Over the years, I have been fairly optimistic about America's economic prospects. Our national culture—with its emphasis on individual opportunity, hard work and striving—combined with a robust business system, devoted to efficiency, growth and profits, generally has put prosperity on a solid footing. Some evident past problems (inflation, for one) were curable, though often at a cost.

Still, I admit that I have grown less optimistic in recent years, because we have been so lax in addressing obvious problems. We may weaken our productive machine by inattention to clear and present economic threats. In the concluding chapter, I mention some of these: an aging society; an uncontrolled health-care sector that is now approaching one-fifth of the entire economy; a world economy that might become dangerously unstable; and an uncritical reaction to the possibility of global warming that may cause us to undertake costly policies that, in the end, do little to affect global warming but do weaken our economy's performance.

I call what I have produced a "reportorial essay." Like my previous book, it makes an argument and presents reporting—facts, evidence—that corroborates the argument. In earlier drafts, the book was perhaps a third longer than its final version, but on the advice of friends and my editor, I eliminated some portions because, though interesting, they did not relate to the central argument. I should also tell you what this book is not. It is not a detailed history of the Federal Reserve, monetary policy or economic policy (including taxes and regulations) in general; nor is it an exhaustive examination of the economic well-being of American families and workers; nor is it a detailed evaluation of American "competitiveness" (technology, worker skills, business efficiency and the like); nor is it an investigation of globalization or, indeed, of worldwide inflation. The story touches on all these subjects, but readers interested in greater detail should go elsewhere. My story uses them as pieces of a puzzle, trying to fit them together so that the final result is a coherent picture of a powerful and misunderstood feature of America's modern history.

ROBERT J. SAMUELSON
MAY 30, 2008

THE

GREAT INFLATION

AND ITS

AFTERMATH

1

THE LOST HISTORY

I

History is what we say it is. If you asked a group of scholars to name the most important landmarks in the American story of the past half century, they would list some or all of the following: the war in Vietnam; the civil rights movement; the assassinations of John Kennedy, Robert Kennedy and Martin Luther King, Jr.; Watergate and President Nixon's resignation; the sexual revolution; the invention of the computer chip; Ronald Reagan's election in 1980; the end of the Cold War; the creation of the Internet; the emergence of AIDS; the terrorist attacks of September 11, 2001; and the two wars in Iraq (1991 and 2003). Looking abroad, these scholars might include other developments: the rise of Japan as a major economic power in the 1970s and 1980s; the emergence of China in the 1980s from its self-imposed isolation; and the spread of nuclear weapons (to China, India, Pakistan and others). But missing from any list would be the rise and fall of double-digit U.S. inflation. This would be a huge oversight.

We have now arrived at the end of a roughly half-century economic cycle dominated by inflation, for good and ill. Its rise and fall constitute one of the great upheavals of our time, though one largely forgotten and misunderstood. From 1960 to 1979, annual U.S. inflation increased from a negligible 1.4 percent to 13.3 percent. By 2001, it had receded to 1.6 percent, almost exactly what it had been in 1960. For this entire period, inflation's climb and collapse exerted a dominant influence over the economy's successes and failures—and much more. Inflation and its fall shaped, either directly or indirectly, how Americans felt about themselves and their society; how they voted and the nature of their politics; how businesses operated and treated their workers; and how the American economy was connected with the rest of the world. Although no one would claim that inflation's side effects were the only forces that influenced the nation over these decades, they counted for more than most people—including most historians, economists and journalists—think. It's impossible to decipher our era, or to think sensibly about the future, without understanding the Great Inflation and its aftermath.

With hindsight, the havoc wreaked by rising inflation is plain to see. Stable prices provide a sense of security. They help define a reliable social and political order. They are like safe streets, clean drinking water and dependable electricity. Their importance is noticed only when they go missing. When they did in the 1970s,

Americans were horrified. During most of these years, large price increases were the norm, like a rain that never stopped. Sometimes it was a pitter-patter, sometimes a downpour. But it was almost always raining. From week to week, people couldn't know the cost of their groceries, utility bills, appliances, dry cleaning, toothpaste and pizza. People couldn't predict whether their wages and salaries would keep pace. People couldn't plan; their savings were at risk. And no one seemed capable of controlling inflation. The inflationary episode was a deeply disturbing and disillusioning experience that eroded Americans' confidence in their future and their leaders.

There were widespread consequences. Without double-digit inflation, Ronald Reagan would almost certainly *not* have been elected president in 1980—and the conservative political movement that he inspired would have emerged later or, conceivably, not at all. High inflation incontestably destabilized the economy, leading to four recessions (those of 1969–70, 1973–75, 1980 and 1981–82) of growing severity; monthly unemployment peaked at 10.8 percent in late 1982. High inflation stunted the increase of living standards through lower productivity growth. And high inflation caused the stock market to stagnate—the Dow Jones Industrial Average was no higher in 1982 than in 1965—and led to a series of debt crises that afflicted American farmers, the U.S. savings and loan industry and Latin American countries.

If inflation's legacy were nothing more, it would merit a sizable chapter in America's post–World War II narrative. But there is much more. Declining inflation—"disinflation"—was equally potent and much less understood. It led to lower interest rates, which led to higher stock prices and, much later, higher home prices. This disinflation promoted the past quarter century's prosperity. In the two decades after 1982, the business cycle moderated so that the country suffered only two relatively mild recessions (those of 1990–91 and 2001), lasting a total of sixteen months. Monthly unemployment peaked at 7.8 percent in June 1992. As stock and home values rose, Americans felt wealthier and borrowed more or spent more of their current incomes. A great shopping spree ensued, and savings declined. By 2005, the personal savings rate (savings as a share of disposable income) was virtually zero, down from 10 percent in the early 1980s. Trade deficits—stimulated by Americans' ravenous appetite for cars, computers, toys, shoes—ballooned. Paradoxically, this prolonged prosperity also helped spawn complacency and carelessness, which ultimately climaxed in a different sort of economic instability: the financial turmoil that assaulted the economy in 2007, 2008 and 2009.

The very belief in the permanence of economic growth undid economic growth. Initially triggered by falling inflation and interest rates, the upward march first of stock prices and then of home values induced speculative dizziness. People began to believe that prices of stocks and homes could only rise. Once that intoxicating mind-set took hold, prices rose to silly and perilous heights, leading to "bubbles" that burst in 2000 (for stocks) and 2007 (for homes). Home loans were extended to buyers with weak credit and with little or no requirement for down payment. The presumption that homes would always be worth more tomorrow than today provided a false sense of security to the lenders and rationalized credit standards that, with hindsight, seemed self-evidently doomed. When these "subprime" mortgages began to default in large numbers, the home-building boom ended, housing prices fell, financial institutions—banks, investment banks—suffered large losses on securities backed by mortgages, and the economy descended into a deep and demoralizing recession.*

The significant point for our story is that the economy's present problems are yet another unappreciated consequence of inflation and its subsequent decline. The immediate cause of the housing collapse lay in lax lending practices; but the backdrop and inspiration for those lax practices were the expectations of perpetually rising real estate values that were sown in the climate of disinflation and falling interest rates. So it is with much else about our economic system that we now take for granted: The connections to the inflationary experience are there, but we simply refuse to see them. Corporate behavior is a good example. In the first decades after World War II, government and big business joined in an unwritten alliance. Government promised to control the business cycle, to minimize or eliminate recessions. Big companies pledged to raise living standards and provide economic security for workers—safe jobs, adequate health insurance and reliable pensions.

But when inflation overwhelmed the government's commitment to manage the business cycle, the implicit social contract broke down. The 1980s became a watershed in corporate practices. If companies couldn't raise prices, they would (and did) cut costs. Layoffs, "restructurings" and "buyouts" for early retirees became more widespread and acceptable. "Capitalism," a word that had essentially

* As revisions for the paperback edition were made in the summer of 2009, the unemployment rate was 9.4 percent (in July), and there was widespread commentary that the recession was ending or soon would.

disappeared from common usage in the early postwar decades, reentered the popular vocabulary. The result was a paradox: Although the overall economy grew more stable after 1982, individuals' sense of insecurity increased, because companies were less bound by the norms of earlier postwar decades to preserve jobs and shield workers from disruptive changes. The "new capitalism" controlled inflation in part by breeding anxiety that kept wages and prices in check. It also tolerated greater inequality—growing gaps between the rich, the middle class and the poor.

"Globalization"—the thickening integration of national economies through trade, finance and information flows—is another example. Although we don't connect that with inflation, we should. Had the U.S. economy remained as in the 1970s, beset by seemingly intractable inflation and ever-worsening recessions, America's confident championing of globalization in the 1980s and 1990s wouldn't have happened. American leaders wouldn't have attempted it; and even if they had, no one would have listened. The restored stability and vitality of the economy, which stemmed from disinflation, empowered U.S. leaders to pursue internationalist policies. The same forces also renewed the dollar's role as the primary global currency used in international business. That companies and individuals thought they could rely on the dollar to buy and sell goods and as a store of wealth promoted both trade and cross-border finance.

The American story of the past half century is thus heavily grounded in inflation and disinflation. Much of what we take as normal and routine either stemmed from their occurrence or was decisively influenced by them. The great shopping spree, the reemergence of capitalism, increased globalization and the 2007–09 financial crisis are but examples. But we have now come to the end of this period. Just what the next economic cycle will bring is an open question that, in some ways, will involve dealing with the sequels of many of the effects of the Great Inflation. The great shopping spree has ended. What will replace it? Globalization seems threatening to many Americans, as does the new capitalism. Will we shape these forces to our advantage or find ourselves whipsawed by them? Can we maintain acceptable levels of economic growth and stability?

At the end of the book, I discuss some of these questions and make suggestions as to how we might respond to them. But a new era hardly renders the Great Inflation irrelevant. To the contrary, its history holds important lessons for the future.

The simplest is this: Inflation, if it reemerges, ought to be nipped in the bud; the longer we wait, the harder it gets to rein it in. The lesson is worth heeding, but as memories of the Great Inflation fade—for many Americans, they don't even exist—it may get lost. Inflation's hazards may seem less menacing, and only by suffering them again will we be reminded of their pernicious power. One of the uses of history is to avoid preventable errors; but to do that, we've got to get the history right. And this brings us to a broader lesson: how we temper and regulate our national enthusiasm for self-improvement. It is a powerful American virtue but one that, from time to time, gets us into immense trouble. Skepticism in the face of seductive appeals for social betterment is not always pessimism or conservatism; often, it is prudent realism.

For double-digit inflation was not an act of nature or a random accident. It was the federal government's greatest *domestic* policy blunder since World War II: the perverse consequence of well-meaning economic policies, promoted by some of the nation's most eminent academic economists. These policies promised to control the business cycle but ended up by making it worse. The entire episode invites comparison with the war in Vietnam, which was the biggest foreign policy blunder in the post–World War II era.★ Similarities abound. Both arose from good intentions—the one would preserve freedom; the other would expand prosperity. Both had intellectuals as advocates, whether economists or theorists of limited war. Both suffered from overreach and simplification; events on the ground constantly confounded expectations. But there is a big difference. One (Vietnam) occupies a huge space in historic memory. The other (inflation) does not.

II

As I use the phrase, "the Great Inflation" refers roughly to the period from the mid-1960s to the early 1980s, when inflation was rising from negligible to double-digit levels. I lived through these years and, as a newspaper reporter and later columnist for *Newsweek* and *The Washington Post,* wrote about what happened. Inflation is not just the rise of a few prices—say, gasoline or clothes. General inflation is the rise of most prices. In any modern economy, measuring true inflation is impossible. There are too many goods and services, and almost everyone buys a slightly different mix of

★ Some would argue that the invasion of Iraq in 2003 was a worse blunder. I leave it to others to settle that dispute.

products and, therefore, experiences slightly different inflation. The best that can be done is to survey the prices of many things that people buy. Every month, the Bureau of Labor Statistics (a part of the Labor Department) sends hundreds of data collectors into 30,000 locations to record the prices of about 80,000 items—including soap, eggs, cars, personal computers, college tuitions, gasoline, drugs—and 5,000 rents. The prices are then weighted by people's consumption habits, as revealed in other surveys and the diaries of about 30,000 individuals. The result is the Consumer Price Index, or CPI, the government's best-known inflation indicator.[1] Virtually all references to inflation in this book use the CPI, precisely because it is so familiar.*

To understand why inflation was so pivotal first requires rebutting the arguments that it wasn't. Conventional wisdom anoints other developments and events as the dominant economic influences of our time. Personal computers and the Internet are favorite choices. So are globalization and the stubborn persistence of sizable U.S. budget deficits. It's also frequently argued that inflation wasn't really an independent event. It was, rather, the outgrowth of other events—the war in Vietnam and the worldwide increases in oil prices in the 1970s. Therefore, inflation really isn't worth considering on its own; it was simply one facet of these other histories. All these views seem plausible. On examination, they are less so.

* Using other inflation indicators would have slightly altered the numbers, though not the basic trends. All prices changes, unless otherwise noted, refer to December-to-December comparisons rather than year-over-year averages. That's how people experience inflation—month-to-month shifts, not annual averages.

Computers and the Internet have undeniably altered everyday life in countless ways. But technological upheavals are a constant refrain in the American experience, and it's unclear whether this latest upheaval matters more than many of its predecessors. In the decades after the Civil War, large-scale industrialization (steel making, sugar and oil refining, cigarette manufacturing, flour milling) created massive cities and slowly transformed America from a rural into an urban society. Is the Internet more important than that? Or than the mass production of automobiles that spawned suburbanization? Or than the advent of telephones, radio and television that transformed mass communications and entertainment? All these technological convulsions and others rivaled—and perhaps exceeded—the Internet and personal computers in their social and economic implications.

As for globalization, it defines the next economy perhaps more than the last. Despite growing international interdependence, the nation-state still dominates economic life, especially for large societies such as the United States. Consider: The United States, Europe, Japan and other advanced economies all have access to the same technologies and management practices. If globalization were so overpowering, then all these economies would be identical, or nearly so; and yet they are not. Their economic performance and living standards differ in many crucial ways, because their cultures, histories, values, politics and economic policies differ. Globalization is just one force that comes into play. It commands our attention mainly because it seems novel.

A similar caveat attaches to U.S. budget deficits. Since the early 1960s, the budget has been in deficit except for five years (1969 and 1998–2001). Still, the federal debt held by the public—the accumulation of all past annual deficits—is actually smaller now in relation to the economy than at the end of World War II. The real budgetary threats lie in the future, when the costs of the retiring baby boom generation could produce much higher taxes, deficits, or both.*

Well, what about the argument that high inflation was the unfortunate spillover of Vietnam and the successive surges of oil prices in 1973–74 and 1979–80? In this telling, inflation was not mainly a failure of government policy or economic theory. It was collateral damage from other events and, therefore, does not deserve much independent attention. Superficially, this seems possible. In the 1960s, it's said, wartime spending created a classical inflationary hothouse: too much demand pressing on too little supply. Wages and prices rose. Later, the global oil cartel (OPEC, the Organization of the Petroleum Exporting Countries) inflicted new damage. But these notions, though plausible, are easily disproved. If Vietnam had been the central cause of inflation, then inflation should have abated as the war wound down (that's what happened after the Korean War). It didn't. And if oil were the source, then energy should have been a major part of higher inflation. It wasn't.

Like many myths, these survive because they contain a kernel of

---

* In 1946, the publicly held federal debt of $242 billion was 109 percent of the country's then Gross Domestic Product of $223 billion—in effect our national income. By 2006, the publicly held debt had grown to $4.8 trillion, but the GDP was $13.2 trillion. The debt was only 36 percent of GDP. But deficits incurred by President Obama in 2009 and 2010, as well as those projected for the next decade, would raise the debt burden substantially. By 2019, the debt-to-GDP ratio could reach 80 percent, estimates the Congressional Budget Office. Other projections are even higher.

truth and because they are politically and intellectually convenient. The Vietnam War did worsen inflation. As early as 1965, two of President Johnson's economists—Gardner Ackley, chairman of the Council of Economic Advisers, and Charles Schultze, then director of the Bureau of the Budget—recommended a tax increase to dampen economic demand.* Johnson didn't propose one, because he (correctly) surmised that Congress wouldn't pass it. Moreover, Johnson wanted both guns and butter. "I believe that we can continue the Great Society while we fight in Vietnam," he said in his 1966 State of the Union message. He feared that, faced with a proposal to raise taxes, Congress might instead cut spending on his new social programs. When Johnson finally proposed a 10 percent income tax surcharge in 1967, Congress didn't enact it until 1968. Still, inflation persisted despite the surtax and (later) the war's end.[2]

The oil story is similar. Along with the standard CPI, the government also publishes separate indexes without energy. Comparing the two shows how much higher energy prices contributed to overall inflation. The answer is "not much." In 1973, before the full impact of the first "oil shock" (which came late in the year), the overall CPI rose 8.7 percent, up from 3.3 percent in 1971. Without energy prices, the increase would have been 8.3 percent. The next year, the CPI rose 12.3 percent; without energy, the increase was 11.7 percent. In 1978—before the leap in oil prices—the CPI increased 9 percent, almost double the 4.9 percent gain of 1976. In 1979, the CPI's over-

---

* The Bureau of the Budget is now the Office of Management and Budget (OMB).

all gain was 13.3 percent; without energy prices, it was still 11.1 percent. Economic research has confirmed what these raw figures—available at the time—showed. "Disturbances in the oil market . . . matter much less than has commonly been thought," wrote economists Robert Barsky and Lutz Killian of the University of Michigan.[3]

The real reason for oil's outsized place in our historical memory is that it scarred the American psyche. In the midst of the Yom Kippur War of October 1973, Arab oil suppliers embargoed oil shipments to the United States; more important, global oil supplies before the war were already tight, putting suppliers in a position to raise prices. From September 1973 to January 1974, the official price of Saudi Arabian oil went from $2.59 to $11.65 a barrel. Although gasoline prices did not rise correspondingly (domestic oil was under price controls), the increase was still 40 percent by March. Americans were shocked; they simply could not grasp how something so basic as gasoline could go up so quickly and unexpectedly. As Daniel Yergin related in his history of oil, *The Prize*:

> [The oil] shortfall struck at fundamental beliefs in the endless abundance of resources, convictions so deeply rooted in the American character and experience that a large part of the public did not even know, up until October 1973, that the United States imported any oil at all. But inexplicably, in a matter of months, American motorists saw retail gasoline prices climb by 40 percent—and for reasons that they did not understand. No

other price change had such visible, immediate, and visceral effects as that of gasoline. Not only did motorists have to shell out more money to fill their tanks, they also passed stations that upped the price of a gallon of gas as often as once a day.[4]

It wasn't just price. When government tried to allocate scarce fuel supplies, long lines at gas stations materialized as drivers feared being caught short. In early 1974, *The New York Times* reported that "people in metropolitan areas have become increasingly suspicious and angry, insecure, devious and often violent . . . all because of a lack of gasoline." In Gary, Indiana, a customer shot and killed a station owner after cutting into line and being refused service. "These people are like animals foraging for food," one dealer commented. "If you can't sell them gas, they'll threaten to beat you up, wreck your station, and run over you with a car." The story repeated itself in 1979–80 when the overthrow of the shah of Iran and the Iran-Iraq War helped send crude prices from about $15 a barrel to a peak of nearly $40. Little wonder that high gas prices—and gas lines—symbolized inflation in the public mind.*[5]

Blaming inflation on an unpopular war or unpopular foreigners disguises the unflattering reality: The main villains were our own poor economic policies. In all of American history, this inflation had

---

* The 2004–08 increase in gasoline prices did not cause a similar reaction, mainly because the government relied exclusively on higher prices to allocate supplies. There were few long gas lines, because motorists knew that they could get as much as they could afford. As previously noted, the oil price increases of 2007 and 2008—unlike those of the 1970s—were heavily responsible for big jumps in the CPI.

no comparable precedent. Sudden bursts of inflation had occurred before, almost always during wars when the government printed more and more money to pay for guns, soldiers, ships and ammunition. The floodtide of cash sent prices upward according to the time-honored formula of all major inflations: Too much money chased too few goods. The unbounded printing of paper money in the Revolutionary War by both states and the national government was one inspiration for the Constitution; the Founders wanted to prevent a recurrence by regulating money. Other wartime inflations—after the Civil War and, to a much lesser extent, World Wars I and II and the Korean War—ended when the wars ended.

What happened in the 1960s and 1970s was different. America's most protracted peacetime inflation was the unintended side effect of economic policies designed to reduce unemployment and eliminate the business cycle. This inflation was a self-inflicted wound that resulted from collective hopefulness and intellectual overconfidence. In 1962, a Hershey bar cost 4 cents, a hamburger 28 cents, a first-class stamp 4 cents and a full-size Chevrolet $2,529. By 1994, when inflation began the last stage of its descent toward the low 1950s levels, the Hershey bar cost 75 cents, the stamp 29 cents, the hamburger $1.65 and the Chevrolet $19,495. Almost everyone and everything was affected.[6]

III

We Americans are progress junkies. We think that today should be better than yesterday and that tomorrow should be better than today. Compared with most other societies, we place greater faith in "opportunity" and the chance to "get ahead." In a forty-four-country poll, respondents were asked to agree or disagree with the following statement: "Success in life is pretty much determined by forces outside my control." More Americans (about 60 percent) disagreed than respondents in any other country. In France, for example, about 60 percent agreed. What made Americans detest rising inflation so much was its assault on the national belief in progress: It challenged Americans' hopeful view of themselves and consigned their destiny to outside forces. We seemed to have lost control, both as individuals and as a society, over our fate. That was inflation's most damaging effect.[7]

In 1979, Daniel Yankelovich—one of the leading students of post–World War II public opinion—wrote this about inflation:

> For the public today, inflation has the kind of dominance that no other issue has had since World War II. The closest contenders are the cold war fears of the early 1950s and perhaps the last years of the Vietnam war. But inflation exceeded those issues in the breadth of concern it has aroused among Americans. It would be necessary to go back to the 1930s and the Great Depression to find a peacetime issue that had the country so concerned and so distraught. From the public's point of view, it [seems] an intractable problem. . . .[8]

At the time, Yankelovich's assessment was uncontroversial. People took it for granted. Now, it seems astonishing—inflation more upsetting than Vietnam or Watergate? How could that be? Those traumatic events remain deeply lodged in public memory, while inflation has mostly vanished. But what distinguished rising inflation from Watergate, Vietnam or even a sharp recession was that it directly affected almost everyone: workers, shoppers, retirees, small businesses, big businesses, state and local governments, nonprofit organizations, the national government. Everybody had to pay higher prices. Some might win from inflation; some might lose. The process seemed capricious and unpredictable. It threatened, or seemed to threaten, people's living standards, their savings. It seemed to envelop the future in a thick, impenetrable fog.

These fears, of course, were not unique to Americans. Lenin is reputed to have said that the best way to destroy a capitalist society is to debauch its currency—indeed, it's probably the best way to destroy any society, because high inflation arrays a government against its citizens. In a recent book, the Swiss economist Peter Bernholz counted twenty-nine hyperinflations in the modern era (basically: since the French Revolution), with hyperinflation arbitrarily defined as price increases of at least 50 percent a month. Among the worst was the German hyperinflation of 1920-23, reaching a unfathomable monthly rate of almost 30,000 percent. At levels well below these, inflation destroys both the economy and public trust. Private virtues—hard work, saving, planning ahead—are neutralized, because savings can be rendered worthless and hard work becomes pointless when pay depreciates so rapidly in value. People devote more time to spending their earnings quickly—as opposed to working and producing—before the paper money becomes entirely useless. In Germany, people carted currency in suitcases and wheelbarrows. Although money was ultimately stabilized, Germany's fledgling democracy (the Weimar Republic) never fully regained "the trust of the middle class that had lost so much to inflation," notes historian Eric D. Weitz.[9]

Even at much lower levels, inflation is profoundly disorienting, because people fear that they can't keep up with prices (even if they often can) and worry that they are losing ground to others who have better protection or who are luckier. Ironically, it was the English economist John Maynard Keynes who best explained inflation's socially corrosive effects. (The irony arises because the U.S. economic policies that led to high inflation were justified in his name. Keynes died in 1946, and so we can never know whether he would have endorsed the policies labeled "Keynesian." Lenin's observation also came from Keynes; there is no independent source.) Initially, Keynes argued, rising inflation stimulates economic activity because businesses assume that the higher prices signal more demand for their products Companies invest and hire more. But soon, inflation disrupts established social and economic relationships. Here is Keynes's central insight:

> [W]hen the value of money changes, it does *not* change equally for all persons and purposes. A man's receipts and his outgoings [incomes and expenses] are not modified in one uniform proportion. Thus a change in prices and rewards, as measured in money, generally affects different classes unequally, transfers wealth from one to another, bestows affluence here and embarrassment there, and redistributes fortune's favors so as to frustrate design and disappoint expectation.[10]

Keynes's perception explains why high inflation is so threatening to middle-class societies. It makes social and economic advance seem a lottery—a lottery that's constantly being replayed so that winners in one round could become losers in the next. Even for those with jobs, it seems to reduce or deny control over their own destinies. Americans increasingly felt that way. In 1973, the CPI rose 8.7 percent; but hourly wages went up only 6.2 percent. Some price explosions triggered public protests. In early 1973, meat prices rose at a scorching annual rate of 75 percent (price controls had just been lifted). Shoppers reacted by staging a weeklong beef boycott; meat sales temporarily dropped by two-thirds. Americans tried to protect themselves against inflation through both public policies and private hedging. By 1975, about 60 percent of union contracts indexed wages to the CPI—as the CPI rose, wages followed. Earlier (in 1972), Congress indexed Social Security benefits to inflation. More families bought homes as inflation insurance. A Harvard economics professor told Peter Kilborn of *The New York Times:* "I see it in the young folk around here, the nontenured faculty. They're buying houses at high prices and taking big mortgages. They wouldn't do it if they weren't counting on inflation."[11]

Mostly, Americans were discouraged. Since 1935, the Gallup Poll has regularly asked respondents "What do you think is the most important problem facing the country today?" In the nine years from 1973 to 1981, "the high cost of living" ranked number one every year. In some surveys, an astounding 70 percent of the respondents cited it as the major problem. In 1971, it was second behind Vietnam; in 1972, it faded only because wage and price controls artificially and temporarily kept prices in check. In 1982 and 1983, it was second behind unemployment (and not coincidentally, the high joblessness stemmed from a savage recession caused by inflation). There was a term to describe the stubborn mixture of high inflation, modest economic growth and high unemployment—"stagflation." The columnist Joseph Kraft was among the first to use it. Writing in the Feburary 25, 1971, *Washington Post,* he said, "the core of stagflation is a sluggishness in economic activity. Unemployment is 6 percent. . . . [The economic] slowdown was at least partially caused by administration actions to restrain inflation. But the rise in consumer prices has not been cut very much. In 1969, the consumer price index rose 6.6 percent. Last year it rose 5.5 percent."[12]

Among government officials, there was indeed a widespread fatalism about reducing inflation. President Carter often seemed forlorn at the prospect. Early in 1980, he was asked at a press conference what he planned to do about inflation. He replied: "It would be misleading for me to tell any of you that there is a solution to it. As you know, this is a worldwide, all-pervasive problem with oil prices having been increased 100 percent during the last 13 or 14 months." His resignation was common. Inflation had so insinuated itself into the fabric of everyday life, the thinking went, that it could not be easily extracted. The standard remedy would be a horrific recession, or a depression, that would reduce wage and price increases. Conventional calculations suggested that a one percentage point rise in unemployment (say, from 6 percent to 7 percent) would reduce inflation only by half a percentage point (say, from 8 percent to 7.5 percent) over a year. To lower prevailing inflation (about 8 percent in early 1979) significantly would "take either an enormous recession or an extraordinarily long one," wrote one well-known economist at the time. The "staggering human costs" signified that "it would probably be precluded politically."[13]

Inflation was rationalized as a reflection of the deeper ills of American society. It was not a cause of our problems; it was a consequence of our condition. Specifically, it was said to show that the nation was becoming ungovernable. Americans had more wants (for higher pay, more government programs, a cleaner environment) than could be met. Inflation "is the symptom of deep-rooted social and economic contradiction and conflict, between major economic groups claiming pieces of the pie that together exceed the whole pie," wrote Yale economist James Tobin, a former adviser to President Kennedy who had advocated the policies that accelerated inflation. Alfred Kahn, a Cornell University economist and top Carter inflation aide, expressed a similar view. "Can a democracy discipline itself?" he asked. "The problem in our economy is that we have persistent, well-organized pressures by each individual and group to preserve his or her absolute position regardless of what happens to the country as a whole." Inflation was portrayed as an impersonal way to regulate this competition. Some groups would get ahead; others would fall behind.[14]

In some ways, the apex of national pessimism occurred in July 1979, when Carter, his popularity sinking, addressed the nation. The talk was subsequently dubbed the "malaise" speech, though Carter never actually used that word. The president spoke of a "fundamental threat to American democracy . . . a crisis of confidence":

Confidence has defined our course and has served as a link between generations. We've always believed in something called progress. We've always had a faith that the days of our children would be better than our own. . . . Our people are losing this faith. . . . For the first time in the history of our country, a majority of our people believe that the next five years will be worse than the past five years.[15]

But Carter did not attribute this loss of faith to the rise of inflation. Though much of his speech concerned energy policy—among other things, he proposed subsidies for synthetic fuels—his basic diagnosis of the country's spiritual crisis was, paradoxically, that Americans were too concerned with "progress," or at least material progress. "In a nation that was proud of hard work, strong families, close-knit communities, and our faith in God, too many of us now tend to worship self-indulgence and consumption," he said. "Human identity is no longer defined by what one does, but by what one owns. But we've discovered that owning things and consuming things does [sic] not satisfy our longing for meaning. We've learned that piling up material goods cannot fill the emptiness of lives that have no confidence or purpose." Government thereby escaped much responsibility for the nation's state of mind. Growing pessimism reflected individual failings.

All these somber musings were, up to a point, believable. Certainly, persistent federal budget deficits attested to politicians' tendency to promise more—more programs, more tax cuts, more individual benefits, and balanced budgets—than they could deliver. Certainly, many Americans craved spiritual meaning. But in the end, these theories were not so much explanations of the country's mood as excuses not to do anything about inflation, and the point at which they became less believable was the 1980 election. "By the summer of 1979, no other issue could rival inflation as a pressure on the American mind, its mood and family planning for the future," the political writer Theodore H. White later observed. Prices were routinely rising at double-digit annual rates, more than twice the 4.9 percent inflation in 1976 inherited by Carter.

Ronald Reagan won in a near landslide—50.7 percent of the popular vote against Carter's 41 percent and "independent" John Anderson's 6.6 percent. Inflation was the dominating concern. Voters didn't know that Reagan could control it; but they did know that Carter hadn't. Later, Carter himself judged that inflation had been the decisive issue against him, more important than his mishandling of the Iranian hostage crisis.★ Exit polls showed that 47 percent of Reagan's voters rated "controlling inflation" as the most important issue, followed closely by 45 percent who valued "strengthening America's position in the world." (Voters were asked about what one or two issues mattered, so more than one answer was possible.) In the Gallup Poll in September, 58 percent rated inflation as the number one problem. In other ways, Carter's economy

---

★ On November 4, 1979—after the shah of Iran had fled into exile and been replaced by a new revolutionary government—young "revolutionaries" seized the U.S. embassy. Carter was unable to secure the release of the fifty-two hostages, a failure widely seen as humiliating to the United States. The hostages were released on January 20, 1981, the day of Reagan's inauguration.

hadn't performed so badly; it had, for instance, created eleven million jobs since his election.[16]

The acute public anxieties of the late 1970s, it turned out, did not spring from a spiritual void or unresolved group conflicts. They came from inflation and its side effects. Once high inflation had been suppressed—that is, once Reagan had chosen to endure the bruising recession that economists had said was politically impossible—the public's mood improved noticeably, even though unemployment declined only slowly. From a peak of 10.8 percent in late 1982, it still averaged 7.5 percent in 1984. But Reagan was easily reelected, and his campaign slogan of "It's morning again in America" was essentially a victory cry over inflation. It signified order and optimism, a sharp contrast to the mood four years earlier.

One study of public opinion surveys found that almost 60 percent of the decline of public confidence in national institutions (government, business, labor) in the 1970s reflected higher inflation and unemployment—and inflation dominated. Wrote public opinion analysts Seymour Martin Lipset and William Schneider: "A high rate of inflation appears to lower the public expectations of the future in all respects: for their own lives, for the country as a whole, for the economy. . . . *Inflation, more than anything else, created the infamous, albeit temporary, 'malaise' of 1979.*" (The italics are in the original.) The "malaise" was man-made.[17]

IV

Of course, inflation's political and psychological fallout cannot be separated from its economic effects. What Americans think of themselves, their lives and their society has always reflected economic fortune. Inflation and disinflation had widespread economic consequences. They shaped business cycles, affected living standards and refashioned the nation's financial system. For the first two decades or so of the half century that began in 1960, rising inflation weakened the economy. Then, over the next twenty-five years, disinflation strengthened the economy's performance until infectious optimism turned into destructive speculation and triggered the savage recession that began in late 2007.

The most obvious influences were on the business cycle. High and rising inflation led to more frequent and harsher recessions, and lower inflation led—until the latest slump—to less frequent and milder recessions. The contrasts are stark, as a few basic statistics indicate. From 1969 to 1982, inflation averaged 7.5 percent and unemployment 6.4 percent. From 1990 to 2007, the comparable figures were 2.9 percent for inflation and 5.4 percent for unemployment. With rising inflation, government slipped into "stop-go" policies that aggravated the economy's instability. When unemployment seemed too high, the Federal Reserve would ease credit; when easier credit then led to higher inflation, the Fed would tighten it. To use a popular analogy, the Fed was constantly "pushing too hard on the accelerator" and then reacting by "jamming too hard on the brakes." Once inflation diminished, so did the destructive "stop-go" policies.

Rising inflation also stunted the growth of living standards. The relevant concept here is "productivity"—economic jargon for efficiency. Productivity is most commonly measured as "output per hour worked" and is the wellspring of higher living standards. The more efficient we are, the higher our incomes or the greater our leisure time. Wages, salaries and fringe benefits rise with productivity. Since 1950, inflation and productivity have seemed inversely related. From 1950 to 1965, inflation was low and productivity was high. Annual gains averaged 3.1 percent. When inflation rose in the late 1960s, average productivity growth deteriorated to 2.4 percent from 1965 to 1970. The years of the worst inflation, 1973–80, were also the years of worst productivity growth, an average of 1.1 percent a year. The increases improved in the 1980s to 1.8 percent, and when inflation descended to 1950s levels, so did productivity growth. The 1995–2005 average was 2.9 percent.*[18]

This was not an accident. No one would contend that inflation single-handedly determined productivity trends. Indeed, productivity responds to so many influences—technology, government policies, competition, risk taking—that economists have never fully explained its movements. Some early gains after World War II un-

---

* In fairness, if I had chosen other end points, the productivity picture would look different. For example, from 1970 to 1995, annual productivity growth averaged 1.7 percent, making it seem that inflation had little effect. It is precisely because the numbers can be arranged to tell many different stories that the subject is controversial. However, my selection is hardly contrived. It is common. In a recent report, for example, the Congressional Budget Office picked similar time periods. (See table 2-2, "The Budget and Economic Outlook 2008–2018," January 2008.)

doubtedly reflected the adoption of new technologies whose introduction had been delayed by the war and the Depression: direct distance dialing (which reduced the need for operators); faster and
bigger planes for commercial aviation; advanced machine tools.
Some recent gains originated with computers and the Internet.

Still, higher inflation almost certainly depressed productivity
growth. One reason was the "money illusion": the tendency to mistake price increases for real gains. As inflation rose, companies' sales
and profits grew rapidly. Managers believed they were doing better
than they were; they paid less attention to the many small daily op-
erational matters that improve efficiency. From 1964 to 1974, after-
tax profits jumped from $41 billion to $95 billion. Because profits
are how most managers evaluate themselves (and are evaluated),
what was the problem?

Simple: The gains mostly reflected inflation. When some companies voluntarily published inflation-adjusted financial statements in
the late 1970s, the results were sobering. In 1978, General Motors
reported that its sales and profits were up 77 percent and 46 percent,
respectively, from five years earlier. Impressive, it seemed. But when
adjusted for inflation, the sales increase dwindled to 20 percent, and
the profit increase disappeared altogether. GM was no fluke. Though
reported profits rose smartly in the 1970s, profit margins—profits as
a share of sales—fell from 17 percent in the 1950s to 11 percent in
the 1970s.[19]

Initially, many executives may not have appreciated what was
happening. But by the late 1970s, only the dullest manager could
not have suspected the reality. Yet many corporate managers were
"not anxious to move to accurate profit reporting" by adopting

inflation-adjusted accounting, *The Wall Street Journal* editorialized in 1979. "They would rather be publicly pilloried for [price] gouging than explain losses and low profits to shareholders." As late as 1981, *BusinessWeek* chided:

> Through more than a decade of inflation, a generation of corporate managements has refused to admit that the earnings reported to shareholders—and frequently cited as "record profits"—are not all that they are cracked up to be. Double-digit inflation has rendered the traditional yardstick of company performance illusory or suspect.[20]

High inflation also hurt productivity growth in other ways. The most obvious was the added time and effort required to make frequent price changes—a phenomenon that economists call "menu costs." (The reference is to the costs of changing a menu.) As inflation rose, whether to increase prices 3 percent or 5 percent became as important to profits as productivity gains. Trying to comply with, or evade, the various forms of wage-price controls also consumed managers' time. Finally, inflation interacted with the tax code to reduce incentives for new, productivity-enhancing investments. Depreciation allowances—a noncash cost covering the aging of machinery and buildings—are intended to help companies pay for new equipment, machines, factories and offices. But the allowances were based on historic costs; inflation eroded their value. As inflation raised replacement costs for new investments, depreciation allowances were increasingly inadequate.

Once inflation diminished, so did these adverse effects. In addition, managers could no longer hide. By the 1990s, many firms complained that they'd lost "pricing power," even as pressures from Wall Street to increase profits intensified. Profits would now rise mostly from increased sales or reduced costs. Managers had to search for new ways to increase productivity.

Interest rates were another crucial mechanism by which inflation reshaped the economy. Interest rates are the price of money: what people and firms pay to borrow. Of all the prices in the economy, interest rates are the most important, because they affect so much else. They overshadow other significant prices—say for wheat, oil or computer chips. In practice, many factors determine interest rates: the supply of savings; the demand for credit; the state of the business cycle; Federal Reserve policies; the nature of financial markets. But inflation and the expectations of future inflation play a large role, because lenders want to be protected against the possible erosion of the value of their money. Higher inflation causes—with an uncertain lag—interest rates to rise; and falling inflation causes—also with a lag—rates to fall. In 1965, 30-year fixed-rate home mortgages averaged 5.8 percent; by 1980, the average was 12.7 percent; and by 2005, it was back down to 5.9 percent. For the same years, commercial banks' "prime rate" offered to the best customers went from 4.5 percent to 15.3 percent to 6.2 percent.[21]

These dramatic swings profoundly affected credit markets, the stock market and the value of land and housing. Remember the S&L crisis? To most Americans, "savings and loan associations"—also known as S&Ls and "thrifts"—are now relics. In 2006, there were only 845 of them, with about $1.5 trillion in assets; by contrast, more than 7,000 commercial banks had nearly $10 trillion in assets. But in 1975, the roughly 5,400 thrifts made about half the nation's home mortgages. S&L managers often lived a "three-six-three" day, wrote economist Lawrence White. They "could take in money at 3 percent on deposits; they could lend it out at 6 percent on mortgage loans; and [they] could be on the golf course by 3:00 in the afternoon." But this cushy arrangement required stable prices, because S&Ls "borrowed short" (short-term depositors could withdraw their funds anytime) and "lent long" (mortgages had fixed interest rates and 30-year maturities). If higher inflation pushed up deposit rates, the S&Ls' borrowing costs might exceed repayment rates on older mortgages. That's what happened.[22]

The S&L crisis is typically cast as a tale of inept government regulation and corrupt lending. S&Ls squandered their funds on ill-conceived housing projects, shopping malls and resorts. This is misleading. The real source of distress was inflation. By 1981, 85 percent of thrifts were unprofitable. As short-term interest rates rose, they faced a dilemma: either raise their own deposit rates, which might make them unprofitable, or face a huge outflow of deposits, which would make them insolvent. The advent of money-market mutual funds in the late 1970s rendered government interest-rate ceilings on deposits at banks and S&Ls ineffective; savers could move their money elsewhere. Only after S&Ls faced this squeeze did inept regulation and lending mushroom. Government liberalized S&Ls' lending authority in the hope that profits on new loans for commercial real estate would offset losses on old mortgages; but speculative new loans simply compounded the losses. The S&Ls' collapse cost taxpayers about $160 billion—the difference between what depositors (protected by federal deposit insurance) were owed and what the failed S&Ls' assets were worth.[23]

The same interactions caused other credit crises. As inflation rose, American farmers borrowed huge amounts, based on the increasing crop and land prices. "Lenders would come out to the farm," one Iowa farmer told journalist William Greider, "and they would say, 'That tractor looks a bit aging.' So the farmer would buy a new one. Why not?" Farmers' income and wealth seemed ample. From 1972 to 1975, wheat went from $1.34 a bushel to beyond $4.00, corn from $1.08 to $3.02. In Iowa, land prices quintupled, from $319 an acre in 1970 to $1,697 in 1982. But when inflation declined and crop prices collapsed in the 1980s, many farmers were crushed by debt. Widespread foreclosures ensued. So did "tractorcades" to Washington and some well-publicized suicides among farmers who lost land that had been in their families for generations.[24]

The so-called Third World debt crisis followed a similar trajectory. In the 1970s, commercial bank loans to Latin American countries barely existed; by 1982, these debts totaled $327 billion. It was reasoned that the rising prices for commodities, a mainstay of their exports, would enable them to pay foreign debts, denominated mostly in dollars. Mexico and Venezuela had oil; Brazil, coffee; Argentina, wheat and meat. But rising interest rates (most loans had "floating" rates that changed automatically) and falling commodity prices in the early 1980s destroyed this logic. In August 1982, Mexico defaulted on $80 billion of loans. Fifteen other Latin countries followed suit. The following years are called "the lost decade," as many Latin nations—burdened with debts they could not repay—suffered slow economic growth and rising poverty.[25]

Unsurprisingly, the swings in interest rates also played havoc with stocks. Half of U.S. households now own stocks or mutual funds. It

is conventional wisdom that the 1990s' "high tech" frenzy was responsible for luring people into the market. This is at best half true.
Go back to the 1950s, and you discover that stocks and stock ownership flourished. From the end of World War II until 1965, the
Dow Jones Industrial Average quintupled. The number of shareholders jumped from 6.5 million in 1950 to 30.9 million in 1970.
But higher inflation halted the market's rise and squelched the enthusiasm for stocks. In August 1979, *Business Week* wrote an obituary.
"The Death of Equities: How Inflation Is Destroying the Stock
Market" was the cover line. "Have you been to an American stock-
holders' meeting lately?" asked one young corporate executive.
"They're all old fogies." Among those under sixty-five, the number
of shareholders had dropped 25 percent during the decade. Poor
performance had alienated younger investors.[26]

In 1982, the Dow was actually lower than in 1965. Inflation made
"investors very cautious," *Business Week* argued. Americans had learned
"that inflation will lead to an economic downturn that will wreck
corporate profitability and stock prices. This happened in 1974,
when the worst recession since the Depression followed the last
burst of double-digit inflation." But in a larger sense, stocks had
fallen victim to the merciless logic of rising interest rates. Stocks,
bonds, bank deposits and money market mutual funds all compete
for investors' dollars. As rates on bonds and other interest-bearing
investments rose, stocks had to stay competitive. Their earnings
yields had to rise; paradoxically, this put downward pressure on stock
prices. In January 1973, the Dow had hit a record of 1,051.70. By
December 1974, it had dropped by almost half to 577.60. In 1979,

when adjusted for inflation, stocks were still down 50 percent from the 1973 peak.

A simple example shows why. Suppose a Treasury bond pays a 5 percent rate. Stocks, being riskier, have to offer a higher yield, say 7 percent. A stock's yield is the company's per share earnings (profits) divided by its stock price. A company with earnings of $7 a share and a $100 stock price would have an earnings yield of 7 percent. Now assume that the interest rate on the Treasury bond jumps to 10 percent. To maintain the 2 percentage point premium over bonds, the stock's earning yield has to go to 12 percent. With $7 per share earnings, the stock's price would fall to $58 ($7 is 12 percent of $58). If profits had risen fast enough, stock prices might have increased; in practice, this didn't happen. Higher inflation sabotaged the stock market.*

---

* Many economists argue that this should not have been so—that investors misjudged inflation's effects on stocks. Inflation, they argued, benefited some companies by eroding the real value of their debt. Investors ignored that. Moreover, investors should have made decisions based on "real" (inflation-adjusted) and not nominal interest rates—and "real" rates were low in the 1970s and high in the 1980s. Perhaps. But two points need to be made. First, the actual connection between shifts in interest rates and changes in stock prices during much of this period (the 1970s, the 1980s and the early 1990s) is incontestable. Higher rates depressed stock prices; lower rates elevated them. The connection was not always automatic, but the broad relationship is obvious. Second, inflation made it harder to predict the future and to estimate "real" values over any extended period. Thus, investors may have been rational in comparing stocks and other investments based primarily on their present returns.[27]

But when inflation broke in the early 1980s—and interest rates began to tumble—the process reversed with the same frenzied logic. Falling rates and rising profits propelled shares upward. By 1986, the Dow had doubled from 1982; by 1989, it had almost tripled; by 1996, it had more than sextupled. Investors flooded the market, well before the "high tech" obsession. In 1989, only 31.6 percent of households owned stocks or mutual funds; by 1998, the share was 48.8 percent. The market's relentless advance convinced many investors, often neophytes, that prices would move inexorably upward, even if there were periodic interruptions. It was this mass conviction that set the stage for the final speculative binge, the "tech bubble." Stocks rose to levels completely inconsistent with historic relationships. At one point, Yahoo!'s stock sold for 2,154 times earnings (profits); by contrast, the historical average price-to-earnings ratio of all stocks was closer to 14 or 15. Even so, the "bubble" was fairly short. One careful study dates its onset to between mid-1997 and late 1998; the market peaked in early 2000.[28]

In the end, inflation transformed the entire financial system. Though often arcane, high finance serves a simple purpose: to channel a society's savings into productive loans and investments. From the Great Depression to the 1980s, the financial system was highly compartmentalized. Banks and S&Ls dominated lending. The S&Ls provided most home mortgage loans; banks made mortgages and business and consumer loans. Blue-chip companies could sell bonds; few other firms could. Few companies raised money by selling new stock; with a stagnant market, only existing shares were traded. Inflation wrecked this system. S&Ls were decimated, banks weakened (mostly by bad farm, real estate and developing country loans).

"Securitization" emerged as a new way to provide credit. Mortgages, auto loans and credit card loans issued by banks and other lenders were bundled into bondlike securities and sold to pension funds, insurance companies and other big investors. Meanwhile, a rising stock market became a place to raise capital, especially for new firms, and to buy control of existing firms that seemed undervalued.

It's true that this new financial system has proven unstable. The first warning was the stock market crash of 1987, when the Dow Jones Industrial Average fell 22.6 percent in a single day (October 19); the decline was short-lived. More damaging was the collapse of the "tech bubble" in 2000. But most destructive of all was the dramatic panic of 2007 and 2008, with its devastating effects on the economy. Banks suffered huge credit losses, especially on mortgage-backed securities. Stocks dropped sharply. The crisis is often blamed on the deliberate abandonment of government regulation: the triumph of "free market" ideology (to critics, free market "fundamentalism"), it's said, led to the replacement of a regulated and stable financial system with a freewheeling, lightly supervised system that succumbed to greed and shortsightedness. Though plausible, this indictment is simplistic and misleading.

For starters, the old system wasn't consciously replaced. It collapsed under the weight of inflation, and its successor was the result less of an elaborate free-market master plan than of a series of opportunistic and, to some extent, necessary responses. "Securitization"— to take an obvious example—aimed to remedy the constricted credit flows from banks and S&Ls. Government regulation wasn't discarded; banks, which became the epicenter of the subsequent crisis, remained heavily regulated. For many years, this evolving financial system performed its textbook role of allocating savings and investments fairly efficiently. Its undoing stemmed mostly from conceit: investors, money managers, government regulators, legislators and academics all overestimated their understanding of how it worked.

The huge profits made in these decades by both professional and amateur investors—profits driven heavily by disinflation and its effects on stock and bond prices—conditioned many to believe in the underlying benevolence of finacial markets. Markets might periodically go to excess, but their virtues vastly overshadowed their vices. Sooner or later, the excesses would correct themselves without too much permanent damage. Markets would revert to a more stable and sensible equilibrium. That was the prevailing wisdom. People saw the opportunities and were blinded to the dangers. They, therefore, misjudged the dangers and became more vulnerable to them. In retrospect, it's easy to see why.

If the value of what you buy (stocks, bonds) is rising and the cost of borrowed money (aka "leverage"—one way to buy stocks, bonds and other financial assets) is falling, it doesn't take a genius to make money. That was the lucrative logic of disinflation. From 1980 to 1990, the value of household stocks and mutual funds rose from about $1 trillion to $2.5 trillion; by 2000, that was almost $11 trillion. Bonuses to Wall Street professionals soared, from about $2 billion in 1985 to roughly $6 billion in 1995 and almost $20 billion in 2000. In a culture where success and intelligence are often measured in dollars, these profits imbued many investment bankers, money managers, regulators, scholars and even ordinary investors with an exaggerated sense of their understanding and mastery of financial markets.[29]

Their error was to mistake disinflation's windfalls for wisdom, and the financial crisis proceeded from this widespread blunder. In some ways, the old financial system was superior to the new. Banks and S&Ls were generally close to local borrowers—homeowners, consumers, businesses—and held most loans in their own portfolios. They had an incentive to make loans only to borrowers with good repayment prospects. With securitization, caution receded. Lenders and borrowers were often widely separated. An "originator" (say, a mortgage broker) might make a loan that would be sold to an investment bank (say, Bear Stearns) that would "securitize" it and sell it to final investors. All the middlemen had incentives to complete transactions from which they earned fees.

The ensuing careless lending practices fed the rise in housing prices, which in turn justified making more loans. If housing prices always rose, even loans that went into default could be repaid by selling the home at a higher value. That many of these mortgages were packaged in exotic and confusing securities ("collateralized debt obligations" being a good example), constructed by overconfident financial "engineers," compounded the financial collapse. Trust and confidence were lost. Panic followed, as banks, investment banks and others no longer knew the true value of many securities or who held them. If regulation seemed lax, with hindsight, the main reason was that regulators shared the conventional wisdom. They were no more prescient than the bankers. Markets seemed to be working. Why interfere? Much aggressive regulation is after-the-fact; it reacts to problems and does not anticipate them.

What matters for our story is that the origins of this crisis lay in the side effects of inflation and disinflation on the financial system.

Great gains inspired perverse behavior. Believing the system less risky, investors and regulators took or condoned more risks in the false belief that they weren't. The traumatic crisis had symbolic as well as substantive meaning. It represented a logical end point to a half-century cycle in which inflation's rise and fall were decisive forces in shaping the economy.

Change, of course, is a permanent characteristic of the American economy, possibly its only permanent characteristic. Had there been no inflation, the economy today would be different from what it was fifteen years ago or fifteen years before that. But there *were* inflation and disinflation. They fostered the instability of the 1970s, the long expansions of the 1980s and 1990s, the swings in productivity growth, the consumption and housing booms and the financial crisis of the first decade of the new century. All of these changes had other causes, and some might have occurred in some fashion anyway. But all were also the by-products of the inflationary experience, which affected everyone and whose influence seeped into many of the economy's nooks and crannies.

V

To take even this truncated tour of the past half century is to confirm the huge effects of inflation—both its going up and its coming down—on national life. It was not a sideshow; it was part of the main show. It shaped politics, the economy, the national mood, financial markets and much more. Which highlights the central puzzle: If inflation's so important, why is it so ignored?

By now, there is a vast literature recounting the American journey in recent decades. Virtually all of it consigns inflation to a cameo appearance.★ It doesn't matter whether the authors are historians or economists; whether they are liberal or conservative; whether they are critics or champions of various presidents; or whether they are the presidents themselves. In *Morning in America: How Ronald Reagan Invented the 1980s* by Gil Troy, inflation does not merit a chapter or an index entry. But neither does it figure much in journalist Haynes Johnson's harsher portrait of Reagan in *Sleepwalking Through History.* In his memoir *Keeping Faith,* Jimmy Carter says that "during the early months of 1980, the most serious domestic problem was inflation"—actually, it was serious for most of his presidency—but devotes only four pages to it. He favors his foreign policy feats, such as the peace treaty between Israel and Egypt. Ronald Reagan regarded economic revival as one of his great triumphs but emphasizes tax cuts, not falling inflation. He, too, prefers foreign policy, especially his negotiations with Mikhail Gorbachev that helped end the Cold War.[30]

We are losing a crucial chunk of history; indeed, its omission creates bad history. Consider the dueling explanations for the economy's impressive performance in the 1980s and 1990s.

Conservatives remember the 1980s nostalgically as Reagan's heroic moment, when he cut taxes, reduced government and revived the economy. The trouble is that much of this story is myth. Although tax rates dropped dramatically (the top rate fell to 28 percent from

★ A striking exception to this inattention is William Greider's masterful *Secrets of the Temple,* an exhaustive and engaging history of the Federal Reserve through the late 1980s.

70 percent), the overall tax burden barely decreased, nor did the size of government. In 1980, total federal taxes were 19 percent of GDP; when Reagan left office in 1989, they were 18.3 percent.* Lower tax rates occurred because budget deficits increased and some tax loopholes were closed. Meanwhile, liberals credit Bill Clinton's policies for the strong economy of the 1990s. But Clinton's policies were the opposite of Reagan's: He raised tax rates (to a top rate of 39.6 percent) and curbed budget deficits. Both stories can't be correct; and in fact, neither is.

The economy performed well in both decades, and the explanation is that the major act of economic policy for both presidents was the containment of inflation. It stabilized the economy and, through the reduction of interest rates and the increases in stock market and real estate wealth, promoted strong consumer spending. Lower tax rates, even after Clinton's increases, may have helped; but they were not the decisive influence. Nor were Clinton's shrunken federal budget deficits. Indeed, budget deficits persisted through most of Clinton's tenure, disappearing only in 1998, more as a result of the strong economy and rising stock prices—which produced an unexpected floodtide of tax revenues—than as a cause. Both ideological accounts of these decades are misleading. The major economic event of this period was the conquest of double-digit inflation.

* Reagan did, however, restrain growth in domestic "discretionary" programs for which Congress must appropriate money annually. These programs dropped from 4.7 percent of GDP in 1980 to 3.1 percent in 1988. Social Security, Medicare and other "entitlements" are not included in this category. Total spending as a share of GDP barely budged.

It's not just our own history that we're missing. The decline of inflation was also a global event. Among many (though not all) economists, government officials and business leaders today, there is a strong belief that high inflation is enormously destructive. Many are old enough to have lived through double-digit price increases and to remember the fallout. To a large extent, the lesson went global. Harvard economist Kenneth Rogoff has compiled figures that show the dramatic nature of the change. In the 1970s, annual inflation averaged 162 percent in Chile, 33 percent in Israel, 9 percent in Denmark, 15 percent in South Korea and 9 percent in France. Early in the twenty-first century, the rates were 3 percent for Chile, Denmark, South Korea and Israel; for France, it was 2 percent. For all developing countries, annual inflation fell from an average of 31 percent in 1980–84 to 6 percent for 2000 to 2006. For rich nations, it went from 9 percent to 2 percent. Crowd behavior makes it easier for all nations to follow low-inflation policies—and harder, though not impossible, for any nation to permit inflation to surge.*[31]

I have already cited one reason for the slighting of inflation: the overemphasis on the role of oil and the war in Vietnam. But there must be other explanations. An obvious one is simply the passage of time. A majority of today's Americans have never experienced double-digit inflation. It was not part of their life, as it was of mine. In 2008, slightly more than 60 percent of today's roughly 300 mil-

---

* Whether these gains might be squandered was unclear in mid-2008, as the hardcover edition of this book went to press. China, Indonesia, India and Saudi Arabia all had 8 percent to 10 percent inflation. See "Inflation's Back," *The Economist,* May 24, 2008, 17.

lion Americans were born in 1962 or later, meaning that the oldest of them would have been only seventeen or eighteen when inflation peaked in 1979 and 1980. They were too young for it to have made much of an impression. Even for some of those who lived through it, the memory of inflation has faded. All this is true and, in a very superficial way, provides a serviceable explanation. But it is unconvincing, because the same arithmetic applies to Vietnam—indeed, more so, since it was an earlier event—and yet Vietnam retains a powerful grip on the national consciousness. Something else must be at work.

Closer to the truth, I think, is a collective failure of communication and candor by the nation's economists. At its base, double-digit inflation was their doing. It resulted from bad ideas that—promoted by many leading economists and converted into government policies—produced bad results. There is now a widespread recognition of this, and although there are many technical studies of inflation and of the period of high inflation, there has not been much in the way of public apologies (from those who were complicit in the error) or reprimands (from those who were not, because they either dissented or were too young). There seems to be an unspoken pact of self-restraint to let bygones be bygones, perhaps out of collective embarrassment or a recognition that dwelling excessively on past failures might compromise economists' opportunities as government advisers and high-level appointees.

Other possible explanations of the neglect are partisanship and historical dramatization. Historians, economists and political commentators—consciously or not—play favorites. People try to fit the facts to their preconceived notions and political heroes. There's a tendency to render judgments for or against one set of policies and actors versus another. Our narratives tend to glorify or demonize our leaders. Inflation does not lend itself well to this sort of story-telling. For starters, when inflation begins, it usually creeps up slowly. To fight it at its earliest stages is, if successful, to engage in a preemptive attack that is largely unappreciated by the public because inflation is not yet highly visible. To fight it at its later stages is to undertake an attack that, even if successful, has awful consequences (higher unemployment, lost incomes) that are unpopular with the public. Either way, it's hard to claim bragging rights. Fighting inflation lacks the drama of a real war or of many of the public crusades and campaigns embraced by political leaders. This may help explain why it figures so little in presidential and political memoirs.

Up to a point, these explanations help resolve the puzzle. But there's a deeper cause, I think, for the oversight. It's the way we do history. To simplify somewhat: Historians don't do economics, and economists don't do history. In general, economists—even when they examine historical events—focus mainly on the economic causes and consequences. They rarely use economics as a springboard to inform a broader historical narrative. Historians suffer the opposite failing. Their landscape consists almost entirely of the political, the social and the personal. Economics baffles and bores them.★ People and ideas are their prime movers. If economic forces intrude, historians typically acknowledge and describe them with-

---

★ Marxist historians are a conspicuous exception to this generalization, because Marx saw economic conflict as the cauldron for much historic change. However, few leading American historians are Marxist.

out trying to explain or analyze them. And journalists? They concentrate on the here and now. They want to know who did what to whom and why—but only today or yesterday.

In short, we compartmentalize. History skimps on economics, and economics skimps on history. The Great Depression—the most momentous economic event of the twentieth century—illustrates the failing. Economists have produced many ambitious attempts to explain its economic causes, ranging from John Kenneth Galbraith's *The Great Crash* to Barry Eichengreen's more recent *Golden Fetters*. From historians, we have many superb accounts of the 1930s, including Frederick Lewis Allen's *Since Yesterday* and Arthur Schlesinger Jr.'s *Age of Roosevelt* trilogy. But we have few syntheses that treat both the economic origins and larger consequences.★ If the Great Depression suffers from this lapse, it is hardly surprising that double-digit inflation—a significant but much lesser upheaval—does too. We are forgetting an important part of our past. It is time to retrieve this lost history.

★ From this blanket indictment, I would exclude David Kennedy's splendid *Freedom from Fear: The American People in Depression and War, 1925–1945*, which succeeds at integrating economic events and explanations into a broader narrative.

2

THE "FULL EMPLOYMENT" OBSESSION

I

You may wonder: How did this happen? If the United States had never before experienced a prolonged peacetime inflation, why did one start in the 1960s? The short answer is the power of ideas. In the 1960s, academic economists argued—and political leaders accepted—that the economy could be kept permanently near "full employment" (initially defined as 4 percent unemployment). Booms and busts, recessions, and depressions had long been considered ugly and unavoidable aspects of industrial capitalism. But once people accepted the idea that the business cycle could be mastered, then the self-restraint that had silently kept prices and wages in check gradually crumbled. New assumptions emerged. If government could prevent recessions, then companies could always count on strong demand for their products. All higher costs (including higher labor costs) could be recovered through higher prices. Similarly, if the economy was always near "full employment," then workers could press for higher wages without facing job loss. If their current employers wouldn't pay, someone else would. Government wouldn't tolerate substantial unemployment; that was its promise. The result was a stubborn wage-price spiral. Wages chased prices, which chased wages. Inflation became self-fulfilling and entrenched. It was that simple.

We know now that the promise to eliminate the business cycle was fated to fail. If it inspired inflationary behavior (as it did), and if rising inflation threatened economic expansion (as it did), then there was an inescapable collision. All this is obvious now, but it wasn't then, at least to most people. For one thing, inflationary behavior emerged slowly. There was not a collective flash, when business executives, union leaders and ordinary workers concluded, "Gosh, government has abolished recessions. No one need worry that huge wage and price increases will ruin our businesses or destroy our jobs." Instead, Americans quietly observed that price and wage gains that, in the past, would have been dangerous were no longer so. Inconvenient bursts of inflation were blamed on onetime events: spending for the Vietnam War or global surges in oil prices. If these temporary causes explained most inflation, then the basic promise—the mastery of the business cycle—remained operative. Unfortunately, most inflation did not stem from temporary causes.

It is hard for us now to recall the single-mindedness with which both Democrats and Republicans pursued "full employment" in the late 1960s and 1970s. Not surprisingly, Richard Nixon, a man of acute political sensitivities, best captured the obsession. "When you start talking about inflation in the abstract, it is hard for people to understand," he commented early in his presidency. "But when unemployment goes up one half of one percent, that's dynamite. . . . The public has had eight years without a recession [in the 1960s]. . . . We can't allow—Wham!—a recession. We'll never get in [office] again." Low unemployment was the be-all and end-all of economic policy; inflation was an inconvenient nuisance. Those priorities endured for more than a decade. Looking back on the Carter presidency (1977–81), Stuart E. Eizenstat, the White House's chief domestic adviser, later confessed:

> The principal fault of the economic policy of the Carter years was a failure to identify the ferocity of the underlying inflationary pressures of the economy. We stuck too long to the stimulative fiscal and monetary policies promised in the 1976 presidential campaign, to end what we called "the Ford recession." In retrospect, we were blind until it was too late to the rising level of inflation. . . . The president's top aides, myself included, and the Democratic party in general, feared and tended to oppose any economic decision which risked restraining growth and causing higher unemployment to fight inflation.[1]

Political ideas often follow the familiar cycle of infatuation and disenchantment. In all infatuations, everything initially seems perfect. Life has a special glow. The future seems full of promise and pleasure. Sooner or later, strains intrude. The romance loses luster.

Sometimes it evolves into a sturdier relationship; sometimes it sinks into recriminations and remorse. So it was with the pledge to abolish business cycles. At first, the performance matched the promise. Slowly, complications arose; there were desperate attempts to retrieve the original promise—mainly through various wage and price controls. People abandon cherished beliefs slowly, usually only when confronted with massive evidence of error. By the late 1970s, such evidence was at hand, and inflation's destructive effects spread disillusion. People no longer believed the original promise.

II

Our story starts with John F. Kennedy's election in 1960. Entering the White House, Kennedy did not have an explicit economic agenda. He certainly did not argue that business cycles could be eliminated—an idea that would have struck most Americans as absurd. But he had campaigned on the vague pledge to "get America moving again." Exactly what that meant in practice was unclear because America had been prosperous in the 1950s, with the exception of a significant recession in 1957–58 (unemployment averaged 6.8 percent in 1958, up from 4.1 percent in 1956). But Kennedy's argument was not just for more prosperity and less poverty. He connected America's economic performance at home with its ability to confront the Soviet Union abroad. "We must recognize the close relationship between the vitality of our own domestic economy and our position around the world," he said in one standard stump speech. "If we stand still here at home, we stand still around the world."[2]

Fifteen years after World War II, that reasoning resonated powerfully with most Americans. The Cold War spawned an unrelenting sense of threat. Democracy and free enterprise were locked in a death struggle with communism and collective ownership. It was not clear then which system would triumph. The Soviets' launch of Sputnik, the first artificial Earth satellite, in 1957 shocked Americans, shaking their faith in U.S. technological superiority. Sputnik made more menacing and credible the Soviets' boasts that they would overtake the United States economically. Kennedy played to these fears, while also appealing to voters' immediate self-interest in greater prosperity. Although he didn't have a program, he did have a disposition to appoint people who did.

Chief among them was Walter Heller, a forty-six-year-old economist from the University of Minnesota who became the chairman of Kennedy's Council of Economic Advisers (CEA). Heller was probably the CEA's most influential chairman ever, not because he was the most brilliant but because he succeeded—more than any other—in getting the president to adopt his ideas. Heller was an aggressive salesman for what ultimately became known as the "new economics," a popular label for Keynesianism. Keynes's ideas already dominated the mainstream among economists, and Heller was determined to put them into practice. By the time he left the CEA in 1964, he had succeeded, probably beyond his wildest imagination. After Kennedy's assassination, Congress had passed a major tax cut—as recommended by his economists—to spur economic growth; and Lyndon Johnson had embraced the idea of active economic management. In 1966, Heller wrote triumphantly:

> Economics has come of age in the 1960s. Two presidents [Kennedy and Johnson] have recognized and drawn on modern economics as a source of national strength and Presidential power. Their willingness to use, for the first time, the full range of modern economic tools [reflects a] . . . narrowing of the intellectual gap between economic advisers and decision makers. The paralyzing grip of economic myth and false fears on policy has been loosened, perhaps even broken.[3]

Heller's enthusiasm typified the times. Conditioned by victory in World War II and postwar technological advances (jet travel, nuclear power, television), Americans were supremely confident in their power to solve problems. Heller was hardly a one-man band. He was simply the conductor, leading an orchestra of like-minded economists: Paul Samuelson of the Massachusetts Institute of Technology, a chief Kennedy adviser in the campaign;* James Tobin of Yale, a member of the CEA; Robert Solow of MIT, a top staff economist on the CEA; Kermit Gordon from Williams College, first a member of the CEA and then director of the Bureau of the Budget; and Seymour Harris, an adviser to the Treasury, formerly of Harvard before moving to the University of California at San Diego. Their collective intellectual firepower was considerable. Three (Samuelson, Solow and Tobin) later won Nobel Prizes in economics; Samuelson

---

* No relation to the present author.

had authored what would remain for many years the leading college economics textbook; and Gordon subsequently became the head of the Brookings Institution, a major Washington think tank. All believed that the American economy could perform better.

In some ways, their conceit was astonishing. Compared to almost any period in U.S. history, the economy had performed impressively since World War II. At war's end, with the Great Depression fresh in people's minds, fears of another economic collapse were widespread. In 1946, 60 percent of Americans thought a depression might occur within a decade. In 1947, Harry S. Truman warned that "the job today is to see to it that America is not ravaged by recurring depressions and long periods of unemployment." Reality stood these worries on their head. Americans enjoyed a prodigious boom, marked by headlong suburbanization and an orgy of car and appliance buying. In the 1950s, the U.S. population grew by 28 million, nearly a fifth. Two-thirds of the growth occurred in the suburbs. "[J]ust as the census of 1890 announced the passing of the frontier, the census of 1960 announced the passing of the great city," one commentator wrote. Couples were breeding enthusiastically. This was the heyday of the postwar baby boom.[4]

Children signaled Americans' renewed optimism and faith in the future. In the 1930s, birth rates had plunged, reflecting widespread gloom. But after the war, America's mood improved along with the economy. By 1960 and allowing for population growth, average per capita incomes were up 24 percent from 1946 and 94 percent from 1929. The recessions that occurred in 1949, 1953–54, 1957–58 and 1960 were, compared with the Depression, mild. The highest monthly unemployment, 7.5 percent in July 1958, was not close to the double-digit levels of the 1930s, when joblessness averaged 18 percent. An altered relationship between the economy and government also bolstered confidence. "Given the experience of the 1930s, it was inconceivable that the government would fail to commit itself to maintaining high employment," the economist Herbert Stein later wrote. Congress made that commitment with the Employment Act of 1946, creating the Council of Economic Advisers to monitor economic conditions and make recommendations to the president. A Democratic Congress had passed the Employment Act, and in the 1950s, a Republican president, Dwight Eisenhower, embraced its precautionary consensus. Eisenhower believed in a balanced budget and stable prices. But he also thought that government had to act— that is, run deficits and cut interest rates—if the economy risked a deep recession or depression. Government would avert calamity.[5] Under Eisenhower, it did.

The Kennedy economists found that approach too cautious. Government could do more, they thought, than merely prevent disasters. Heller and others believed that they could keep the economy expanding perpetually and operating close to "full employment." When unemployment was too high, government could stimulate spending and production. It would cut taxes, increase federal spending—even plan a deficit—and reduce interest rates. This was essentially sophisticated "pump priming." If too much priming aggravated inflation—pushing up prices because demand was greater than supply—then the process could be reversed. Taxes and interest rates could be raised; federal spending could be cut; the budget could swing to surplus. The economy would slow; inflation would subside. This sort of "activist economics" cast economists as public-spirited engineers who could deliver everlasting prosperity. Not co-incidentally, their power and prestige would ascend.

"Fine-tuning" is what this approach was ultimately called. Some of the Kennedy-Johnson economists later complained that the label was a journalistic simplification and exaggeration. Not so. In 1965, President Johnson—no doubt reading words that his economists had written or approved—declared, "I do not believe that recessions are inevitable." As late as 1970, Arthur Okun, a Yale economist who served on Johnson's CEA from 1964 to 1969 (with a year as chairman) wrote, "Recessions are now considered to be fundamentally preventable, like airplane crashes and unlike hurricanes." Many of these economists promoted "fine tuning," by whatever name. The Great Depression had profoundly influenced them. "Words and statistics cannot convey to people who did not live through it and do not remember it anything like an adequate picture of the Depression," as one put it. "We saw the unemployed, the breadlines, the foreclosed homes, the abandoned farms directly, and not through statistics or television film."[6]

In classical economics, business cycles were inevitable but self-correcting. Recoveries would occur spontaneously through automatic shifts in wages, prices and interest rates. Lower prices would spur more buying; lower wages would spur more hiring; lower interest rates would spur more borrowing. Yet, this hadn't happened in the 1930s. Only Keynes seemed able to explain why. As he argued, wages might be "sticky" and not decline sufficiently in a slump. Even at low interest rates, gloomy businesses and investors might not borrow more. Thus, spontaneous adjustments wouldn't always correct serious economic downturns. Unless government intervened, economies might settle into a high-unemployment stagnation. Keynes infused economics with political relevance and scholarly energy. "We were attracted to the subject [economics] by the happy combination of intellectual excitement and the promise of dramatic social improvement," Tobin wrote.[7]

By the 1960s, the American Keynesians believed that technical advances in economics allowed them to go beyond the master. Before World War II, economic statistics were primitive—reports on the economy's output (Gross Domestic Product), unemployment and inflation became routine only in the 1940s and 1950s.* It was then thought possible to estimate the economy's "potential output"— what could be produced when all companies operated at maximum capacity and all willing workers had jobs.† New computer-driven eco-

---

* The concept then widely used was Gross National Product, or GNP, rather than today's Gross Domestic Product, or GDP. The two are virtually identical. The main difference is the classification of income of foreign-owned enterprises. In GNP, U.S. income of foreign-owned firms was excluded and overseas income of U.S. multinational firms was included. GDP reverses that: It includes the U.S. income of foreign-owned firms (say, a Japanese auto plan operating in Ohio) and excludes income of American firms operating abroad. I have used GDP—the current convention—in the text to avoid unnecessary confusion.

† On paper, the calculation was simple. Output equaled the number of hours people might work multiplied by average productivity (output per hour worked). Suppose, for example, the economy's "potential output" had been $100 billion this year and that both productivity and "hours worked" were increasing at rates of 2 percent a year. Then, potential output in the second year would increase by 4 percent (2 percent for extra labor and 2 percent for higher productivity). It would be $104 billion.

nomic models aided the process. These models showed how different economic variables (consumer spending, interest rates, housing construction) interacted with each other. The models could, it was thought, therefore, provide accurate forecasts. They could determine how far the economy was straying from "potential output." They could also predict recessions and inflation, it was believed. Thus, corrective policies could be adopted. If the economy was below full employment, it could be nudged up. If it were in an inflationary zone, it could be nudged down. With better information and theories, economics seemed a reliable form of social engineering.

Conditioned by the Depression, the Kennedy-Johnson economists didn't worry much about inflation. From 1958 to 1961, unemployment had averaged 6.1 percent annually while inflation was only 1.5 percent. Joblessness seemed the pressing problem. Modest inflation was viewed as a "cost-push" phenomenon: Some industries (steel, autos, rubber), dominated by a few firms and with unionized work forces, had enough independent market power to push wages and prices higher. By contrast, "demand-pull" inflation—too much demand raising all prices—seemed unthreatening. The Kennedy economists took comfort in the "Phillips Curve," which purported to show a stable relationship between unemployment and inflation. A society could select what "mix" of inflation and unemployment it preferred. The curve was named after New Zealand economist A. W. Phillips, who in 1958 had first plotted a historical relationship between unemployment and wages for England. (Wages closely tracked prices.) When economists Paul Samuelson and Robert Solow examined the U.S. data, they concluded that there was a favorable "menu of choice." They suggested that 3 percent unemployment might exist with a permanent inflation of about 4.5 percent. This seemed a socially and economically desirable mix.★[8]

Actually, Samuelson and Solow had called 3 percent unemployment a "non-perfectionist's" goal, implying that in time it might move even lower. The optimism was telling: The Kennedy-Johnson economists were not much plagued by self-doubt. They saw themselves as missionaries for the collective benefits available from modern economics. A new era was at hand, if only political and public resistance could be swept away. "[T]he major barrier to getting the country moving again lay in the economic ignorance and stereotypes that prevailed in the land," Heller wrote. "[M]en's minds had to be conditioned to accept new thinking, new symbols, and new and broader concepts of the public interest." The trouble was that many of the "stereotypes" that produced "ignorance" were not held just by the general public but also by its political leaders, including Kennedy.[9]

First among the stereotypes was widespread belief in the virtue of balanced budgets; this made it harder to use the premeditated deficit as a tool of economic management. As a general principle, Americans believed that debt was bad. That included government debt. They typically likened the government's finances to their own. People shouldn't "live beyond their means." Neither should government. Moreover, insisting that politically painful taxes pay for politically pleasurable spending checked the growth of government.

★ A certain amount of unemployment is unavoidable—people just entering the labor market from school or after childrearing; people changing jobs. This is usually called "frictional unemployment."

These views dated to the start of the republic, though they were often breached in wars and depressions, when deficits were accepted as practical necessities. It was hard to pay for costly wars by immediate and huge tax increases; big tax increases or spending cuts when the economy was collapsing were similarly difficult. But such expediency did not extend to running deficits consciously during periods of peace and relative prosperity. By these precepts, using budget deficits aggressively to achieve full employment was precluded.

A second strand of "ignorance" was the popular hostility toward inflation. People liked stable prices; the Keynesian economists recognized that. But they believed that most Americans had made it an undesirable fetish. Just a bit of inflation—the prospect held out by the Phillips Curve—would be more socially constructive. It would permit more expansive economic policies, lower unemployment and greater output. The benefits were well worth the costs. There was "a vast exaggeration of the social costs of inflation," Tobin wrote as late as 1974. In 1962, Kennedy's first CEA designated 4 percent unemployment as a temporary target for "full employment." By the U.S. Phillips Curve, that implied the country would run a permanent inflation rate of about 3 percent to 4 percent. The presumption was that most people would adjust to slightly higher inflation without much resentment or serious economic or social side effects.[10] It was crucially presumed that inflation would be stable and not accelerate.

A final obstacle to active economic management involved gold. At the time, the United States was pledged to convert dollars held by foreign governments into gold at a rate of $35 an ounce. This commitment, reached at an international conference in 1944 at

Bretton Woods, New Hampshire, aimed to make the dollar suitable as international money to be used for foreign trade and to settle debts among nations. The dollar would be as good as gold. If U.S. inflation eroded the dollar's value, then foreign governments might deplete U.S. gold reserves by presenting their dollars for redemption. To prevent that, the United States would have to slow its economy by raising interest rates or running budget surpluses. Inflation and imports would abate. Fewer dollars would go abroad (Americans paid for their imports with dollars), and foreign governments would have more confidence in the dollar. That was the concept of the Bretton Woods international monetary system. But to the Kennedy economists, this logic might sabotage "full employment" policies at home. Ransoming the domestic economy to gold, they thought, was self-defeating. Better to drop the gold guarantee.

To achieve their goals, Kennedy's economists had to remove all these political obstructions—and the job started at the White House itself. Kennedy instinctively disliked budget deficits, as did many other officials in his administration. There was no unanimity of views, because Kennedy didn't want unanimity. "I simply cannot afford to have one set of advisers," he once remarked. So he didn't. Not surprisingly, C. Douglas Dillon, a Republican who was the Treasury secretary, opposed *deliberate* deficits. Moreover, ditching the antideficit prejudice was politically risky. Republicans routinely attacked Democrats as spendthrifts, addicted to deficit financing. In Congress, fiscally conservative southern Democrats held many key positions. Especially important was Senator Harry Byrd of Virginia, chairman of the Senate Finance Committee, which would consider any tax legislation. Advocating deliberate deficits would vindicate

Republicans and alienate southern Democrats. And for what? Even Kennedy initially doubted the political appeal of Heller's ideas. "The 94 percent employed," he noted privately early in his term, "couldn't care less about the 6 percent unemployed."[11]

By late 1962, Kennedy had changed his mind. Although the budget was already in deficit, he proposed a huge tax cut in early 1963. In part, the conversion reflected the man himself. Kennedy saw himself as a cautious experimenter, open to new ideas. "[T]he economists never had a President so willing to listen to them," wrote Hugh Sidey of *Time* magazine. "Kennedy trusted hard facts, not hunches." The economists deluged him with facts that "the politicians could not match . . . , and so the pragmatic Kennedy turned to the economists." The economy's lackluster performance aided his conversion. A recession in early 1961 had raised unemployment to 6.7 percent. But in mid-1962, joblessness stopped declining and remained stuck at about 5.5 percent—roughly where it had been in 1960. In June 1962, Kennedy gave a commencement speech at Yale University that tentatively endorsed the "new economics." He denounced economic "myths," including the "myth" that budget deficits were automatically bad. Still, Kennedy didn't decide on a major tax cut until late in the year. What finally persuaded him was the enthusiastic reaction to a speech in December before the Economic Club of New York, in which he portrayed a tax cut as lifting "the burden on private income and the deterrents to private initiative imposed by our present tax system." The audience, mainly of Republican businessmen, reacted warmly. "If I can convince them," Kennedy said, "I can convince anyone."[12]

Actually, he couldn't. Once the proposal went to Congress, it languished. Republicans labeled it "the biggest gamble in history." Although some business groups backed Kennedy, public support was underwhelming. In October 1963, the House of Representatives had finally passed a bill, 271–155, but prospects for Senate action were unclear. After Kennedy's assassination in November, one opinion poll found "fiscal irresponsibility" to be the most unpopular aspect of his administration. No one can ever know what would have happened had Kennedy lived. The proposal's approval the next year resulted partly from national guilt over his death and partly from Lyndon Johnson's mastery of the legislative process. But once it did pass, it seemed an unquestioned triumph. The economy expanded 5.3 percent in 1964 and 5.9 percent in 1965. The unemployment rate dropped to 5 percent by the end of 1964 and to almost 4 percent a year later. Inflation remained at less than 2 percent in both years. If this was not economic paradise, what would be?[13]

Capitalism seemed to have arrived at a better and permanent future. To mark the moment, *Time* magazine put Keynes on its cover at the end of 1965. Symbolically, the "new economics" had evolved from an obscure academic theory into a pillar of populism. It was widely embraced, if not completely understood. The United States had, said *Time,* "discovered the secret of steady, stable, non-inflationary growth." The economy was in the fifth year "of the most sizeable, prolonged and widely distributed prosperity in history." Keynesianism had first convinced economists, then the public and, finally, conservative businessmen. "They believe that whatever happens, the Government will somehow keep the economy strong and rising," *Time* said. There were some signs that inflation was inching up, but

Time was confident (as were most of the economists interviewed) that it could be contained without too much trouble.[14]

III

Politics, as much as economics, had changed. Henceforth, recessions and slumps would not be treated as unfortunate but inevitable occurrences. Political leaders would be blamed because (it was now assumed) competent governments could control the business cycle. Although the "new economics" was Democratic dogma, many Republicans grasped its popularity and embraced it. "Full employment" became the bipartisan standard against which economic success was measured. After being selected by Richard Nixon for a spot on his Council of Economic Advisers, Herbert Stein was asked by the president-elect what the administration's most serious economic problem would be. Inflation, replied Stein. Nixon objected: "[He] immediately warned me that we must not raise unemployment," Stein wrote later. "I didn't at the time realize how deep this feeling was or how serious the implications would be. . . . [T]he country valued continuous high employment above price stability." Nixon particularly valued it, because he believed that he had lost the 1960 election because an economic slowdown had cost him crucial votes. But the sentiment was widespread.[15]

The result of this mind-set was that the same mistakes were repeated for fifteen years: Inflation was underestimated; policies to "stimulate" the economy (tax cuts, budget deficits, easy money) were overused; and wage-price controls, either "voluntary" or mandatory, were seen—despite constant failure—as a reasonable way to reconcile "full employment" with low inflation. Wishful thinking triumphed. People believed what they wanted to believe. By 1966, inflation had risen to 3.5 percent, which—by the standards of the 1950s—was high. But it "wasn't as big a thing as it should have been [in our minds]," economist Charles Schultze, director of the Bureau of the Budget under President Johnson, said later. Government and private forecasters regularly underestimated inflation. "In every single year of the 1970s, the consensus forecast [of inflation] made late in the previous year *understated* the actual value of inflation," reported economist J. Bradford DeLong of the University of California at Berkeley.[16]

The learning curve was remarkably flat. Successive presidents, Congresses and their advisers engaged in the same self-defeating behavior, very much like a compulsive eater who knows gorging is bad but can't stop. Why didn't Nixon learn from Johnson, or Carter from Nixon? One explanation is that presidents regarded economics as an obscure and technical subject that required them to lean heavily on their advisers—and mainstream economists revised their thinking slowly. Having claimed in the 1960s that they could improve the economy's performance (and having, thereby, enhanced their status), they were reluctant to admit that they had vastly overstated their case. Striving to redeem the original and unrealistic promise, they followed one round of bad advice with another and then another. Ideas ruled the roost, and the ruling ideas were wrong. Because they had created public and political expectations that couldn't be met, the effort to do so ultimately made matters worse.

But there was another cause of failure. Controlling inflation was an afterthought for most presidents. It was not central to what they or their political parties sought—not central to their ambitions for the country or for themselves—and so it was dealt with on the fly. When it got bad, they could not ignore it, but their responses were careless and casual—mostly "crisis management." Most presidents' first impulse was to prevent inflation from frustrating other goals (including "full employment"), not to sacrifice other goals to suppress inflation. The result was that these presidents did not devote to inflation the time or rigor required to develop an independent judgment as to what could or should be done. Instead, they went along with what seemed most convenient.

Imagining himself the heir to Franklin Roosevelt, Lyndon Johnson had embarked on his Great Society. It included more than Medicare, Medicaid and "the war on poverty."* He wanted to rebuild cities, transportation systems and much more. (Both the Department of Housing and Urban Development and the Department of Transportation were created under Johnson.) Vietnam and inflation threatened Johnson's ambitions. From the end of 1964 to early 1968, the number of U.S. troops in Vietnam rose from 23,000 to more than 500,000. The war's costs competed directly with funding for the Great Society. Johnson understood the dilemma, writing later: "[I]f I left the woman I really loved—the Great Society—in order to get involved with that bitch of war on the other side of the world, then I would lose everything at home. All my programs. All

---

* Medicare and Medicaid were, respectively, government health insurance for the elderly and the poor. Congress created both in 1965.

my hopes . . . all my dreams." Inflation, in this analogy, was at best a bad date. Combating it by slowing the economy would shrink tax revenues (inflation was a time-honored way of paying for wars) and further erode Johnson's popularity.[17]

When Nixon and then Carter entered the White House, their political agendas didn't include controlling inflation. Nixon's great ambitions were in foreign policy and politics. He wanted to disengage honorably from Vietnam and later decided to open relations with China. He also hoped, as historian Allen Matusow of Rice University has observed, to engineer the first major political realignment since the Great Depression. Republicans could become the majority party, Nixon thought, by fusing their traditional base of economic conservatives with disenchanted southerners and blue-collar Democrats who'd become estranged from liberalism by the lifestyle, sexual and racial upheavals of the 1960s. Carter was determined to erase the taint of Watergate, restore rapid economic growth and—later—mediate peace between Israel and Egypt. For both men, inflation was an annoying distraction They paid attention only when there was no alternative.[18]

Nixon's initial economic policy, dubbed "gradualism," promised to reduce inflation almost painlessly. In 1967, Johnson had finally proposed a temporary increase of income taxes, which Congress reluctantly passed in 1968. When Nixon became president in 1969, the budget had moved into surplus for the only time since the early 1960s (and, as it turned out, the only time until 1998). Interest rates had also risen. The idea of "gradualism" was that a slight economic slowdown and the resulting "slack" (unemployed workers, spare industrial capacity) would gradually reduce wage and prices pressures.

Unemployment, which was 3.4 percent when Nixon moved into the White House, would rise to just above 4 percent—slightly more than "full employment." Competition among workers and companies for jobs and sales would curb inflation without a recession. Most Americans would hardly notice. Nixon's economists expected these good results in 1969 and 1970. What happened was different. In 1970, there was a mild recession. Unemployment reached 6 percent by December. Inflation barely diminished. It was 6.2 percent in 1969 and 5.6 percent in 1970.

To the public and Nixon, "gradualism" was a flop. In the 1970 elections, Republicans didn't make the gains Nixon had wanted (they gained three Senate seats and lost nine in the House). "Without the economic drag, [we] would have carried both the House and Senate," he told White House aide H. R. Haldeman after the election. Discouraged, Nixon switched Treasury secretaries at the end of 1970, replacing David Kennedy, a mild-mannered banker, with John Connally, the flamboyant ex-governor of Texas, a conservative Democrat who had been in the same car with John Kennedy when he was assassinated. Nixon saw Connally as a partner in building a new majority and even imagined him as his presidential successor. Connally's first job was to counteract harsh Democratic attacks. To embarrass Nixon, the Democratic Congress had passed legislation in August 1970 empowering the president to impose wage-price controls. No one expected Nixon to use the power, because the president and his advisers publicly opposed controls. Nixon's dislike for controls was visceral. During World War II, he had served with the Office of Price Administration—an agency that oversaw wartime controls—and came to detest the rationing and inefficiencies of wage-price regulation. For Democrats, the law was a public relations sledgehammer. It allowed them to attack Nixon for the slowdown's failure to suppress inflation; therefore, they could also hold him responsible for excessive unemployment.[19]

Nixon ultimately stunned—and delighted—the nation when he announced a ninety-day wage-price freeze on August 15, 1971, as part of a program to let the dollar depreciate and abandon the commitment to pay foreign government gold for the dollars they held. The decision simply disregarded the administration's previous hostility toward controls. In June, Connally had announced the four "no"s of administration policy: no controls; no wage-price board (that is, no voluntary controls); no tax cut to stimulate the economy; and no increased federal spending (for the same purpose). With hindsight, it's easy to think that Nixon adopted controls for crass political reasons: He wanted to cut inflation so he could stimulate job creation and ensure his reelection in 1972. That's certainly part of what happened. Both the federal budget and Federal Reserve policy turned expansionary in late 1971. By June 1972, unemployment had dropped to 5.5 percent from 6.1 percent in August 1971. Nixon—consumed by political calculation and obsessed with being reelected—understood the implications. He surely intended controls to improve his prospects.

Still, his reversal was not entirely an act of political self-interest. In a broader sense, he merely surrendered to the overwhelming forces of public opinion and conventional wisdom. Nixon "abandoned gradualism only after practically every prominent Democrat, most professional economists, a growing number of Republicans, much of the corporate community, [his own economists] and the public demanded he do so," wrote historian Matusow. One poll found that 75 percent of the public approved; only a short time earlier 73 percent had disapproved of his economic policies. In the end, imposing controls helped him win reelection, but when they were removed—after becoming unpopular and unmanageable—inflation exploded into double digits.[20]

Considering the history—Nixon's and, earlier, Johnson's failure to control inflation—the wonder is that the Carter administration fared even worse. But it did. By early 1980, inflation was running almost 15 percent annually. The explanation was not mysterious: "Full employment" remained the obsession. Blaming inflation's worst outbursts on the Vietnam War and oil price explosions—onetime events that exonerated normal economic policies—resulted in a ruinous complacency. Just before Carter took office, the nonpartisan Congressional Budget Office (CBO) issued a report titled *The Disappointing Recovery*. It expressed concern that the unemployment rate might exceed 6.5 percent by late 1978. It suggested policies (tax cuts, spending increases) to improve job prospects. Carter was considering just such a "stimulus" plan. Inflation was then about 6 percent, but the report did not discuss how it might be reduced. At a congressional hearing, CBO director Alice Rivlin said that Carter's "stimulus" program would have only a "fairly small" effect on inflation. The CBO forecast that by the end of 1978, inflation would be between 3.8 percent and 5.8 percent.[21]

All these forecasts were wildly inaccurate. By the end of 1977—before Carter's "stimulus" program had had much effect—unemployment was down to 5.4 percent and inflation was up to almost 7 percent. But both Rivlin's view and Carter's policies reflected mainstream thinking. At the same hearing, Paul McCracken, the first chairman of Nixon's Council of Economic Advisers, supported a "stimulus" program, arguing that the inflation risk would be "acceptable." Later, testifying before another congressional committee, Reginald Jones, then the head of General Electric, was even more emphatic in favoring a "stimulus" program. "[T]here is so much slack in the economy right now that we believe a fairly sizable program of permanent tax cuts and job oriented programs would not cause unmanageable inflation or deficits [but] rather would strengthen the economy against future inflation and deficits," he said.

IV

Looking back, it's tempting to assign culpability for all these serial blunders. Certainly, the presidents, economists and advisers who shaped economic policy from the 1960s through the late 1970s could not take much pride in their handiwork. The nation's economic performance steadily deteriorated. Every president from Kennedy through Carter contributed to the failure with one possible exception: Gerald Ford. Almost from the moment of Nixon's resignation in August 1974—disgraced and facing impeachment over Watergate—Ford focused on inflation. In September, he convened a White House conference on inflation, which he declared "our domestic enemy number one." The White House issued WIN buttons (for "Whip Inflation Now"), though these later inspired scorn because they coincided with an unfolding recession that proved to be unexpectedly harsh.★ But the recession did reduce inflation from 12.3 percent in 1974 to 4.9 percent in 1976. Ford's head was in the right place, and a second Ford administration might have cut it further. We will never know.

But it is misleading to blame individuals, when the real source of error lay in prevailing doctrines. It was the power of ideas that ordained failure, not the shortcomings of individuals. All these presidents and their advisers embraced the same basic concepts that, despite modest differences and disagreements, inevitably led them to make bad decisions in the name of a good cause. Different people adopting the same ideas would have ended up in virtually the same place. For the political logic of the "new economics" virtually guaranteed inflation that would, almost automatically, become too great to be halted painlessly.

The impatience to get unemployment as low as possible was fatal. Politicians would demand policies that would promote job creation until there was a reason to stop—the outbreak of serious inflation being the only obvious limit. If that point were 4 percent unemployment, economists' first estimate of "full employment," then fine. If it was lower, better. Economists admitted that their estimates were imprecise, leaving considerable leeway to probe until actual limits

---

★ At the September 5, 1974, White House conference, for example, Otto Eckstein—a Harvard professor, former member of Johnson's CEA and head of a major forecasting firm—predicted that unemployment would peak "a little beyond 6.5 percent." In fact, the peak was 9 percent in May 1975.[22]

were reached. The fact that unemployment tended to decline before inflation rose (reflecting a "lag" between tight labor markets and higher wages) only made the policy more hazardous. The obsession with lowering unemployment meant that, even if there had been no Vietnam War or oil price explosion, there would have been high inflation. The outcome was built into the system.

Everything rested on an illusion, the Phillips Curve: the notion that there was a fixed trade-off between unemployment and inflation. If true, that meant a society could consciously decide how much of one or the other it wanted. If, say, 4 percent unemployment and 4 percent inflation seemed superior to 5 percent unemployment and 3 percent inflation, then a society could choose the former. The trouble was that the trade-off didn't exist, except for brief periods. In an important paper in 1968, economist Milton Friedman explained that, if government tried to hold unemployment below some "natural rate," the result would simply be accelerating inflation. Economist Edmund Phelps of Columbia University developed the concept almost simultaneously. By their logic, governmental efforts to push unemployment down to unrealistic levels were doomed to failure.

Lower unemployment would occur for a brief period because workers didn't anticipate higher inflation. Their wage demands would lag behind price increases, making labor cheaper in "real" terms and causing companies to hire more people. Once workers recognized higher inflation—that is, once their inflation expectations shifted—they would demand higher wages, reducing the incentive of firms to engage in extra hiring. Unemployment would then return to its "natural" level, except that inflation would now also be higher. The only way that government could hold unemployment below the "natural rate" would be to increase inflation indefinitely, so that workers were repeatedly fooled about their wages.★ Even targeting the "natural rate," Friedman warned, was difficult, because it couldn't be accurately estimated in advance and might change over time, being affected by workforce characteristics (age, education levels, attitudes) and laws and institutions (minimum wages, unemployment insurance). A country with generous unemployment insurance, for example, might have a higher "natural rate" than one with stingy insurance: Unemployed workers in the first would have less reason to take new jobs they didn't like.

What would actually happen in the 1970s—the constant acceleration of inflation—was all foretold by Friedman and Phelps. But good ideas could not spontaneously displace the bad until actual experience demonstrated the differences, especially because the bad ideas were politically more attractive than the good ones. By the end of the 1970s, inflation was mainly a political and psychological phenomenon that could be reversed only if the underlying politics and psychology changed. Americans—workers, shoppers, small business owners and corporate executives—came to believe that inflation, as much as they hated it, was a semipermanent way of life. Government wouldn't suppress it, because doing so would involve large, politically unacceptable social costs—higher unemployment, lower

---

★ Economists have renamed the "natural rate" the NAIRU, which stands for the "non-accelerating inflation rate of unemployment"—a baffling label that attests to economists' ability to devise exclusionary jargon that confuses almost all noneconomists.

incomes and profits. As long as people believed this, meaning as long as they harbored high inflationary expectations, they would act in ways that made an acceleration of inflation self-fulfilling. Workers would seek wage increases compensating for past inflation, plus a little more, and companies would meet these expectations, because they believed they could pass the higher labor costs along in higher prices. Inflation would feed on itself, and if government permitted it by creating ever-larger amounts of money, it would be unstoppable.

3

THE MONEY CONNECTION

I

A mong Washington's prominent public landmarks, the Federal Reserve is not in the first rank. Located near the Lincoln Memorial and constructed in classical style, its plain-looking exterior belies an elegant interior of marbled lobbies and staircases, befitting its role as the symbolic citadel of the American economy. Through its influence on interest rates and the money supply, "the Fed"—as it's colloquially known—was a prime accomplice in the Great Inflation. Its responsibility stemmed from the truism that all major inflations involve "too much money chasing too few goods." America's worst peacetime inflation occurred because the government, through the Fed, created too much money.

The Fed didn't light the fire, but it did supply the oxygen that kept the fire burning, and once it refused to supply the oxygen, the fire diminished. Without the Fed's acquiescence, the Great Inflation could not have occurred.

It was Milton Friedman who popularized the argument that inflation "is always and everywhere a monetary phenomenon in the sense that it can be produced only by a more rapid increase in the quantity of money than in [economic] output." Friedman's dictum merely restated the classical "quantity theory of money," which dates at least to the Scottish philosopher David Hume (1711–1776). The basic concept is intuitively obvious, as a simple example shows. Suppose a society produces ten widgets and has a money supply of $10. Then the price of each widget is $1. If the money supply doubles to $20 and the country still produces ten widgets, each widget fetches $2. The result is 100 percent inflation.* For minor inflations, there may be other causes: demand outrunning supply (because, say, population temporarily grows faster than food production) or monopolistic business and labor practices. But Friedman's dictum applies to all inflations exceeding a few percentage points annually, and it certainly applied to America's. As commonly defined in the 1950s and 1960s, the money supply consisted of circulating cash and checking

---

* In this illustration, I have ignored the turnover of money, what economists call "velocity." The same money can be—and is—used to finance many transactions. Although velocity is important for technical debates about economic policy, it merely modifies—and does not disprove—the quantity theory of money. In general, higher inflation increases money velocity. People spend their money more rapidly because they don't want to hold on to something whose value is constantly cheapening.

accounts in banks. In the 1950s, money-supply growth of 23 percent mainly accommodated the needs of an expanding economy. By contrast, growth was 44 percent in the 1960s and 78 percent in the 1970s. Inflation worsened accordingly.[1]

Just why the Fed acceded to double-digit inflation is a central part of our story. The most poignant explanation came from Arthur Burns, Fed chairman from 1970 to 1978. When Nixon appointed him, Burns was one of the nation's most respected economists. A pipe-smoking former professor at Columbia University, he was considered the preeminent expert on U.S. business cycles and had headed the National Bureau of Economic Research, a prestigious scholarly body. Despite these impressive credentials, Burns's performance as Fed chairman was dismal. During his tenure, inflation rose from 5.9 percent to a peak of 11 percent in 1975. In 1978, it was still 7.7 percent. The economy also suffered its then-worst post–World War II recession from 1973 to 1975. Burns knew that his reputation had been tarnished, perhaps ruined. In September 1979, he gave a long lecture called "The Anguish of Central Banking." It was a defense, an apology and an effort to rescue his legacy. ("Central banks" refer to government-created banks, like the Fed, that generally regulate a nation's money and financial system.)[2]

Burns conceded that the Fed "had the power to abort inflation at its incipient stage fifteen years ago or at any later point." If inflation is too much money chasing too few goods, the Fed could have fought it by supplying less money. Indeed, the Fed had stepped "hard on the monetary brake" in 1966, 1969 and 1974, Burns said. Unfortunately, the initial effects were a slower economy and higher unemployment—cardinal sins in the new political climate. So each time the Fed had relented too quickly before inflation was broken, bowing to criticism from Congress and the administration. The Fed couldn't, Burns argued, defy public opinion. Post–World War II prosperity, he said, had "strengthened the public's expectation of progress." The Employment Act of 1946 required maximum employment. Congress had created new social programs (food stamps, Medicare) and expanded old ones (Social Security). The Fed had to provide the money to pay for the new benefits. The Fed could not flout "the will of Congress to which it was responsible." The Fed's role in fostering inflation was, therefore, "subsidiary." The real villains, claimed Burns, were "philosophic and political currents" that created inflationary pressures. Defeating inflation required a new "political environment."

There was much truth to Burns's account. The social and political climate had shifted; the Fed could not stay completely aloof. Although the Fed is nominally "independent" and its members are not elected, they cannot regularly defy broad public expectations. They must either do what government leaders want or persuade them that the Fed's policies are desirable, even if unpleasant. Barring this, the Fed's "independence" is vulnerable. The seven Fed governors are nominated by the president and approved by the Senate; the selection and approval (or disapproval) of new appointees allow political leaders to register dissatisfaction and exercise influence. If that fails, the president and Congress can curb the Fed's power by modifying its legal status. So Burns's thesis was half correct. What was misleading was his implication that the Fed was dragged against its will into fostering inflation. In reality, it was complicit. The Fed shared and followed the (mistaken) beliefs about managing economic growth and achieving "full employment." Only belatedly did it recognize its errors.

The process by which the Fed influences the economy is akin to printing money but, in practice, is slightly more complicated. To increase the money supply, the Fed buys U.S. Treasury securities from banks and other dealers. The Fed deposits the money to pay for them in the bank accounts of the sellers. This is new money—in effect, created out of thin air. Banks and other sellers now have more money. If banks wish to convert these new deposits into currency (paper money), they can get dollar bills from the Fed. One way or another, banks have more to lend. Credit is more ample; the money supply expands. Short-term interest rates tend to decline. To reverse the process—squeeze money and credit—the Fed sells Treasury securities to banks. Presto, money goes out of circulation as banks make payment for these securities to the Fed. Banks have less to lend; credit availability shrinks; interest rates tend to rise.★ What matters is how these powers are exercised and for what purposes.

We now think of the Fed as a bastion of economists. Ben Bernanke, the present Fed chairman, once taught at Princeton. His predecessor, Alan Greenspan, was a private economic forecaster. Many other economists have become Fed governors, and the Fed's huge economic staff churns out a constant stream of studies. But this was not always so. For decades, bankers and business executives dominated. William McChesney Martin, Jr., Fed chairman from 1951 to

---

★ As a technical matter, the changes in deposits are usually made in the accounts that commercial banks have at one of the twelve regional Federal Reserve banks.

1970, was so skeptical of economic forecasts that he forbade the staff from making them until 1966. Fed officials saw their role as preventing bank panics and policing credit markets. The Fed did share central banks' traditional hostility to inflation; Martin said the Fed's job was to take away the punch bowl just as the party gets going. But the Fed also strove to stabilize interest rates so that the government could more easily sell its bonds. To some extent, these goals conflicted. "Until the 1970s, the Treasury sold all notes and bonds at fixed interest rates, and the Fed followed an 'even keel' policy, holding rates fixed during the weeks surrounding [debt offerings]," writes economist Allan Meltzer of Carnegie Mellon University, author of a history of the Fed. The Fed's mission changed as economic ideas changed.[3]

The mid-1960s were a watershed, when the Fed's orientation shifted. Pressured from without and from within, it gradually adopted the ambitions and analytical framework of the "new economics." In 1965, Sherman Maisel, a professor at the University of California at Berkeley, became the first academic economist to be appointed a governor since Adolph Miller (1914–36). Staff turnover elevated many younger Keynesian economists to positions of influence. In making policy, the Fed gradually deemphasized financial conditions and adopted the Keynesian goals of aiming for maximum performance. If the economy seemed below potential output and full employment, the Fed would try to narrow the gap by reducing interest rates and increasing money growth. If the economy seemed above its targets—risking higher inflation—then the Fed could raise interest rates and tighten money growth. The Fed turned "activist," says Athanasios Orphanides, a former Fed economist who exhaustively studied the period. It would try to steer the economy along its most productive path. The prevailing analogy was that an economy that had ample "slack"—meaning unemployed workers and spare industrial capacity—could not generate higher "demand-pull" inflation. People still looking for jobs would hold down wages; companies competing for extra sales would hold down prices. "Most of the economics profession was convinced that the model worked fairly well," said Orphanides.[4]

But, as we now know, it didn't. In targeting "full employment" and "potential output," the Fed consistently overestimated both. As Orphanides has shown, the errors were huge. Before 1977, the Fed reckoned "full employment" to be an unemployment rate between 4 percent and 4.5 percent. In fact, later estimates put the actual figure closer to 6 percent. Below that threshold, the labor market would turn increasingly inflationary as employers bid for scarce workers. The Fed also overestimated productivity growth: gains in output from greater efficiency. For most of the 1970s, economists in and out of government assumed continuation of the productivity growth of the early postwar decades, generally 2.5 percent to 3 percent annually. In fact, productivity growth for much of the late 1970s barely exceeded 1 percent a year.

The consequences of these mistakes were devastating. All during these years, the Fed's policies were too expansionary. The "slack" in labor and unused capacity assumed to exist often didn't. In early 1976, as the economy emerged from the deep 1973–75 recession, the economy was reckoned to have an "output gap"—aka, "slack," or the difference of what it was producing and what it might—of 12 percent. This was massive; later estimates put the output gap at a modest 2 percent. In early 1979, the output gap was estimated at about 2 percent; later estimates indicated there was none. In effect, the Fed was deliberately driving the economy into territory that, if reached, would generate ever-higher inflation. The Fed is often said to "step on the accelerator" to increase economic growth and "apply the brakes" to slow growth. Too often in the 1970s, the Fed stepped on the accelerator because it believed it was on an economic super-highway. There was little danger in speeding up. In reality, its blurred vision meant that it was actually speeding along a dirt road, littered with gravel and boulders. If it didn't apply the brakes, there would be a crack-up.[5]

When inflation inevitably worsened, the Fed reacted—acknowl-edging that it had left the highway—by tightening money and credit. Slowdowns or recessions (those of 1966, 1969–70 and 1973–75) ensued. But unfailingly, these responses were inadequate, because (as Burns noted) they were abandoned too quickly. Inflation abated briefly, and then the errors were repeated. It is possible to argue that if the Fed had gotten its assumptions about "full employment" and "potential output" correct, it could have operated successfully with the same basic economic model. Policy would have been less expan-sive and more restrictive. The economy would have been less infla-tionary and more stable, as a study by Orphanides and Fed economist John C. Williams suggests. Superficially, the blunders seem mostly technical: the economic equivalent of a bridge collapsing because engineers miscalculated its load capacity.[6]

But this verdict is too narrow. The larger truth is that all the er-rors were in the same direction—in the direction of trying to accel-erate economic growth and achieve "full employment." The Fed's mistakes reflected the powerful political and intellectual imperatives of the time, which reinforced one another. What was politically convenient was also rationalized intellectually. The Fed told itself that it could accomplish what political leaders and the public wanted it to accomplish. It is necessary to understand why the Fed was so vulnerable to these new pressures. There were many reasons, the most basic of which is almost always overlooked.

II

It was the changed nature of American money. Inflationary policies became possible only because the gold standard, which prevailed for most of American history, had collapsed during the Great Depression of the 1930s. Since the Depression, the United States has operated under a new money system—"fiat money," created by government—that differed fundamentally from everything that had preceded it. Although the Federal Reserve was at the center of the change, the new circumstances and their full implications were poorly grasped. In earlier periods, the ambitions of the "new economics" would have run afoul of the gold standard, which limited the amount of money that could be created. Paper money had to be backed by gold reserves. But because the gold standard was implicated in causing the Depression—the greatest economic calamity in U.S. history—it was discredited and abandoned. Its destructive vices obscured its virtues. Once the limits it imposed were gone, new limits were needed, but the people in charge only barely recognized the need and had no experience in creating them.

This transformation of American money is a little-known tale that, aside from its inherent interest, is crucial to understanding the inflationary experience. Economic texts tell us that money serves three roles. Most important, it is a means of buying and selling (a "medium of exchange"). This obviates the need for barter and promotes specialization: farmers, factory workers, doctors and engineers can concentrate on what they do best, because they can buy whatever else they need. Specialization, made possible by money, is the basic source of economic progress. Money is also a way of pricing (a "unit of account") and of preserving wealth (a "store of value"). All of these roles require trust. People must believe that whatever serves as money has some predictable and enduring value. In many ways, the history of money is an unending tension between creating trust and pursuing other goals—paying armies; mediating between debtors and creditors; promoting economic growth and regulating business cycles—that may erode trust.

Before the Great Depression, American money was a constantly shifting hodgepodge of gold and silver coin (known as "specie"), paper currencies and bank deposits. For most of this time, paper currencies were supported by gold, meaning that someone with a $10 paper note could go into a commercial bank or an office of the U.S. Treasury and exchange it for $10 in gold coin. At times, silver also backed currencies; we were then on a "bimetallic standard." Tying paper money to precious metals was thought to check the human tendency to print too much currency and, thereby, depreciate its value. The faith was almost theological. Listen to Hugh McCullough, the Treasury secretary following the Civil War: "[G]old and silver are the only true measure of value. They are the necessary regulators of trade [meaning business]. I have myself no more doubt that these metals were prepared by the almighty for this very purpose, than I have that iron and coal were prepared for the purpose in which they are being used."[7]

The reliance on gold and silver was written into the Constitution and reflected the unhappy experience with paper money at the state level under the Articles of Confederation and in the Revolution, when "continentals" issued by the Continental Congress to pay soldiers and suppliers were printed in such quantities that they quickly became worthless. The Constitution reserved to the national government a monopoly to mint gold and silver coin; states were prohibited from printing paper money or designating anything aside from gold and silver as "legal tender"—that is, lawful payment to fulfill contracts. Despite these strictures, paper money flourished in the nineteenth century. At first, it was issued by state-chartered banks, which (not being states) seemed uncovered by the constitutional prohibition. These bank notes were usually backed by gold or silver; if asked, banks were obliged to exchange specie for their paper. The Civil War ended the use of state bank notes when Congress created national banks that could issue "national bank notes," also backed by gold. But Congress also issued $450 million in "greenbacks," paper money not backed by gold, to pay for the war. (The Constitution, though implying the federal government should not issue paper money, did not expressly ban it.)[8]

What was termed the "money question" in the nineteenth century was often at the center of politics and covered much of what we now call "economic policy": how to promote growth and stability and how to distribute the economy's gains. Money, banking and economic expansion were interconnected, because banks issued paper money and made loans—and both money and credit affected economic expansion. Before the Civil War, proponents of "hard money" of gold and silver coin (most prominently, President Andrew Jackson) argued that paper currencies fostered speculation, which led to bad loans, bank panics (depositors tried to redeem their money in gold—and there wasn't enough to go around) and then depressions. On the other hand, paper money was more convenient than coin and, when not overissued, seemed to stimulate business and commerce. As early as 1723, a young Ben Franklin noticed that when the colony of Pennsylvania issued paper money, employment and construction improved.[9]

One drawback of a gold-backed system was that government had (by design) only a limited influence over money and credit conditions. Both responded to the metal's availability. When gold was discovered in California in 1849, the money supply automatically increased. If Europe had a poor harvest, U.S. grain sales abroad would bring in more gold, received in payment for American wheat. If Europe had bumper crops, gold inflows would slacken—or there would be outflows as Americans paid for imports. Government could influence money conditions only by supplementing gold with silver or by being more or less restrictive with paper money. There was much arbitrariness. After the Civil War, complaints intensified because population and economic production expanded more rapidly than money. Prices declined. Farmers felt oppressed, arguing that falling crop prices reduced their incomes and made it harder for them to repay debts. From 1881 to 1892, a bushel of wheat dropped from $1.15 to 79 cents. The money farmers borrowed had to be repaid in dearer, not cheaper, dollars.*[10]

The discontent climaxed in the 1896 presidential election, when William Jennings Bryan, the Democratic nominee, argued for more silver coinage to supplement the scarce supply of gold. His speech, regarded as one of the great masterpieces of American oratory, captured the prevailing passions:

> You come to us and tell us that the great cities are in favor of the gold standard; we reply that the great cities rest upon our broad and fertile prairies. Burn down your cities and leave our farms, and your cities will spring up again as if by magic; but destroy our farms and the grass will grow in the streets of every city in the country.... Having behind us the producing masses of this nation and the world ... we will answer their demand for a gold standard by saying to them: You shall not press down upon the brow of labor this crown of thorns, you shall not crucify mankind upon a cross of gold.[11]

William McKinley won that election and, just coincidentally, new gold discoveries and refining technologies expanded the country's supply. Unfortunately, scarce gold was not the nation's only money

---

* There is a scholarly debate about whether falling prices actually made farmers worse off, because some of their costs (farm tools, clothes) were also falling. However this debate is resolved, it does not alter the reality of agrarian discontent. Many farmers felt they were worse off.

problem. Under the national banking system, money was "inelastic" in that it didn't automatically increase to meet seasonal needs or the temporary demands created by bank panics—when depositors wanted either gold or currency. The main seasonal demands were agricultural. Cash and credit needs peaked in the spring (when farmers needed funds for planting) and the fall (when buyers needed funds to pay for harvested crops). Seasonal credit demands and financial panics were sometimes connected. If rural banks withdrew their deposits from New York City banks, those banks would cut their overnight loans ("call loans"), which were widely used to buy stocks. This could trigger a fall in stock prices, as investors and speculators sold to repay their debts. Bank runs could occur for many reasons (bad loans, shady management, rumors or sheer fear). Major bank panics occurred in 1873, 1884, 1893 and 1907. They could cause or worsen economic slumps if depositors suffered losses and banks cut lending.[12]

No bank can cope alone with an unchecked panic, because no bank has enough ready cash (whether gold or paper money) to repay all depositors at once. The only way to stop a panic is to pay many depositors quickly enough to convince the others that the bank is sound—and that they need not withdraw their money. The national banking system had no official mechanism to provide these emergency supplies of cash. During panics, bankers sometimes improvised. They cooperated to create synthetic cash ("clearinghouse receipts"), which they would accept among themselves. After the panic of 1907, Congress established the Federal Reserve in 1913 to provide a safety net that would meet the extra demands for cash created by panics and normal seasonal swings. When pressed for funds, commercial banks could borrow from one of the twelve regional Federal Reserve banks, receiving a new form of paper currency, Federal Reserve notes. Still, the Federal Reserve System remained anchored to gold. The Fed had to maintain a gold reserve equal to at least 40 percent of the outstanding Federal Reserve notes. It could not create infinite amounts of currency.

The gold standard did not effectively end until the 1930s. Like almost everyone, Franklin Roosevelt didn't know what caused the Depression, but he was determined not to wait idly on events. He feared that gold imposed a straitjacket on the banking system and credit creation. If Americans hoarded gold, the economic crisis might deepen. On March 6, 1933, two days after his inauguration, Roosevelt barred banks from paying it to depositors. On April 5, he outlawed "hoarding"—Americans had to redeem all gold coins above $100. "They came with little bags, briefcases, paper bundles, boxes or bulging pockets," reported one newspaper. Roosevelt also devalued the dollar in terms of gold. For years, it had been $20.67 an ounce; the government would buy or sell gold at that price. On January 30, 1934, he set a price of $35 an ounce for foreigners. In practice, the nearly 70 percent devaluation meant that the gold backing for the paper currency was so ample that money and credit could expand without encountering legal restrictions. After that, gold no longer played a major role in guiding the U.S. economy. The remaining connections were progressively severed.*[13]

---

* For some decades, there remained requirements that the Fed have a specified "gold cover"—that is, gold backing for a given portion of the paper currency. But these restrictions were consistently lowered and

American money had undergone a fundamental transformation. For our story, this upheaval was fateful. The gold standard was hardly ideal. Had it remained, the U.S. economy and those of other countries would probably have fared worse after World War II than they did. Growing economies need more money and credit. The gold standard limited money and credit, reflecting the metal's rigid and unpredictable supply. But this vice was also, to some extent, a virtue. It imposed limits on money and credit creation that prevented runaway inflation. The removal of these limits created an entirely new situation, requiring new understandings and obligations. Inflation would no longer control itself. It had to be controlled—and so the ideas, beliefs, motives and behaviors of people charged with controlling it mattered. They had to understand why preventing it was important and that it was their job to do so. These responsibilities got lost.

III

They were submerged by both economic theory and practical politics. On the one hand, the Kennedy-Johnson economists—and most of the early Keynesians—regarded Federal Reserve policy

---

finally eliminated. Likewise, the United States as part of the Bretton Woods agreement in 1944 pledged to redeem dollars for gold at $35 per ounce. This promise exerted slight influence on American policies in the 1950s and 1960s. President Nixon renounced it in 1971. (See pages 98–99 for details.)

(what we call "monetary policy") as playing a subordinate and supporting role to shifts in government taxes and spending (what we call "fiscal policy"). Although the two would work in tandem, monetary policy would take its cues from changes in fiscal policy. Implicitly, this discouraged and devalued independent thinking and action. What also discouraged independent action were the repeated efforts—all ultimately failures—to suppress inflation through various forms of voluntary and mandatory wage and price controls. Presidents Johnson, Nixon and Carter all tried this approach. The basic idea was simple: If wages and prices wouldn't stay down on their own, then they could be cajoled, pressured or ordered down. Whether intended or not, these efforts relieved the Federal Reserve of the prime responsibility for preventing or reversing inflation.

Controls' failure should have surprised no one. In a complex economy—and a democratic society—it is difficult to devise rules that cover all situations and simultaneously seem fair and practical. Controls have to be flexible enough to accommodate economic realities (some prices vary seasonally; imports can't be covered, and so forth) but not so flexible that they seem capricious. The dilemma: If exceptions to the controls aren't made, they may collapse economically (if some prices are set too low, for example, shortages will result); but too many exceptions may cause the controls to collapse politically. People see their wages or prices as fixed while those of others aren't. Feeling victimized or suspecting favoritism, they then defy or evade the controls. With dropping public support, controls need intrusive enforcement; but that seems heavy-handed—a police state—and invites a popular backlash.

Historically, the United States had resorted to compulsory controls only in wars, notably World Wars I and II and the Korean War. In war, the problem is straightforward: The surge of military needs—for equipment, fuel, soldiers—requires that substantial production and labor be diverted from civilian to defense use. Somehow, government must outbid civilians to buy what it wants. The simplest way is to raise taxes and subtract directly from consumer purchasing power. Another way is to borrow heavily, raising interest rates and crowding out private borrowing. A final way is to print (or create) money—inflation. Because government spends the money first, it buys at lower prices; as the money circulates, consumer prices rise and living standards fall. Prices for scarce goods rise. Given these unpopular choices, government controls—rationing and limits on wages and prices—can be an attractive alternative. Government restricts civil production directly and holds down inflation by legal restrictions. In wartime, there's a clear political and moral rationale for controls, as economist Hugh Rockoff has noted. If prices alone allocate limited civilian goods, the heaviest burdens fall on the poor, because they can least afford the higher prices.[14]

In his *Drastic Measures: A Study of Wage and Price Controls in the United States,* Rockoff concluded that the controls worked reasonably well in both world wars. They restrained inflation without spawning massive inefficiencies or widespread public anger. The wars themselves explained this success. Patriotism counted. People tolerated restrictions and anomalies that, in peacetime, would have provoked outrage. In World War II, meat, gasoline, clothes, sugar, coffee and some other consumer goods were rationed. The War Production Board allocated industrial supplies—steel, copper, aluminum—to factories. Wages were controlled; unions renounced the right to strike. Still, some black markets, notably for meat, developed. Rent controls were sometimes evaded; to get scarce apartments, there were under-the-table payments. Some products were adulterated. Of twenty candy bars examined by *Consumer Reports,* nineteen shrank in size from 1939 to 1943; the disguised price increase was 23 percent. After the war, pent-up demand meant that the selective removal of price controls resulted in huge price increases. Freed from the no-strike pledge, unions sought to catch up with prices and capture what they saw as excessive profits. In 1946, strikes occurred in the auto, steel and coal industries, among others. By November, President Truman ended controls; without popular support, they were unworkable.[15]

The trouble with peacetime controls is that they face all the wartime vices without any of the wartime virtues. They are still complicated and cumbersome, but they lack patriotic props. The controls—voluntary and mandatory—of the 1960s and 1970s also had a fundamentally different purpose. It was not to reallocate production "fairly"; it was to maximize production and employment without the bother of inflation. To succeed, these controls required almost inhuman self-restraint—companies, workers and unions had to renounce their immediate self-interest in raising prices and wages while tolerating the mistakes, inconsistencies and absurdities of government regulations and bureaucrats.

The first precursor of controls emerged in the 1962 report of the Council of Economic Advisers, which advocated wage-price "guideposts." The focus was on unionized industries—steel, autos, airlines, trucking—usually dominated by a few firms. Unions (it was said) could exact big wage increases that companies could then pass along in higher prices. This market power could produce modest inflation even if the economy wasn't at "full employment." The guideposts aimed to "mobilize public opinion and government persuasion to bring wage and price decisions of high-powered labor and business units into closer conformity with competitive behavior," Walter Heller later wrote. Translation: The threat of bad publicity would substitute for genuine competition. In its 1964 report, the CEA fixed a number to the concept—3.2 percent. Businesses (the argument went) could raise wages 3.2 percent a year without raising prices. That represented estimated annual productivity growth. Greater efficiencies would cover the added labor costs without penalizing profits.[16]

President Johnson strove to enforce the guidelines. His delusion was that he could talk businesses and unions out of inflationary behavior so that the problem would just go away. "Jawboning" was the word used at the time, and Johnson was zealous at it. In 1965, the steelworkers and major steel companies—then a dominant industry—were close to an agreement that would have breached the guideposts. A flagrant violation would have rendered the guideposts meaningless. Johnson summoned the negotiators to Washington, provided his own mediators and insisted on wage increases within the guideposts and no price increases. When the negotiators capitulated, he announced his success live on all three major networks (ABC, CBS and NBC). Later, when Bethlehem Steel raised structural steel prices $5 a ton, Johnson attacked its executives as unpatriotic; they backed down. The episode "confirmed the belief in our minds and Johnson's that the President could get anyone to agree and that we could exert enormous influence over labor negotiations in the future," wrote his aide Joseph Califano.[17]

The confidence was misplaced. Even Johnson could not single-handedly persuade and bully the entire economy the way he had the U.S. Senate while majority leader. But he tried. For a while, he became America's firefighter in chief, rushing everywhere to douse inflationary flames. When aluminum companies raised prices in late 1965, he ordered the government to sell aluminum from its strategic stockpiles to break the increases. It did. When copper companies boosted prices later, he released more stockpiles, controlled exports and suspended an import duty. Informed that copper prices were set in world markets and that Chile was a major supplier, Johnson was undaunted. "Find out what will get [the president of Chile] to roll the price back," Johnson commanded. Ultimately, the U.S. copper companies rescinded their price increases. With hindsight, some of his forays seem almost comical. Califano recalled:

Shoe prices went up, so LBJ slapped export controls on hides to increase the supply of leather. Reports that color television sets would sell at high prices came across the wire. Johnson told me to ask RCA's David Sarnoff [RCA was then a major TV manufacturer] to hold them down. Domestic lamb prices rose. LBJ directed [Defense Secretary Robert] McNamara to buy cheaper lamb from New Zealand for the troops in Vietnam. The President told CEA [Council of Economic Advisers] and me to move on household appliances, paper cartons, newsprint, men's underwear, women's hosiery, glass containers, cellulose, [and] air conditioners. . . . When egg prices rose in the spring of 1966 and Agriculture Secretary Orville Freeman told him that not much could be done, Johnson had the Surgeon General issue alerts as to the hazards of cholesterol in eggs.[18]

All this was for naught. The slight effects on individual prices and wages were overwhelmed by the emerging economic boom, which put upward pressure on all wages and prices. By early 1966, unemployment was very low (3.7 percent in February), and businesses were planning a huge 19 percent increase in spending on plants and equipment. In this climate, "jawboning" could not do much. In 1966, average hourly earnings rose 4.5 percent, a big jump over the 3.2 percent average from 1960 to 1965. Johnson might have embraced policies—a tighter budget, higher interest rates—to muffle the boom directly. But he wanted neither higher taxes nor higher interest rates. "Jawboning" seemed an alternative. It ended in August 1966, when a major union, the International Association of Machinists and Aerospace Workers, defied the president and negotiated wage gains of nearly 5 percent. The union's president boasted that the settlement "destroy[s] all existing wage and price guidelines." So it did.★[19]

★ LBJ secretly considered imposing mandatory wage-price controls, despite the absence of explicit legislative authority to do so. He planned to use general authority to declare a national emergency under the 1917 Trading with the Enemy Act. He abandoned the idea, dissuaded by the "vehement opposition expressed by those who had helped administer economic controls during World War II and the Korean War," according to Califano.

Despite this experience, economists actually warmed toward "incomes policies"—another euphemism for controls—in the early 1970s, because such policies seemed the only way to reconcile the promise of "full employment" with acceptable levels of inflation. The rationale shifted subtly. With "guideposts," the emphasis had been on the market power of a few highly visible industries. Now, the aim of "incomes policies"—whether voluntary or mandatory— was to permit the orderly suppression of inflation. Everyone would come down together: workers in wages, businesses in prices. No one would gain an advantage. A common analogy involved spectators at a football game. If a few stood up to get a better view, then almost everyone else would ultimately have to stand up (that was rising inflation). But if everyone sat down simultaneously, then all could enjoy a good view (that was falling inflation). On paper, "incomes policies" seemed imaginative, pragmatic and public-spirited. They would prescribe a gradual decline of price and wage increases. In practice, incomes policies and controls were unworkable. Worse, they falsely suggested that there was an administrative solution to inflation.

Although Keynesian economists championed these proposals, they were not alone. Symbolic of the shift was the conversion of Arthur Burns, by then chairman of the Fed. Once critical of the guideposts, Burns said in a speech in May 1970 that the economic rules had changed and that some "incomes policy" might be necessary. Wages and prices rose in good times but didn't decline much in bad. Despite the then prevailing recession and higher unemployment, he noted, wage increases had barely abated. "Market forces" had lost power. Society's success in ensuring prosperity (given that another depression was not a "serious threat") had fostered "cost-push" inflation. Because the unemployed soon expected to be re-hired, their wage demands didn't decline. Companies stuck with surplus inventories were "less likely to cut prices to clear the shelves—as they once did. Experience has taught them that, in all probability, demand will turn up again." Government intervention was needed to break the spiral.[20]

Burns's conversion reflected a growing yearning for a legalistic remedy to inflation—a hope that it could, with bold leadership, simply be swept away. The shift in mood culminated in Nixon's mandatory controls the next year. The trade-off between high inflation and joblessness seemed to have worsened. Unemployment around 6 percent seemed too high, and yet inflation remained stubborn. In July, a series of labor negotiations resulted in inflationary settlements. Steelworkers won first-year increases of 15 percent, prompting an 8 percent price increase. High inflation had weakened U.S. exports, and a deteriorating trade balance threatened huge gold withdrawals by foreign governments.* Treasury Secretary Connally—like Nixon, an acute political animal—changed his mind about wage-price controls. On August 15, 1971, Nixon simultaneously repudi-

---

* In the summer of 1971, Britain and France converted $800 million into gold, reducing U.S. gold stocks below the symbolically important level of $10 billion. In August, the British indicated they wanted additional assurances that their $3 billion of dollar reserves could be converted at existing exchange rates. Once that became public, the expectation was that demand for gold would overwhelm the limited U.S. supply. In his speech, Nixon closed the gold window.

ated the U.S. pledge to pay gold to foreign governments at $35 an ounce and announced his ninety-day wage-price freeze.[21]

The history of Nixon's controls can be quickly summarized: They worked; they weakened; they collapsed. After the freeze came Phase II, a testimonial to controls' complexity. It had a Price Commission, a Pay Board (to consider wage agreements) and committees for health services, state and local governments and interest and dividends. To focus on the biggest actors, exceptions to the rules soon multiplied. In early 1972, retail firms with less than $100,000 in annual sales were exempted. In January 1973—the election safely past—Nixon started dismantling controls in Phase III. Prices, artificially suppressed, rose rapidly. Overruling most advisers, Nixon imposed a second freeze. It was a disaster. With grain prices set in uncontrolled world markets, food processors were squeezed between rising feed costs and fixed selling prices. There were meat scarcities; cattlemen withheld animals from slaughter. One chicken hatchery drowned 43,000 baby chicks in barrels; that was shown on national television. "It's cheaper to drown 'em than . . . to raise 'em," the manager said. People were shocked. Nixon lifted the freeze on August 12. The remaining controls lapsed in April 1974, when congressional authority expired. In 1974, inflation was 12.3 percent. The harsh 1973–75 recession reflected inflation's erosion of purchasing power.[22]

Carter's efforts to grapple with inflation were as fumbling and futile as Nixon's—perhaps more so. After a series of unsuccessful anti-inflation advisers and programs, Carter embraced an incomes policy in October 1978. It consisted of "voluntary" wage and price standards, whose complexity made Nixon's controls look simple. In the first year, pay increases were not supposed to increase by more than 7 percent; but in the second, the limit was actually raised to a band from 7.5 percent to 9.5 percent. However, many workers (low-income employees and workers covered by existing contracts) were excluded; by one estimate, that was two-fifths of the labor force. Price standards were equally complicated. To strengthen compliance, the administration investigated the pricing behavior of twelve industries, including meatpacking, cement and shoes. A subsequent study by the General Accounting Office concluded that the program had had "no discernible effect on inflation."[23]

Indeed, all the programs of wage and price restraints actually made matters worse by obscuring the essential nature of inflation. The deplored behavior of wage and price increases of firms, unions and workers were not themselves the causes of inflation. They were not spontaneous and independent events—as they were often portrayed—reflecting economic power, selfishness or self-interest. They were, rather, the consequences of lax money and credit policies, centered at the Federal Reserve. Companies and workers were merely defending themselves against and, in some cases, exploiting an inflation that was not of their own making. By the late 1970s, this truth was becoming increasingly apparent. But the prominence given to the various wage and price controls reinforced the political climate in which the Federal Reserve would simply follow the signals provided by the White House and Congress.

Everyone wanted an easy escape from inflation. When Carter announced his wage-price standards in October 1978, he pointedly rejected deploying the traditional economic response to runaway inflation. A recession "would not work," he said. Tom Wicker, a well-known columnist for *The New York Times,* had written in 1977 that the government should relax its "reliance on indirect fiscal and monetary policies" in controlling inflation. Fed governors and their staff had to be affected by this climate. After all, they read the papers, went to receptions and testified before Congress. Not surprisingly, G. William Miller—a businessman who replaced Burns as Fed chairman in 1978—warned of the "limitations of monetary policy as the main bulwark against inflation." As long as that attitude prevailed, there was little chance that anything significant would be done to reduce inflation.[24]

IV

Through its history, the Fed has made many small errors but only two major blunders. The first was permitting the Great Depression; the second was fostering the Great Inflation. It is instructive to compare the two because, although the details differed dramatically, the origins of the failures were remarkably similar. Both ultimately stemmed from mistaken ideas that informed the intellectual and political climate and, thereby, the Fed's policies. The failure was not so much of inept individuals as of the faulty doctrines.

In the 1930s, credit and purchasing power shriveled. From 1929 to 1933, 10,797 banks (42 percent of the nation's total) failed. The fear—and reality—of bank runs caused banks to curb new loans, which worsened the economy and dampened depositors' confidence. The Fed could have minimized the collapse by feeding money and credit into the banking system. It failed to do so, because prevailing economic thinking, governed by the gold standard and the so-called "real bills" doctrine, rationalized timidity. To bolster the economy, the Fed did cut interest rates, but at crucial moments, it refrained from aggressively rescuing the banking system—providing more funds to deter the runs—because it feared that supplying too much money would drain the system of gold. Americans and foreigners would trade in their extra dollars for coins or bullion. Too much paper money would subvert faith in gold.[25]

The "real bills" doctrine reinforced the timidity. A "bill" is a short-term business loan. The "real bills" doctrine held that the Fed should provide credit only for productive loans: loans that increased output of goods and services. But in a collapsing economy, this meant the Fed had little reason to increase money and credit. "The Federal Reserve Act was written on this basis [the "real bills" doctrine]," explained Allan Meltzer, author of an extensive history of the Fed. "It talks about lending to industry, commerce, agriculture. The idea was that if you lent on productive credit, you'd never get inflation because it would provide inventories or capital. The capital would produce more output [and that would prevent prices from rising]." But in the Depression, loan demand had collapsed. The "real bills" doctrine provided no rationale for expanding credit to stimulate recovery. "They [Fed officials] didn't do anything," said Meltzer, "and they thought they were doing the right thing."[26]

The mistake with inflation was almost the exact opposite. The impulse was to push money and credit onto the economy in the hope that the result would be accelerating growth and declining joblessness. This justified more and more money and credit creation. Periodic efforts to suppress inflation were halfhearted and not sustained, just as in the early 1930s the efforts to mitigate the banking crisis were halfhearted and not sustained. By and large, the Fed was aware of the dilemmas, but in both cases, there was a strong bias in one direction or the other. In the 1930s, it was too stingy in supplying money and credit; in the 1960s and 1970s, it was too profligate. Down both paths lay ruin. What ultimately governed their decisions was the conventional economic wisdom.

With inflation, personal political pressure, sometimes crudely applied, pushed the Fed powerfully in the same direction. Presidents knew their political fortunes rested on the economy and were willing to run inflationary risks to preserve low unemployment. After the Fed raised its discount rate in December 1965—against President Johnson's wish—the president privately excoriated Fed chairman Martin at his Texas ranch. "You've got me in a position where you can run a rapier into me, and you've done it," Johnson said. "You went ahead and did something I disapproved of and can affect my entire term here. . . . I just want you to know that's a despicable thing to do." The incident did not embolden Martin to oppose Johnson again. Nixon was only slightly less subtle with Burns. Burns often informed Nixon of Fed decisions—nothing necessarily wrong with that—but Nixon frequently reminded Burns that the president's political fortunes depended heavily on the Fed's ability to increase economic growth. Just after nominating him as Fed chairman in December 1969, the president privately said, "I'm counting on you, Arthur, to keep us out of recession." At an Oval Office meeting in October 1971, barely a year before the 1972 election, Nixon was equally blunt: "I don't want to go out of town fast." No one could have missed the message.[27]

By the late 1970s, the Fed had maneuvered itself into a political and intellectual cul-de-sac. The advent of fiat currency had transformed its chief responsibility into guarding the stability of the nation's currency. Yet both the public at large and the nation's political leaders saw the Fed as an essential instrument in achieving rapid economic growth and maintaining "full employment." The Fed had adhered to economic doctrines that promised to accomplish both these goals, but in practice, it was achieving neither. There seemed to be no way out, and there wouldn't be until both economic ideas and political objectives changed. In the 1980s, that is what happened.

4

A COMPACT OF
CONVICTION

I

We know that double-digit inflation ended. What now seems unremarkable (so unremarkable that people hardly recall it) appeared impossible then. If you had asked Americans in the fall of 1980, with inflation at 11 percent or more, the odds of reducing it to less than 4 percent by the end of 1982, the response would have been a collective howl. High inflation seemed too entrenched for mere mortals to conquer. It had become a staple of daily life. Economic sophisticates and ordinary people alike shared these views. In 1981, interest rates on 30-year Treasury bonds averaged about 13.5 percent; on 30-year fixed-rate mortgages, they were 15 percent. At those rates, bond investors were signaling that they had lost faith in the government's ability to control inflation. They were protecting themselves against future price increases of 10 percent a year or more. The high interest rates would cover the erosion of their original investment and provide an annual return of, say, 2 to 4 percent. That all these sober judgments proved wrong provides a lesson in history.[1]

Broadly speaking, there are two theories of history. One is the "great forces" theory, which holds that changes in science, technology, population and ideas (from religion to politics) are the prime movers. Most people—kings, generals, bankers, presidents and intellectuals—are simply swept along by these strong tides. The other is the "great leader" theory: Leaders take charge; they bend events to their will, for good or ill. Both theories are, of course, correct—but neither is entirely correct. People are mostly hostage to larger forces that they do not fully understand or control. Most political leaders, business executives and intellectuals follow the strongest current, pretending they are charting their own course. But there are moments when history submits to powerful leaders— a Washington, Madison, Napoleon, Lenin or Hitler. They alter history. The subjugation of inflation was, on a smaller scale, one of those moments.

It was principally the accomplishment of two men—Paul Volcker and Ronald Reagan. If either had been absent, the story would have unfolded differently and, from our present perspective, less favorably. High inflation would have remained longer, with greater adverse consequences. Reagan and Volcker, chairman of the Federal Reserve Board from 1979 to 1987, forged an accidental alliance that was largely unspoken, impersonal and misunderstood. Between the two men, there was no particular personal chemistry. Nor was there any explicit bargain—you do this, and I'll do that. Even while the alliance flourished, it sometimes seemed a mirage. Although Reagan supported Volcker, many officials in his administration openly criticized him. But the alliance was genuine, a compact of conviction. Both men believed, mostly as a matter of faith, that high inflation was shredding the fabric of the economy and of American society. The country could not thrive if it persisted. Buttressed by these beliefs, they broke with the past. Each had a role to play, and each played it somewhat independently of the other.

The division of labor was this: Volcker assaulted inflation, and Reagan provided political support. Volcker took a sledgehammer to inflationary expectations. He raised interest rates, tightened credit and triggered the most punishing economic slump since the 1930s.★ In December 1980, banks' "prime rate" (the loan rate for the worthiest business borrowers) hit a record 21.5 percent. Mortgage and bond rates rose in concert. By the summer of 1981, consumers had trouble borrowing for homes, cars and clothes. Many companies couldn't borrow for new investment. "Because of higher interest rates, people can't afford to remodel homes, and I can't afford to carry my inventory," the owner of a small building supply company in Barnesville, Minnesota, told *Time* magazine in early 1982. Industrial production dropped 12 percent from mid-1981 until late 1982. In many industries, declines were steeper. In autos, it was 34 percent

---

★ As noted earlier, the Fed directly affects only one minor interest rate, the so-called Fed funds rates on overnight loans between banks. But its ability to tighten or loosen credit can indirectly affect other rates.

(from June 1981 to January 1982) and in steel it was 56 percent (from August 1981 to December 1982). By 1982, the number of business failures had tripled from 1979. Construction starts of new homes in 1982 were 40 percent below 1979 levels. Worse, unemployment exploded. By late 1982, it was 10.8 percent, which remains a post–World War II record.[2]

Gluts crushed the economy. There were surpluses of almost everything—workers, cars, office space, steel—with the glaring exception of credit. Business and labor had to respond to the unanticipated distress conditions. Facing lower profits, losses or bankruptcy, companies fired workers, cut wage increases and pressed for lower prices on everything they bought. Workers had to accept the reality that they could no longer command annual wage gains of 7, 8 or 10 percent. It was a buyers' market. Typical was the trucking industry, which had been "deregulated" under the Carter administration. The Interstate Commerce Commission (ICC) no longer set freight rates or limited the number of trucking companies or the cities they could serve. Given the dearth of freight, price competition was ferocious. New nonunion companies undercut high-cost unionized firms. In early 1982, the teamsters union, representing most unionized drivers, agreed to an unprecedented three-year wage freeze. But that didn't satisfy many weaker firms. "Events that will occur in the next few weeks will determine whether our company will continue in business or go down the drain into financial ruin," the president of Hemingway Transport Inc., a midsized firm, wrote to its 1,500 workers in early 1982. He urged them to approve wage cuts. About half the trucking companies that had participated in the nationwide bargaining with the teamsters now broke free of the national contract.[3]

"Pattern bargaining"—where most companies in highly unionized industries accept the same basic wage structure—was crumbling. The fact that many wages were formally tied to inflation through cost-of-living clauses or informally through management practices meant that declining price increases led to declining wage increases. Disinflation (the decline of inflation) was dramatic. At the end of 1980, wholesale prices for finished goods—the costs of factory products to distributors and stores—had risen 11.8 percent from the previous December. By 1982, the annual increase was only 3.7 percent; in 1983, it was a mere 0.6 percent. In 1980, wholesale auto prices rose 9.6 percent. The increases for 1982 and 1983 were 5.8 percent and 2.2 percent. Furniture prices had risen 9.6 percent in 1980; the gains for 1982 and 1983 were 4.2 percent and 3.4 percent. In 1980, labor costs had jumped 10.5 percent; by 1983, the gain was 5.2 percent. Volcker's approach was not subtle. The Federal Reserve bludgeoned the economy until inflation subsided.[4]

It is doubtful that, aside from Reagan, any other potential president would have let the Fed proceed unchallenged. Certainly Carter wouldn't have, had he been reelected, nor would his chief Democratic rival, Senator Edward M. Kennedy. Both would have faced intense pressures from the party's faithful, led by unionized workers—especially auto- and steelworkers—who were big victims of Volcker's austerity. Nor is it likely that any of the major Republican presidential contenders in 1980 would have acquiesced, including George H. W. Bush, Senator Howard Baker and John Connally.

The rise of unemployment transcended people's expectations. As Senate majority leader, Baker pleaded with the Fed to "get its boot off the neck of the economy." At lower unemployment levels, Nixon and Carter had agitated for pro-job policies. As a Nixon aide, Connally sang in that chorus. Later, the administration of George H. W. Bush criticized the Fed for policies it thought too restrictive, despite much lower joblessness than in the early 1980s. The obsession with unemployment called for a dramatic presidential response. A reasonable expectation was that Reagan would provide it. He didn't.[5]

Reagan's initial economic program promised to reduce the money supply to curb inflation. He was the first president to make that part of his agenda, and he never retreated from it. As the economy deteriorated, he kept quiet. He refused to criticize Volcker publicly, urge a lowering of interest rates or work behind the scenes to bring that about. Nor was there veiled criticism in Reagan's rhetoric. The silence was not an oversight, because periodically, when the president did speak, he supported Volcker. At a press conference on Feburary 18, 1982—with unemployment near 9 percent—Reagan called inflation "our number one enemy" and referred to fears that "the Federal Reserve Board will revert to the inflationary monetary policies of the past." The president pledged that this wouldn't happen. "I have met with Chairman Volcker several times during the past year. We met again earlier this week. I have confidence in the announced policies of the Federal Reserve."

On April 3, Reagan inaugurated weekly Saturday morning radio addresses that have since become a presidential institution. His first subject was the economy. "Our greatest success has been in conquering inflation," he said. "It's no longer double digits. For the last five months, it's been running at four and a half percent." In a brief exchange with reporters afterward, one asked about the continuing rise in unemployment. Reagan rejected standard policies to stimulate a recovery:

> The way out of it is not the way that's been tried on most recessions that have taken place in these last few decades: hyping the money supply, artificially stimulating the money supply, stimulating government spending, as if somehow that will be an aid to the economy—and up, of course, goes inflation when you do that.[6]

Reagan's patience enabled the Federal Reserve to maintain a punishing and increasingly unpopular policy long enough to alter inflationary psychology. Since the mid-1960s, economic slowdowns had only temporarily dampened inflation. The Federal Reserve had repeatedly relaxed its anti-inflationary policies prematurely. Companies and workers became conditioned to rising prices and wages in an advancing economy. So, once the economy recovered, inflation accelerated again, ultimately exceeding levels reached in the previous expansion. The pattern was well-established. From 1965 to 1966—a slowdown, not a recession—inflation retreated slightly, from 3.5 percent to 3 percent; but as the economy reaccelerated, inflation reached 6.2 percent by 1969. After the 1970 recession (and the imposition of wage-price controls in 1971), inflation dropped to 3.3 percent in 1971—and then zoomed to 12.3 percent by 1974.

The next recession, ending in 1975, reduced inflation to 4.9 percent in 1976—but it jumped to 13.3 percent in 1979. This time was different.[7]

On paper, what Reagan did or didn't do shouldn't have mattered, considering that the Federal Reserve is legally independent. It does not report to the president; the Fed chairman is not a member of the cabinet and cannot be fired by the president. But it must conform to broader political and social pressures, however ambiguous and ever-changing these may be. "The Federal Reserve is meant to be independent of parochial political interests," Volcker has said. "But it's got to operate—I think of this as a kind of band, sometimes wide, sometimes narrow—within the range of understanding of the public and the political system. You just can't go do something that is just outside the bounds of what people can understand, because you won't be independent for very long if you do that. But you also ... have a real opportunity to affect where the band of understanding is. You do have a role as a teacher or leader."[8]

Reagan counted, because the Fed needed political protection. One threat to Volcker's policies was congressional action forcing the Fed to relent. Like any bureaucracy, the Fed tries to placate its adversaries, sometimes by giving ground to them. The paradox: To safeguard its independence, the Fed may sacrifice its independence. Imminent congressional action might have forced the Fed to retreat. In the 1960s and 1970s, "Fed bashing" was common. Higher interest rates were the usual complaint. Lyndon Johnson once expressed the populist view: "It's hard for a boy from Texas ever to see high interest rates as a lesser evil than anything else." As Volcker's policies took hold, they predictably provoked a backlash. Representative

Henry Gonzalez, a Democrat from Texas, was a relentless critic, accusing all the Fed governors of being "arrogant and wanton users of great powers, the handmaidens of the malefactors of great wealth . . . ruining the country and its citizens."[9]

There was an outpouring of bills and resolutions to impeach Volcker, roll back interest rates or require the appointment of new Fed governors sympathetic to farmers, workers, consumers and small businesses. Representative Jack Kemp, a prominent Republican "supply-sider," wanted Volcker to resign. In August 1982, Senator Robert C. Byrd of West Virginia, the Democratic floor leader, introduced the Balanced Monetary Policy Act of 1982, which would have forced the Fed to reduce interest rates. It seemed possible that the Fed's liberal and conservative (mostly supply-sider) critics would coalesce in a grand coalition. To be sure, some of these proposals were ritualistic, intended to advertise their sponsors' displeasure more than to be enacted. But if Reagan had endorsed any of them, their prospects would have improved instantly, and the Fed would have become a huge, semidefenseless target.[10]

The question remains why Reagan was so steadfast in his support. Volcker believed that public opinion had shifted. Americans' growing fears of runaway inflation made them more tolerant of the hardships necessary to suppress it. Though this was probably true, it could not be seen in Reagan's popularity ratings, which collapsed. Early in his presidency, Reagan's approval had reached a high of 68 percent in May 1981. By April 1982, it was 45 percent (46 percent disapproved); by January 1983, it was 35 percent, the low point (56 percent disapproved). Reagan was condemned as both heartless and headless. As the economy sank, he was advancing an economic program of across-the-board tax cuts, widely portrayed as favoring the rich, and spending cuts, widely portrayed as hurting the poor. The deep tax cuts contributed to huge budget deficits, which in turn were blamed (along with the Fed) for high interest rates. Reagan was portrayed as spearheading an economic assault against ordinary Americans.[11]

Press coverage was murderous. On April 21, 1982, CBS broadcast a documentary by Bill Moyers, *People Like Us*. It condemned Reagan's policies for letting Americans slip "through the safety net." A Hispanic woman in New Jersey had been cut from welfare; a church-run food bank in Milwaukee was swamped. Though criticized as one-sided—actual cuts in social programs were modest, and Moyers ignored inflation—the documentary "set the tone for television coverage," noted *Washington Post* reporter Lou Cannon, Reagan's best biographer. Reagan, a student of television, was acutely aware of the effects of all the bad publicity. "In a time of recession like this," he noted in one interview, "there's a great deal of psychology in economics. And you can't turn on the evening news without seeing that they're going to interview someone else who lost his job, or they're outside the factory that has laid off workers and so forth— the constant downbeat that can contribute psychologically to slowing down a recovery that is in the offing." Print stories were also highly critical. "Reagan's America: And the Poor Get Poorer," said a *Newsweek* cover story in early 1982.[12]

It would have been easy to succumb to these pressures. The fact that Reagan didn't was a matter of personality and beliefs, not cold calculation (all the calculations suggested the opposite). There was a view of Reagan then—and still is among some—that he was a moron or a figurehead. He was too ill-informed, dim-witted and detached to make intelligent decisions. Others decided for him, or events dictated outcomes. This view is wrong, but it can be artificially fitted to selected facts. Unlike some recent presidents—Nixon, Carter and LBJ spring to mind—Reagan avoided micromanaging. On economic matters, he did not immerse himself in complex details. In his irregular meetings with Volcker, he said little and offered almost no advice. "Reagan never asked him to ease or tighten the money supply," said Martin Anderson, a top economic adviser who sat in on the meetings until he left the White House in 1982. Anderson thought that the two men developed "a surprising amount of goodwill." Not really. Volcker later wrote that he and Reagan never had "much personal rapport." The president "was unfailingly courteous, but he plainly had no inclination either to get into really substantive discussions of monetary policy or, conversely, to seek my advice in other areas." Outwardly, Reagan confirmed critics' unsympathetic stereotype.[13]

What they missed was his leadership style. It was to set broad goals, delegate responsibility and, when necessary, resolve conflicts. On inflation, Reagan was clear-eyed. "[U]nlike some of his predecessors, he had a strong visceral aversion to inflation," Volcker later said. Reagan was "influenced by people like [economist] Milton Friedman [an informal adviser] and understood that inflation was always a monetary phenomenon"—it was "too much money chasing too few goods," said William Niskanen, a member of Reagan's Council of Economic Advisers. "He was the first president who understood that. . . . He knew that controlling inflation by regulation [controls] was absurd." Reagan generally surrounded himself with capable subordinates and gave them much autonomy. He viewed

Volcker in this light. "Reagan's attitude was that Volcker was a very sound professional, doing his best," said Anderson.[14]

Still, pressures for change mounted. Reagan's supply-side supporters—who believed that his cuts in tax rates would stimulate more work, investment and economic growth—argued that Volcker's recession would discredit their policies. Treasury Secretary Donald Regan periodically criticized Volcker on technical issues and personally disliked him. Congressional Republicans worried about the 1982 elections. Reagan persevered. In the fall of 1981, some members of Reagan's Presidential Economic Advisory Board (a group of outside economists, academics and business leaders that met about four times a year) suggested that Reagan ought to prod the Fed to relax. Reagan disagreed. "He said he would not do something to help the chances of Republicans in Congress in 1982 only to have to see the need for restrictive policies afterwards," according to economist Jerry Jordan, a member of the CEA. At a cabinet meeting later that fall, similar concerns were raised. Again, Reagan was not persuaded.[15]

Reagan's indestructible optimism, especially for the country's future, was liberating. He believed that correct decisions would turn out well. He was also convinced that reducing inflation required some high unemployment. "Bellyache," he called it. "I'm afraid this country is just going to have to suffer two, three years of hard times to pay for the [inflationary] binge we've been on," he once said privately. After the 1976 election, Reagan occasionally referred to "bellyache" publicly, but his political advisers persuaded him to avoid the phrase. Finally, the fact that his huge deficits were also blamed for high interest rates may have restrained him. He couldn't easily attack Volcker without inviting attacks on himself.★ But Reagan understood his political predicament. Just before his weekly radio address on November 20, 1982, he quipped: "My fellow Americans, I've talked to you on a number of occasions about economic problems and opportunities our nation faces, and I'm prepared to tell you, it's a hell of a mess." It was a sound check, but the mike to the press room was open.[16]

II

In some ways, Reagan and Volcker were polar opposites. Reagan made his career on the public stage; Volcker made his behind the scenes. One was a master of uplifting rhetoric; the other was an expert in studied obscurity. "You would make a very excellent prisoner of war," a frustrated congressman once told Volcker, "because you wouldn't tell the enemy a thing." But what Reagan and Volcker shared was a reflexive loathing of inflation and an absolute faith that the country needed their policies. "You have to start with the conviction that price stability is better than inflation and that 'better' means better for economic growth and stability in the long run and better for everybody," Volcker once said. He dismissed academic economists' elaborate arguments that a little bit of inflation might be

---

★ The contribution of high budget deficits to interest rates was probably exaggerated. Once the Fed eased policy, short-term interest rates declined, even though budget deficits remained large and other credit demands were increasing.

good. Like Reagan, Volcker was imbued with a strong sense of purpose. "He is not confident about himself in some ways, but in his field he is more sure of himself than anybody I have ever known," his wife, Barbara, said in 1982. "It may sound egotistical, but I believe that he thinks he is the only man in the country who can do the job. It is the culmination of everything he has done in his professional life."[17]

That he got the opportunity was an accident. The son of a professional city manager—of Teaneck and Cape May, New Jersey—Volcker had shuttled between government and the private sector. He'd graduated from Princeton in 1949 with a major in public affairs (what we now call public policy) and then received a master's degree in public economy from Harvard. After working at the Federal Reserve Bank of New York as a research economist, he'd been hired by the Chase Manhattan Bank. In 1962 he moved to Washington to work for Robert Roosa, his boss at the New York Federal Reserve and Kennedy's undersecretary of the Treasury for monetary affairs. He returned to Chase in 1965 before becoming Nixon's Treasury undersecretary for monetary affairs in 1969. In 1975, he was named (at Arthur Burns's urging) president of the New York Federal Reserve Bank. When appointed by Carter in July 1979 to head the Fed, Volcker, then fifty-one, was well-known among bankers, economists and foreign economic officials (he was a main architect of Nixon's dollar devaluation in 1971). But to the public, he was a virtual nobody.[18]

Carter had turned to Volcker as an afterthought. In the summer of 1979, the president sought to reinvigorate his administration before the 1980 election. After a ten-day retreat at Camp David, he addressed the nation on television (his "malaise" speech) and then purged five cabinet members, including his Treasury secretary, Michael Blumenthal. Unable to find a replacement for Blumenthal among outsiders—Carter had asked Reginald Jones, head of General Electric, and David Rockefeller, head of Chase Manhattan—he selected G. William Miller, the ex-chief of Textron, a New England conglomerate, who had been Fed chairman since 1978. The White House had a close relationship with Miller, and his acceptance left a vacancy at the Fed. Though Volcker was on the short list, he was not a favorite among Carter's aides, who thought him too conservative (though he was a Democrat) and not a "team player." With Miller present, Carter and Volcker conferred at the White House on Tuesday, July 24, less than a week after Blumenthal's dismissal the previous Thursday. Volcker emphasized the Fed's independence and, gesturing toward Miller, said, "You have to understand, if you appoint me, I favor a tighter policy than that fellow." Volcker left feeling that he had talked himself out of a job. It was unsuccessfully shopped to others, including A. W. "Tom" Clausen, head of the Bank of America. The next morning at around 7:45, Carter called and asked Volcker to accept.[19]

The truth was that the president had little choice. The initial favorable reaction to his speech had faded, because the administration seemed in disarray. "When the president asked for the resignations of his Cabinet unexpectedly, the financial markets became very jittery," Stuart Eizenstat, Carter's chief domestic adviser, said later. "Interest rates were already high and the markets did not really know what was going on. They were thinking of the European model where governments fall." To leave the Fed job open would have compounded the sense of drift. Inflation was worsening, and the economy seemed to be weakening. For much of the year, many economists, including the Fed's staff economists, had been predicting a recession.[20]

Still, Volcker's regime started badly. In August, he convinced the Fed governors to raise the discount rate (the rate on Fed loans to commercial banks) and did so again in September. But the second vote was only 4-3, and the narrow margin was seen as proof that Volcker had already lost political control and couldn't undertake further anti-inflationary actions. Prices of metals—gold, copper, silver, platinum—rose sharply, as investors fled dollars that they expected to lose value. From early August to late September, gold prices increased from about $300 an ounce to nearly $450 and copper prices from about 90 cents an ounce to $1.20. In late September, Volcker flew to Belgrade in what was then Yugoslavia for the annual meetings of the International Monetary Fund (IMF) and the World Bank, the major global economic agencies. There, he heard loud complaints from foreign countries about the dollar's plunging exchange rate.* Investors were switching into other currencies whose value (they thought) would hold up better. Volcker had already asked the Fed staff to prepare plans for a new approach to control inflation. On October 5 and 6, he hosted a telephone conference call and then a secret meeting of the Federal Open Market Committee (FOMC) to consider a radical shift in the Fed's anti-inflation strategy.†[21]

---

* He also attended Arthur Burns's lecture "The Anguish of Central Banking," which reinforced his determination to break the inflationary spiral.

† The FOMC is the Fed's key decision-making body on monetary policy. It consists of the seven Federal Reserve governors and five of the

As a practical matter, the Fed can regulate money and credit in one of two ways—setting its price (interest rate) or its quantity (the money supply). In either case, control operates through the provision of bank reserves. As noted earlier, when the Fed wants to add to bank reserves, it buys U.S. Treasury securities. The payments for these securities are deposited in banks and increase the banks' reserves. The greater a bank's reserves, the more it can lend.★ Selling Treasury securities does the opposite; it decreases bank reserves. Until October 1979, the Fed had targeted interest rates—namely, the Fed funds rate governing overnight loans between banks, the only market rate it controls directly. The Fed increases or decreases reserves until supply and demand produce the desired rate. What Volcker proposed was shifting the focus from interest rates to the basic money supply: cash plus checking accounts, known as M1. The Fed would no longer try to guess the "right" price for money. It would instead provide a given amount of bank reserves, which through subsequent borrowing and spending would translate into a given amount of money.† If inflation was too much money chasing too few goods, squeezing the amount of money would squeeze inflation.

---

twelve presidents of regional Federal Reserve banks. The president of the New York Fed is permanent; the other four are rotating, although all the presidents participate in the policy discussions.

★ Reserves are funds that a bank must, by law, hold as cash or deposits at one of the twelve regional Federal Reserve banks and are usually a fixed proportion of various types of deposits. The more reserves a bank has, the more deposits it can have and the more loans it can make.

† The relationship between a given amount of bank reserves and a sub-

When announced, the Fed's new procedure was widely seen as a capitulation to "monetarism"—the view, championed by Milton Friedman, that the Fed could prevent inflation and minimize recessions by increasing the money supply by a modest and predetermined amount every year, say 3 percent or 4 percent, which theoretically would permit noninflationary economic growth. This interpretation, though plausible, was wrong. Volcker accepted the monetarists' diagnosis of inflation (too much money chasing too few goods) but not their prescription (a simple rule for money growth). The practical problems were too great, he thought. Defining money wasn't easy. Beyond cash and checks, should it include savings accounts and money market mutual funds? Moreover, there were times—a financial panic, for instance—when the Fed might need to depart from a simple money rule. But Volcker had concluded that a temporary shift to monetarist tactics was the sort of dramatic policy jolt that might quell inflation.

For much of the 1970s, the Fed had tried to control the money supply by regulating interest rates, but this approach clearly hadn't worked. One reason, Volcker felt, was that it involved too much human discretion. Fed officials disliked raising rates, for personal and political reasons. It was unpopular; it might trigger a recession. On paper, all the Fed had to do was find a rate that permitted expansion and prevented inflation. Never easy, that task became harder once inflation rose. Rates that once seemed "high" might be low after adjusting for inflation. A 7 percent Fed funds rate was historically high,

---

sequent amount of money—however defined—is known as the "money multiplier." A highly technical concept, it is not entirely predictable.

but if inflation was 7 percent, then the "real" rate (after inflation) was zero. People could effectively borrow for free. Volcker felt that the Fed was always playing catch-up, raising rates too little, too late. In the late 1970s, it had tolerated "real" rates that were low or negative.

The new approach exempted Fed officials from having to make explicit and politically sensitive decisions on interest rates. Volcker also believed that the Fed no longer knew what "the right rate" might be, even in theory. Regulating the amount of bank reserves would allow rates to find their own level. If demand for loans and money was high, rates would rise, perhaps spectacularly. If not, they might fall. Once the Fed adopted its new approach, the Fed funds rate jumped immediately to 13.8 percent in October, up from 11.4 percent in September.[22]

With hindsight, October 6, 1979, was a milestone: the Fed's true declaration of war against inflation. Volcker had shifted priorities. Lowering unemployment would take a backseat, at least temporarily, to getting inflation down. We know that the war succeeded, but while it proceeded, it was—like most wars—full of uncertainties, setbacks and surprises. The commanding general (Volcker) and his troops (the rest of the Fed) often didn't know precisely what was happening to the enemy (inflation) or on the broader terrain of battle (the economy). Nor was the outcome preordained. There were two types of problems: one technical, the other political.

As Volcker and others feared, the mechanics of controlling the money supply were confusing. As the recession grew more severe, Americans piled up cash. In economic jargon, there was a rush to "liquidity." "[P]eople were scared," wrote William Greider in his sweeping narrative of the Fed, *The Secrets of the Temple*. "Under siege, millions of players in the private economy, families and businesses, were storing larger balances in their checking accounts. . . . They weren't spending their money so quickly." As a result, the relationship between bank reserves (which the Fed could control directly) and the money supply (which the Fed could influence only indirectly)—the so-called money multiplier—became more erratic. For long stretches, the Fed had trouble hitting its money-supply targets. Sometimes its aim was too low, sometimes too high. Later, in 1981, the introduction of NOW accounts (checking accounts that paid interest) muddled the meaning of M1, which was defined as cash plus checking accounts. Since the Depression, checking accounts had not paid interest. But now part of M1 would consist of funds that had previously resided in interest-paying savings accounts. How should NOW accounts be treated, as savings or checking?*[23]

But the bigger problem was political. By striking out on its own against inflation, the Fed was testing the limits of its "independence." When Volcker acted, he had not sought the blessing of the Carter administration. On his way to the IMF–World Bank meetings, he had merely informed Treasury Secretary Miller and Charles Schultze, chairman of the Council of Economic Advisers, of his plans. Though unhappy, they had not objected, and even if they had, it is doubtful that Volcker would have desisted. But it is one thing to act, another to persevere. Under the best of circumstances, the new policy could not succeed instantly. It would push up interest rates without immediately pushing down inflation. It was unveiled at an

---

* To deal with the confusion, the Fed created two money-supply definitions, labeled at the time M1-A and M1-B.

awkward political moment, the eve of a presidential election year when the incumbent was running to keep his job. Facing a grim economic outlook, Carter embarked on his own program.

The result was a bizarre episode that, ironically, underlined the extraordinary nature of Reagan's subsequent patience. In early March 1980, Carter proposed a dramatic new economic package designed to show that he could control both inflation and the federal budget. He recommended additional spending cuts—his initial budget had elicited skepticism—and asked the Fed to impose credit controls on bank lending to businesses and consumers, including credit card debt. Volcker opposed the controls as cumbersome but reluctantly went along—and persuaded other Fed governors—as part of an unstated political bargain. The Carter administration hadn't objected to his October 6 policy. Now it was Volcker's turn to reciprocate. "Volcker understood that just as Carter was doing unpleasant things for himself, cutting up his own budget, which would alienate his liberal constituencies," said CEA chairman Schultze, "so he too, Volcker, would have to do something he wasn't quite anxious to do."[24]

Everything backfired. The controls were supposed to relieve pressure on interest rates and avoid a recession without relaxing the assault on inflation. This is not what happened. The Fed—disliking the controls—had designed them to be nearly innocuous. Exempted were the biggest categories of consumer lending, home loans and auto loans. There were only modest restraints on credit card borrowing. Still, the effect was devastating. Addressing the nation on television, Carter had denounced overwrought consumer borrowing. Americans took heed; many stopped using credit. "Some people sent me credit cards," recalled Alfred Kahn, Carter's anti-inflation czar. "[They] wrote irate letters to the effect that Sears Roebuck was still soliciting credit card accounts. They said, 'that's unpatriotic.' " Visa lost 500,000 accounts in a few months. The economy went into a tailspin. From March to June, inflation-adjusted consumer spending dropped at an astounding annualized rate of 9.8 percent. Unemployment rose from 6.3 percent in March to 7.6 percent in July.[25]

Though it was ultimately self-defeating, Carter's behavior showed how unlikely it was that he—or anyone beside Reagan—would have meekly accepted Volcker's prolonged austerity. Recall that unemployment was just above 6 percent when Carter acted. What would have happened when it reached 8 percent or 10 percent? (By December 1981, the jobless rate was 8.6 percent.) There was another lesson, too: To succeed against entrenched inflation, policies had to be harsh. The credit controls, like the earlier incomes policies, were supposed to make anti-inflationary policies work without hurting. Controls would simply choke off inflationary credit. No one would really suffer. This was a delusion. Politicians wanted to quell inflation without serious social disruption. In early 1979, the House Banking Committee issued a report whose key recommendation was that "anti-inflationary policies must not cause a recession." At a hearing in early 1980, Representative Henry Reuss, a respected Democrat from Wisconsin, had warned Volcker: "The Federal Reserve cannot cure inflation with monetary shock treatment and it shouldn't try."[26]

The reality was that only a recession, "shock treatment" or something similar could cure double-digit inflation, precisely because

Americans had come to believe that inflation was indestructible.★ The assumption could be dislodged only by actual experience that disproved it. Companies had to see that they could no longer raise prices as before because, if they did, they might sacrifice sales or go bankrupt. Workers had to understand that high and rising wage increases were no longer automatically in the cards. These realizations came slowly. Among some economists, there was a theory that the mere adoption of a "credible" anti-inflationary program would cause inflation to recede. Recognizing that steep price and wage increases would be self-defeating, businesses and workers would refrain. Volcker soon discovered that the theory was hollow. Shortly after October 6, he met with some chief executives of medium-sized firms. He asked for reaction to the Fed's program. One CEO announced that he had recently signed a three-year labor contract with annual wage increases of 13 percent—and was happy with the result. Only bitter experience would purge inflationary expectations and behavior.

"Credibility" had to be won through suffering. That was essentially the Volcker program. Although October 1979 was the departure point, the genuine assault on inflation did not begin until about a year later. "We were put back six, nine months because of the credit card [episode]," Volcker later said. The brief recession trig-

---

★ Some candid politicians acknowledged this. Senator William Proxmire, a Democrat from Wisconsin and a recognized economic expert, said after Volcker's announcement: "This policy is going to cause pain. Anybody who says we can do it without more unemployment or more recession is just deceiving you or is deceiving himself."[27]

gered by Carter's program temporarily reduced inflation, interest rates and the money supply. But the effects were fleeting. Once the controls were lifted in July—a natural response to the recession— the economy recovered. So did inflation and growth of the money supply. Indeed, during the recession, the Fed had tried to increase the money supply. A study by economists Marvin Goodfriend of the Federal Reserve Bank of Richmond and Robert G. King of Boston University agreed with Volcker on timing. "The true onset of the Volcker disinflation dates to Nov. 1980 or slightly later," they concluded.[28]

For almost two years after that, the Fed held the economy in a vise. As the recession deepened, the pressures to relent intensified. Among home builders and car dealers, the Fed assumed almost demonic status. Home builders sent small two-by-fours to the Fed to protest unsold homes; car dealers sent keys of unsold cars. One issue of *Tennessee Professional Builders* featured a wanted poster for Volcker and the other Fed governors, who were accused of the "cold-blooded murder of millions of small businesses" and killing "the American dream of homeownership." As the recession deepened, members of the Federal Open Market Committee experienced the pressures personally. Frederick H. Schultz, vice chairman of the board of governors and an ex-banker and venture capitalist from Florida who had been appointed by Carter, later put it this way:

Did I get sweaty palms? Did I lie awake at night? The answer is that I did both. I was speaking before these groups all the time, home builders and auto dealers and others. It's not so bad when some guy gets up and yells at you, "You SOB, you're killing us."

What really got to me was when this fellow stood up and said in a very quiet way, "Governor, I've been an auto dealer for thirty years, worked hard to build up that business. Next week, I am closing my doors." Then he sat down. That really gets to you.[29]

Lyle Gramley, another governor who had been a Fed staff economist, felt similarly. "It was a very sobering experience for me to realize that what I do and decide has horrendous effects on the lives of millions of people," he said. Increasingly, members of the FOMC found old friends treating them with hostility. By the spring of 1982, the worsening recession caused some commentators to mutter the word "depression"—which, to those who remembered the 1930s, constituted a dire warning that the economy's downward momentum might become uncontrollable. Testifying before the Senate Budget Committee on March 2, economist Edward Yardeni of the broker E. F. Hutton warned that there was a 30 percent chance of a depression and that, if the economy did not begin to recover by May, the odds would go to 50 percent.[30]

Evidence of economic carnage was everywhere. By spring, bankruptcies were running at 280 a day, a post–World War II high. Some of the fallen were well-known corporate names: Braniff International, the airline; Lionel, the maker of toy trains. International Harvester, a big producer of farm equipment (tractors, combines) and heavy-duty trucks, was in desperate condition. Farm equipment sales dropped 31 percent in 1982, and the company posted a huge $822 million loss. The company survived only by shuttering its farm equipment business and concentrating on trucks under the new name of Navistar International. Disturbingly, the recession was harsher than expected. The Fed's staff economists had expected a recovery by mid-1982; so had many private economists. But it wasn't happening. Recalled Gramley:

> Early in the year, I was making speeches predicting an upturn in the economy in the second quarter [April–June], and when that didn't happen, I said by mid-year. By June and July, with each passing statistic, it became increasingly evident that the turnaround wasn't going to be there.... Our expectations were thoroughly disappointed. The gloom and doom was beginning to spread.[31]

But arrayed against that was the fear that if the Fed relaxed too soon it would forfeit its claim to "credibility"—the public belief that it would not tolerate higher inflation. It was "credibility" that, in turn, would purge inflationary psychology and re-create the self-regulating discipline that would restrain wage and price increases. If the Fed repeated previous errors, easing money and credit too soon, the whole gruesome episode might be in vain. Compounding the difficulty was the money supply's erratic behavior. In early 1982, its growth reached or exceeded the upper limits set by the Fed. Usually, rapid money growth signified a strong economy, accelerating inflation, or both. But interest rates were high, unemployment was rising and inflation was falling. The puzzle might reflect the public's swollen appetite for higher cash balances as protection against the slump. Who knew? The Fed faced a dilemma: Abandoning its money-supply targets—which symbolized the war against inflation—might seem an act of surrender; but adhering to them closely, trying to cut money growth even more, might drive the economy into an even deeper slump.

All these crosscurrents converged at the FOMC's June 30–July 1 meeting. It is sometimes said that the Fed eased decisively at this meeting. That didn't happen. The outcome was more ambiguous: The FOMC decided not to tighten any more—and it hoped to ease. To be sure, many FOMC members were alarmed. At the meeting, Volcker relayed information that Mexico might default on bank loans. The ensuing losses would weaken many major U.S. banks, which were big lenders to Mexico. In Oklahoma, a small bank (Penn Square) was on the brink of failure, having made many bad energy loans on the false premise of permanently high oil prices. By itself, that wasn't worrisome. But many bigger banks—including Continental Illinois and Chase Manhattan—had participated in the same loans, which meant they, too, faced large losses. All this raised the specter of a financial chain reaction, much like what happened during the Great Depression, when bad loans curtailed bank lending—which weakened the economy, causing more bad loans and further curtailed lending.

Companies were squeezed from both ends. Higher interest rates increased their debt burden; sagging sales diminished their capacity to pay. Local bankers feared mounting loan defaults. Edward Boehne, president of the Philadelphia Federal Reserve Bank, warned, "[Bankers] now think that customers they never really thought about as being problems are going to be a problem over the next six months." Among some FOMC members, the pleas to relax credit verged on desperation. "The economy can't stand higher rates because the financial fabric of the country won't tolerate higher rates," said Governor Charles Partee, who—like Gramley—had been a Fed staff economist. Governor Nancy Teeters, a former chief economist of IBM and earlier a Democratic congressional staff economist, was more blunt. "I want to get interest rates down," she said. "We need to signal the market that we have eased." Lower rates would lighten the debt burdens of many firms whose short-term loans had "floating" rates.[32]

Up to a point, Volcker agreed. "The problem is not the desirability of getting rates down," he said. But there was a catch: "The question is whether by reaching too fast for that objective we may not be able to keep them down." Because interest rates incorporate inflationary expectations, the failure to dispatch inflationary psychology could result in Pyrrhic victory; once inflation revived, rates would rise. Other FOMC members expressed similar doubts. The result was a standoff: no tightening, no big easing, but a predisposition to ease. Then, in succeeding weeks, the unexpected happened. The money-supply figures came in lower than expected. Interest rates dropped naturally. The given supply of bank reserves was more than adequate to support the existing money supply. The fierce bidding for overnight loans among banks (for Fed funds) so that banks could meet their reserve requirements subsided. Indeed, reserves might be increased—policy loosened—without breaching the money-supply targets.

On July 15, the FOMC held a conference call. Most of the discussion was highly technical, focused on the official money-supply targets for the next year. By deciding not to reduce the targets, the Fed edged toward an easier policy. As Volcker later explained:

[I]t was sometime in July that the money supply suddenly came within our target band. The Mexican crisis was brewing. The economic recovery had not appeared. I thought, ahah, here's our chance to ease credibly.[33]

Although the economy would not begin expanding again until early 1983, the Fed had relaxed its assault on inflation and committed itself to ending the recession. The country seemed to have turned the corner Volcker had so long sought. On July 19, the Fed cut its discount rate—the rate at which commercial banks could borrow from the Fed—from 12 percent to 11.5 percent, reflecting declines in the Fed funds rate. By December, there would be six more discount rate cuts; these signaled that the Fed approved the decreases in market rates. On August 17, economist Henry Kaufman of the investment bank Salomon Brothers, long christened "Dr. Doom," predicted that interest rates would drop, a reversal of his previous position. The stock market responded with a 38.8 point increase in the Dow, then the largest one-day increase ever. Stocks rose about 50 percent in the next six months, as money came out of money market mutual funds and saving certificates and investors responded to lower interest rates and the prospect of economic recovery. By September, the money-supply figures had accelerated again, but Volcker stayed with his decision to ease. In October, the Fed officially demoted the significance of the money-supply figures, saying that they were too unpredictable to use as guide for daily policy.[34] By December 1982, the increase in the CPI over the previous twelve months had dropped to 3.8 percent.

All during these years, Volcker projected an unshakable determination to suppress inflation. At six feet seven inches, he was not merely tall; he had presence. "Volcker's character—the strong, silent type—became the public symbol for the wrenching discipline being imposed on the American economy," wrote William Greider. "He was physically imposing, a head taller than most everyone else, including the President. He spoke in a brooding Germanic manner that was intimidating by itself. His intellectual self-confidence was daunting and so were his silences." Volcker hadn't isolated himself—he testified before congressional committees, met with senators and congressmen, addressed hostile private groups (home builders, for instance). His forcefulness strengthened the moral case for—and the public acceptability of—attacking inflation. "He's not insensitive," Fed vice chairman Frederick Schultz said later. "But he is a tough guy." Sometime in the summer of 1982, he concluded that the Fed had squeezed the economy as much as was economically and politically possible. Unemployment was rising; banks were shaky; Congress was restless—and threatening to curb the Fed's powers. "If we get this one wrong," Volcker warned at the FOMC's October meeting, "we are going to have legislation next year without a doubt. We may get it anyway." It was a close call, but they didn't.[35]

III

Even now, the social costs of controlling inflation seem horrendous. Over a four-year period (1979–82), the U.S. economy's output barely increased. It nudged ahead in the first two years and then fell back in the last two. Since 1950, there had been nothing like that. Unemployment peaked in 1982 near 11 percent—a figure that, a few years earlier, would have been widely judged as inconceivable. Although lower inflation benefited most people, the casualties were numerous and broadly dispersed geographically and socially: small business owners, overextended farmers, industrial workers. The number of business failures in 1982 (24,908) was nearly 50 percent higher than any other year since World War II, and it would double to 52,078 by 1984. From 1979 to 1983, farm income declined almost 50 percent. Behind the statistics were countless individual stories. As late as October 1983, *Newsweek* quoted Michael Wilk, a thirty-one-year-old technician who'd lost his job at an auto parts company outside Detroit eleven months earlier. He'd been unable to find new work. "I go from feeling depressed to not caring about anything and back again," he said. "Sometimes I'm so paralyzed by it all that I just sit and stare out the window."[36]

But against these heartbreaking costs, there were larger long-term gains. When Reagan left office, Americans still worried about inflation, but it no longer gripped them with fear. Inflation was one problem among many, not a scourge shredding the social fabric. Once the recession lifted, the economy and productivity growth revived impressively. Of all Reagan's economic achievements, this was the most definitive. Indeed, the rest of his economic record was mixed. Although he reduced tax rates and simplified the tax code, federal government spending as a share of national income barely changed during his two terms; tax burdens did drop, and budget deficits rose.*

---

* In 1980, total federal taxes were 19 percent of GDP; in 1988, Reagan's last full year in office, they were 18.1 percent of GDP. Over the same

By contrast, the taming of inflation reinvigorated the economy as nothing else; the expansion lasted from early 1983 until the late summer of 1990. At the time, it was the second longest peacetime expansion in U.S. history. The Volcker-Reagan campaign discredited many of the ideas that had misgoverned national economic policy for nearly two decades. The notion that the Federal Reserve couldn't control inflation was discredited. The notion that a little less unemployment could be exchanged for a little more inflation was discredited. In their place, a consensus slowly developed that "price stability"—a vague term that both Volcker and his successor, Alan Greenspan, defined as inflation so low that it barely affected people's decisions—was desirable and would promote a more stable and productive economy. The consensus was not immediately obvious, but it developed in time.

It is worth reflecting upon the happenstance that contributed to this achievement. The fact that Congress and the public focused heavily on Reagan's tax and budget proposals—seen as the centerpieces of the administration's economic program—in 1981, and even 1982, spared the Federal Reserve and Volcker some of the early criticism they might otherwise have received. That almost everyone underestimated the severity of the 1981–82 recession meant that its power to suppress inflation was also underestimated. This poses an intriguing question: Would Volcker and Reagan have proceeded so forcefully knowing in advance the recession's full wrath, or would they have flinched? These questions can never be answered, but

---

years, federal spending fell from 21.7 percent of GDP to 21.1 percent of GDP. The deficit rose from 2.7 percent of GDP to 3 percent.

what seems certain is that without Reagan and Volcker, the assault on inflation would have been less concerted and less successful. The irony is that, despite the success, relations between the Reagan administration and Volcker never became close or warm. Reagan nominated him to a second four-year term as Fed chairman in 1983, despite opposition from some White House officials. He was not reappointed in 1987. Volcker has said he had promised his wife (who remained living in New York) not to take a third term, but many top administration officials wanted him gone.

Whatever the full story, the achievement of Reagan and Volcker was profound—and it was as much about politics as economics. One of the dilemmas of a democratic society is how to take actions that, though immediately painful and unpopular, seem essential to the society's long-term well-being. Coping with double-digit inflation posed precisely this problem. Any realistic program was bound to hurt millions of Americans, almost all innocent victims. This was so obvious that in the late 1970s a frontal assault on inflation seemed impossible.★ In this sense, Arthur Burns's political diagnosis was en-

---

★ It's worth emphasizing how much the Volcker-Reagan approach disregarded conventional economic wisdom. Most economists believed that a determined effort to reduce inflation to low levels would require horrendous unemployment, surpassing the levels even of the Great Depression. Six respected economic models examined in the late 1970s predicted that, on average, an extra percentage point of unemployment (above the "natural rate") maintained for a year would reduce inflation by only 0.3 percentage points—about a third of a percent. By this math, achieving the inflation reduction that actually occurred in the early 1980s would have required average unemployment of about 20 percent

tirely accurate. Economists and politicians dealt with the dilemma by proposing many unrealistic solutions, from wage-price controls to credit controls to a gradual squeezing of the money supply. All promised fairly painless ways to defeat inflation. Abstractly, all seemed plausible. In reality—meaning in the world of ordinary people and businesses—they weren't. Their appeal was political and psychological. They made their adherents feel and look good. They could pretend to be addressing a serious problem when they were actually evading it.

By contrast, Volcker's approach lacked sophistication. Its chief virtue was that it might actually succeed. But it could not succeed unless it had time to work, and time is what Reagan supplied. It is another unanswerable question as to whether Reagan would have independently pressured a Fed headed by someone else to undertake the same ruthless attack. But presented with it, he provided unwavering support. The ultimate accomplishment of Reagan and Volcker was to show that government could govern and, in so doing, they restored—at least temporarily—Americans' confidence in their leaders and political institutions.

---

for two years, much higher than actually occurred (average unemployment was 7.6 percent in 1981 and 9.7 percent in 1982) and comparable to the levels of the Great Depression. (See Arthur M. Okun, "Efficient Disinflationary Policies," *American Economic Review* (May 1978): 348–52.)

5

CAPITALISM RESTORED

I

What Volcker and Reagan wrought now seems an-
cient history: an isolated episode with little relevance to our present condition. This is utterly
wrong. For every nation, there are crucial demarcation points that
fundamentally alter society. The greatest of these for the United
States was the Civil War. Before, slavery was legal and the sovereignty of individual states (their right to secede) was an open question. After, both issues were settled. The Great Depression and
World War II created another massive chasm. Before, Americans
contented themselves with a small national government that had a
tiny army and whose budget was barely 3 percent of national in-

come. After, the United States had become the world's major power, and government was a colossus—with a huge army and enormous spending—that had a budget equal to a fifth of national income. In our era, the fall of double-digit inflation is one of those separation points, though on a smaller scale. It's a gorge, not a canyon. But ordinary life was much different on each side of the gorge.[1]

Something profound and pervasive occurred: what I call the restoration of capitalism. Much of what we now take for granted—what we consider routine and normal—originated in the tumultuous transition from high to low inflation. The very viciousness of the Volcker-Reagan recession, which transcended what most Americans expected or considered politically tolerable, forced people to reconsider what was realistic and desirable. It set in motion events and forces that altered attitudes and behavior. On the one side of the gorge, Americans imagined—despite all the setbacks of the 1970s— a new society that would fuse the best features of enlightened business and benevolent government. Their magical alliance would create a universal affluence that would gradually purge poverty and social injustice. This was the great post–World War II progressive project.* On the other side of the gorge was a starker society that

---

* I first called this the great "liberal" project. But that word suggests that only Democrats embraced it. Although an extension of the New Deal, the vision also reflected the social consensus that emerged from World War II—that government and business should work together for the common good, just as in the war. By the 1960s, this view commanded wide support. President Nixon embraced it. "Progressive" seemed a better term.

had reverted to the rough-and-tumble existence of a more market-driven economy with greater inequalities and individual insecurities. On the whole, this remade economy was more stable and productive than its predecessor. But it also bred a new set of discontents, because it seemed—to many—more crass and cruel. Americans felt less protected by corporate and governmental goodwill and more exposed to assaults from intense competition, advancing globalization and aggressive finance. At every turn in this history, inflation's aftermath played a central role. Disinflation promoted competition, globalization and finance. In turn, these developments altered common assumptions, norms and expectations, including how companies behaved toward their workers and shareholders.

To say that capitalism was "restored" does not mean that it reverted to what it had been in the 1920s or 1930s. "Capitalism" is a term of art. There's no precise definition, though there are some basic requirements. A capitalist system must permit private property, must tolerate relatively free markets and must endorse the social value of economic risk taking—meaning that people who take greater risks or who work harder can earn greater rewards. Up to a point, inequality is accepted as a necessary and desirable incentive for talent, effort and innovation. Although the United States has always met these broad criteria, capitalism is also a spirit, and after World War II, the spirit waned. The Great Depression had discredited capitalism, which was blamed for the collapse. Almost everyone—political leaders, corporate managers, union bosses, ordinary workers—wanted a fairer and more stable system. American business leaders were especially loath to return to the bitter politics of the 1930s.

The prodigious wartime production of tanks, planes and ships had partly refurbished their reputation, and they wanted the rehabilitation to continue.

So capitalism was not celebrated in the early postwar decades. Indeed, the very term fell into disuse, supplanted by the less inflammatory phrase "mixed economy." This signified a sharing of power between government (which would provide a social safety net, regulate business and prevent depressions) and large corporations (which would improve technology, produce goods and services and provide stable employment for their workers). People did not glorify "profit maximization" or "risk taking" but praised "modern management." The predominant image was not of economic entrepreneurs or "robber barons" but of organized masses of skilled specialists—engineers, marketers, accountants. It was this model of progress that, if not entirely destroyed, was badly damaged in the 1980s, because it presupposed that major corporations are far stronger than they actually are. That notion, understandable in the 1950s when U.S. companies dominated the world, could not survive in the 1980s.

The overconfidence inspired the false faith that large companies are immortal and can protect themselves and their workers from harm. The faith faded as competition intensified from all directions: domestic rivals, foreign rivals, new technologies and altered business models. One telling statistic: In 1980, the typical large U.S. firm in the top fifty of its industry by sales had a one-in-ten chance of falling from that position within five years; by 1998, the odds were one in four. Companies that once dominated their industries (IBM, Sears Roebuck, United Airlines)—and whose dominance was taken for granted—lost ground. In 1970, it was unimaginable that corporate giants such as American Telephone and Telegraph, Bethlehem Steel and Digital Equipment Corporation would cease to exist. They were invincible, the nation's major phone company and the second largest steel and computer firms, respectively. But all are gone, weakened until they were merged out of existence.*[2]

Our economic vocabulary reflects these changes. We now talk routinely of corporate "downsizing," "restructuring" and "outsourcing"— all words and phrases that barely existed before 1980.† These euphemisms for shutting, selling or streamlining business operations— and, in the process, firing workers, relocating them or pushing them brusquely into early retirement—depict a new managerial sensibility. Of course, people were fired before 1980. But among large corporations, the ideal was lifetime employment. Some firms like IBM achieved it. At many companies, career workers could expect to remain for decades. When business was bad, big companies

---

* The name American Telephone and Telegraph—AT&T—remains. But the corporation that had the name was effectively taken over by SBC Communications, Inc., the former Southwestern Bell, in 2005 with the surviving company retaining the AT&T name.

† A LexisNexis search of *The New York Times* finds that "downsizing" was hardly used in the early 1980s—an average of only seven times annually from 1980 to 1984. From 1995 to 1999, the annual average was 284, or nearly once a day. "Restructuring" was more common—probably because it referred to all manner of corporate reorganizations—but its count has also doubled. The annual average in the 1980–84 period was 512; for 1995–99 it was 1,101.

sometimes placed workers on temporary layoff, to be recalled when the economy recovered. Many firms permanently dismissed workers only as a last resort. That is no longer the case.

No one planned this new economic order. It mainly evolved from events and trends. Of course, it differs fundamentally from the celebrated "new economy" of the late 1990s. That was mostly a state of mind. It seemed to promise through its signature technologies— personal computers, the Internet, cell phones—endless economic growth and rises in living standards. To anyone with a sense of history, this was always a mirage. The "new economy" recalled the "new era" of the 1920s and the "new economics" of the 1960s, when fresh ideas and business practices also promised to eliminate business cycles and guarantee ever-improving prosperity. Oversold, all were fated to disappoint. In early 2000, the stock market reached its peak. From giddy highs, many tech stocks crashed: Amazon.com dropped 92.7 percent, from $75.25 to $5.51; Yahoo 96.4 percent, from $238 to $8.45; and Cisco 90.1 percent, from $82 to $8.12. All told, stocks lost roughly half of their value, a decline of $8.5 trillion from their March 2000 high to the October 2002 low. In 2001, the economy went into a brief recession, even before the September 11 terrorist attacks on the World Trade Center and the Pentagon. So much for the "new economy."[3]

What actually occurred was more ambiguous and durable. As inflation receded as a source of macroeconomic instability, some of the insecurity and instability flowed down to the level of the individual firm. The protections premised on corporate invincibility succumbed to market pressures that had been considered suppressed. It was precisely the weakening of these market forces that inspired the widespread belief, in the early decades after World War II, that capitalism had been permanently reformed and improved. The old capitalism was being deemphasized and being replaced by a more orderly and humane version.

The reappearance of unruly forces—or recognition that some had never disappeared—reaffirmed the survival of traditional capitalism or, depending on your point of view, caused it to be resurrected. Either way, there were changes in perceptions about how the economic system actually worked, as opposed to how we thought or wished it worked. There was more emphasis on individual accomplishment, accountability and wealth—and less on collective reponsibilities. Greed gained respectability, many said, blaming Reagan. But this was misleading. Widespread changes in how the economy operated counted for more than the president's agenda. It's worth remembering that, for all of Reagan's antigovernment rhetoric, no major federal program was abolished in his two terms.

II

As economics, the prevailing explanation of the inflation of the 1970s—that it reflected a society whose wants had outrun the nation's capacity to fulfill them—was self-serving, simplistic and wrong. It was a monetary problem that could be fixed by monetary means. But as sociology and politics, the conventional wisdom was fairly accurate. High inflation was one unintended result of a broader, if largely uncoordinated, movement to remake capitalism into a more harmonious economic system. By controlling business cycles, government would enable companies to become more caring. Relieved of fears of deep recessions or depressions, firms could establish long-term employment relationships that provided stable jobs, fair wages and ample fringe benefits. Perversely, this new social contract became a conveyor belt for higher inflation. Because the notion of "fair" wages compensated for past inflation, the reformed capitalism institutionalized a wage-price spiral. Not surprisingly, the repression of inflation—signaling that business cycles endured—undid some of these changes and practices.

Capitalism's early postwar reconstruction focused on jobs, because that was what concerned most people. Going back to the 1920s, some large firms (Eastman Kodak, Sears, Metropolitan Life) had experimented with "welfare capitalism," which aimed to provide job stability and more benefits, mainly pensions and profit-sharing plans. These companies were exceptions. In general, the prewar job market was treacherous. "People moved around a lot," the economic historian Sanford Jacoby has said. "You got laid off and you moved on. And workers were wont to quit just as employers were quick to lay off." Wages were set mainly according to local labor market conditions (if there were surplus welders, their wages suffered, regardless of skill). Many foremen could hire and fire at will. Turnover was high, and hardly anyone had "rights" on the job or the "right" to a job. One autoworker recalled bitterly:

The annual layoff during the model change was always a menace to the security of workers. Along about June or July it started. The bosses would pick the men off a few at a time. . . . In October and November, we began to trickle back into the plants. Again the bosses had full say as to who was rehired first. Years of service with the company meant nothing. . . . [W]orkers had no assurance of that he [*sic*] would be called back at any specific time.[4]

In the 1950s and 1960s, these arbitrary practices receded. There was a greater faith that workers' "relationship with the Organization [was] for keeps" because if they were "loyal to the company . . . the company would be loyal" to them, as William Whyte wrote in his 1956 bestseller *The Organization Man*. This partly reflected the increasing power of unions, which had received new legal protections in the Depression and World War II to organize and conduct collective bargaining. By 1950, union membership reached 15 million; that was more than four times its 1930 level and more than a quarter of nonfarm employment. Terrified of being organized, many nonunion firms mimicked union bargaining preferences in their employment policies, emphasizing job security, seniority, increased fringe benefits and pay scales that narrowed the gap between the top and bottom.[5]

Particularly influential were settlements in the massive auto industry, starting with landmark agreements between the United Auto Workers and General Motors in 1948 and 1950. The 1950 contract guaranteed automatic wage increases covering inflation (a cost-of-living adjustment, or COLA) and an "annual improvement factor" (first 2 percent, then 3 percent after 1955), a pension and half the costs (later increased) of health insurance. The union gave up the right to national strikes between contracts for these hefty benefits; GM could make large investments knowing that, once a contract was in place, the investments could be used. When the 1950 five-year contract was signed, *Fortune* magazine dubbed it the "Treaty of Detroit": "GM may have paid a billion for peace but it . . . has regained control [over the] long range scheduling of production, model changes, and tool and plant investment." Ford and Chrysler made similar agreements, as did other unionized industries (steel, aluminum, chemicals). The resulting "pattern bargaining" in these industries meant that major firms didn't compete on labor costs. Auto companies had similar labor costs; steel companies had similar costs; tire companies had similar costs.[6]

Many large nonunion firms followed suit. Wages and salary increases compensated for inflation plus something. There were more generous fringe benefits: paid vacations, health insurance, pensions, sick leave. From 1950 to 1970, the number of Americans with group health insurance quadrupled from 22 million to 83 million. Wages and salaries were increasingly set through so-called internal labor markets in an effort to achieve results that seemed "fair." For many nonunion workers, that meant being paid according to elaborate job evaluations, an approach pioneered by the Hay Group, a consulting company. Companies adopted point systems to set comparable compensation for comparable workers. Points were awarded for skill, seniority and the nature of the job. The idea was for, say, a mechanical engineer and accountant with similar education levels, responsibilities and experience to be paid roughly the same, so that neither felt misused.[7]

Corporate executives saw themselves as managers—not capitalists—who harnessed the productive potential of huge organizations for the public good. A DuPont advertising slogan captured this attitude: "Better Living Through Chemistry." As early as 1927, speaking at the Harvard Business School, General Electric chairman Owen Young had compared large firms to public utilities with responsibilities to the whole society. After the war, many executives embraced this way of thinking. Aside from shareholders, companies had to satisfy other "stakeholders"—workers, local communities and political leaders (who represented public goals). There was an ideology of management. Studies found a gap in opinion between business leaders in large and smaller firms. The first accepted social responsibilities, while the second "repeated free market rhetoric and denied any commitment to a broader group of stakeholders," wrote Ernie Englander of George Washington University and Allen Kaufman of the University of New Hampshire.[8]

The best-known theoretician of the ideology of management was Harvard economist John Kenneth Galbraith, whose 1967 bestseller *The New Industrial State* synthesized its central assumptions. Galbraith split the modern economy into two distinct sectors: a traditional sector of small and often family-owned businesses—stores, farms, dry cleaners, machine shops; and the "new industrial state" of megacorporations. The traditional sector abided by the standard laws of economics. Competitive markets set prices; firms were born and died; businesses were at the mercy of the market. By contrast, megacorporations enjoyed virtual immortality. With only a few big firms, many industries benefited from near-monopoly market power. Through massive advertising, companies could condition consumers to buy their products and could—without many competitors—set optimal prices. They controlled new technologies, because only they could muster the resources to hire the required engineers and scientists, undertake research and development and build new plants. Finally, they could pay for most new investments with retained profits and depreciation, as opposed to borrowing from banks or selling stock. Thus, managers escaped much discipline from lenders or shareholders.

Old-style capitalism was dead. Profits were assured. Demand would remain high, because government economic management would keep it high. If costs rose (often reflecting higher wages, imposed by unions), they could be passed along to consumers. Modest inflation was inconvenient, not crippling. These large firms were "the heartland of the modern economy. . . . nearly all communications, nearly all production and distribution of electric power, much transportation, most manufacturing and mining, a substantial share of retail trade, and considerable amount of entertainment. . . . [M]ost work [is] done by five or six hundred firms." Their triumph, Galbraith wrote:

assaults the most majestic of all economic assumptions, namely that man in his economic activities is subject to the authority of the market. Instead we have an economic system which, whatever its formal ideological billing, is in substantial part a planned economy. The initiative in deciding what is to be produced comes not from the sovereign consumer who, through the market, issues the instructions that bend the productive mechanism to his ultimate will. Rather it comes from the great producing organization which reaches forward to control the market that it is presumed to serve and, beyond, to bend the customer to its needs.[9]

Hardly anyone talks this way anymore. Some of Galbraith's arguments were simply wrong. He contended, for example, that entrepreneurs—individuals who invent or commercialize new technologies, products or services—were economic relics. Megacorporations controlled innovation. That was never true. In 1920, start-up RCA (not General Electric) pioneered radio; in the 1960s, start-up Xerox (not IBM) pioneered paper copying. Even as Galbraith wrote, Ray Kroc was starting the giant-to-be McDonald's, and David Packard and Ed Hewlett were creating a major electronics firm. Later, Bill Gates and Steve Jobs ended IBM's domination of the computer industry, and Sam Walton revolutionized retailing with Wal-Mart. All were classic entrepreneurs. Similarly, Galbraith underestimated the power of consumer sovereignty. A case in point: In 1985, Coca-Cola tried to replace its long-standing formula with something that, its marketers thought, had more appeal. Customers rebelled; the company sheepishly restored the old formula, renamed Coke Classic.[10]

But inflation and its side effects also demolished much of Galbraith's intellectual superstructure—and the parallel assumptions held by many corporate managers. From the Volcker-Reagan recession, many Americans, and particularly corporate managers, learned that the business cycle had not yet been tamed. Firms could no longer assume they could pass higher costs, including higher labor costs, on to customers. If they tried, profits might suffer, because some customers could not afford higher prices and other customers might buy less. So there were practical pressures to hold down prices, and high-cost firms faced a profit squeeze. In extreme cases, they might go bankrupt. The whole cost-plus mind-set of managers began to submit to new realities. There was a hardening of thinking.

Greater competition reinforced the effect. "[I]t is impossible to understand why the American economy was so good in the 1990s—and why America did better than other countries—without understanding the role that more intense competition has played," writes economist Paul London. Much of this resulted from deliberate government policies to check inflation. Until the late 1970s and early 1980s, the railroad, trucking, phone and airline industries were regulated. Government agencies restricted competition and set prices. These industries were considered to be "natural" monopolies, or something close, which would operate more efficiently with limited or no competition.* Many economists disputed this logic, which often dated from the Great Depression when prices were falling and government policies tried to prop them up. Heavy regulation, the economists argued, suppressed innovation, encouraged inefficiency, and led to cost-push price increases that the government agencies ratified, because the alternative—letting companies go bankrupt—was unthinkable. By the mid-1970s, presidents, members of Congress and policy makers, desperate to control inflation, began to listen. Gradually, regulation of these industries was abolished.[11]

As a result, huge segments of the economy that had been sheltered from competition now faced lower-cost rivals. Foreign

---

* Truckers and airlines were regulated during the Depression, when falling prices plagued both industries. The Interstate Commerce Commission regulated railroads and truckers; the Civil Aeronautics Board, the airlines; and the Federal Communications Commission, AT&T, the nation's telephone near-monopoly.

competition did the same for other industries: steel, automobiles, machine tools, televisions, clothing. In the early decades after World War II, few Americans imagined being challenged by Europeans let alone Japanese (known for cheap toys and transistor radios) or, heavens, the Chinese (then called "the Red Chinese," a sworn enemy). Galbraith essentially ignored the whole subject of foreign competition. Some increase of competition was inevitable as Europe and Japan recovered from the destruction of World War II. But the great intensification of the 1980s stemmed from the dollar's steep ascent on foreign exchange markets. As inflation fell, the dollar's exchange rate rose, because overseas investors regained confidence in the currency. A higher dollar made foreign imports cheaper and U.S. exports more expensive. The upshot: severe pressures on many U.S. industries to reduce costs and increase efficiency.

Even without these changes, executives encountered new threats from the stock market. Galbraith was correct in concluding that managers were insulated from shareholders. In their classic 1934 book *The Modern Corporation and Private Property,* Adolf A. Berle, Jr., and Gardiner Means had noted that most managers could ignore disgruntled shareholders. The rules for electing corporate boards were rigged in favor of management. Unhappy shareholders couldn't easily evict a firm's directors or executives; the simplest solution was to sell their stock. But this insulation thinned in the 1980s with the emergence of the "market for corporate control." As interest rates fell and stock prices rose—again, reflecting lower inflation—investment syndicates borrowed huge amounts and bought all the stock of underperforming firms. The idea was to flip the company: overhaul management, improve performance and resell the shares at a higher price. (Because borrowing is known as "leverage," these transactions are called "leveraged buyouts," or LBOs.)★ Some conglomerates— firms with many separate businesses—were tempting targets; they could often be operated more efficiently if split up into smaller operating units. But the threat of being acquired made most corporate chiefs feel vulnerable. They had "to reduce waste and boost productivity and profitability" or face a takeover, economist Roger Alcaly has noted. A low stock price could jeopardize their jobs. By one study, a quarter of 1,000 large firms received a hostile takeover bid sometime in the 1980s.[12]

In some sense, companies became more capitalist because they had no choice. They either adapted—or faded and failed. The belief structure held by corporate managers and popularized by Galbraith crumbled as competition increased and corporate independence decreased. Top corporate executives, who once enjoyed the tenure of college professors, could be dumped. In October 1992, Robert C. Stempel, General Motors' CEO, resigned after only twenty-seven months on the job, dispatched by disgruntled directors. The company wasn't moving fast enough, the directors thought, to reverse big losses. The change, said *The New York Times,* fulfilled what many experts had urged "for hidebound American corporations: the breakup of the clubby atmosphere in corporate board rooms, where top executives rarely face tough grading on their performance and

---

★ This strategy is known as "private equity." Major private equity firms include Kohlberg Kravis Roberts and Co., the Carlyle Group and the Blackstone Group.

directors rarely take direct action." In January 1993, IBM CEO John F. Akers was forced out. Despite 100,000 job cuts since 1986 (so much for lifetime employment!), the firm had lost $5 billion in 1992. In March, IBM named its first outside CEO, Louis Gerstner, Jr. Just a few years earlier, the expulsion of top executives at two blue-chip firms was unimaginable.[13]

As competition increased and shareholder passivity decreased, companies were quicker to cut jobs and costs. There was a de-emphasis of "internal labor markets" in favor of local wages, which were often lower. In one well-publicized case in 1995, IBM cut the salaries of executive secretaries, because they were "way out of kilter" with local rates. Most of all, unions lost power because they were concentrated in manufacturing and service industries (autos, steel, trucking, telecommunications), which faced heavy competition from imports or nonunion companies with lower labor costs. Unionized firms shed workers and curbed wages and benefits; so the union sector contracted and the remaining unions were less influential. By 2005, only one in thirteen private industry workers belonged to a union, down from one in six in 1983.[14]

A new economic order had come into being mostly as a reaction to unanticipated events. The "mixed economy" that had seemed fairly placid and predictable increasingly resembled a Darwinian free-for-all. The softening of capitalism that had started after World War II stopped and, to some extent, went into reverse. Companies revised hiring, firing and compensation practices. Workers shifted assumptions about what they could expect. Inflation was usually not the immediate cause of these changes, but its side effects—on regulation, stock prices, exchange rates and the business cycle—often were. The result was to strip away many illusions that, in the first decades after the war, had fostered the belief that capitalism had been so thoroughly improved that it had changed into something else entirely. Once these illusions disappeared, many of capitalism's basic characteristics reemerged: intense competition, constant change, the clamor for higher returns. And all these developments were amplified by a parallel set of changes abroad: what we now call "globalization."

III

To a degree unimaginable in 1980, capitalism has gone global. Supply chains and production networks span continents. We live in a world where an American can buy a Ford that assembled in Mexico with a transmission from Japan and half its other parts from non-U.S. sources. Finance spills across national boundaries. A routine *Wall Street Journal* story in 2005—"Foreign Stocks Get New Push"—would have been a fairy tale a quarter century earlier. Most surprisingly, countries such as China and Russia have adopted some form of capitalism. In our mind's eye, globalization is easily explained. Capitalism bested communism, and nations copied the winner. Lower transportation and communication costs tied countries closer together. But this story has glaring omissions. Globalization required a strong America, and a strong America required that inflation be subdued. As a result, capitalism's prestige increased, and the dollar was restored as a dependable currency for trade and international finance. The persistence of higher inflation would have stunted globalization.[15]

Historically, global trade and finance have flourished when a single nation acts as their promoter and protector by providing an open market for goods, a stable world currency and a military umbrella for commerce. Before World War I, Britain played the part. After the war, it was too weak to do so again. Globalization's subsequent foundering in the 1920s and 1930s proves that it depends on more than technology. It also needs a political and economic framework. After World War II, the United States provided that leadership. This first phase of globalization—then simply called "free trade"—was seen as a way to prevent another Depression (protectionism abetted the 1930s collapse) and combat communism (prosperity in Europe and Japan would strengthen democracy). The strategy succeeded. From 1950 to 1970, world trade grew roughly by a factor of five. Tariffs dropped dramatically. Before the war, U.S. tariffs averaged about 50 percent; now they're less than 5 percent. But this initial globalization need not have continued. By the late 1970s, rampaging inflation had weakened the U.S. economy and eroded American leadership. We can never know exactly what would have occurred if the erosion had continued, but we can speculate.[16]

Imagine what would have happened in the 1980s if America had remained plagued by stubborn inflation, frequent recessions and meager income gains. Even if the Soviet Union had collapsed (not a certainty), the United States wouldn't have been a good advertisement for capitalism. America would have seemed an ailing giant. Indeed, a burgeoning scholarly and popular literature had already reached that conclusion. In *The Rise and Fall of the Great Powers* (1987), Yale historian Paul Kennedy made the argument by comparing the United States to other lapsed superpowers, particularly the Hapsburg and British empires. In *Trading Places* (1988), Clyde Prestowitz—an expert on Japan—argued that Japan had already overtaken the United States. It had higher savings rates and seemed to have assumed leadership in many critical industries (electronics, steel, autos). "[T]he American Century is over," Prestowitz wrote in the book's 1989 paperback edition, and "the trading of places by Japan and the United States . . . has become a *fait accompli.*"[17]

We forget how prevalent those views were. At home and abroad, the United States was portrayed as lagging in technology, living standards and economic growth. Only in the late 1980s and early 1990s, just as the Soviet Union collapsed, did it become clear that these widespread criticisms did not fit the evidence. People could see that America's economic vitality had been prematurely and erroneously discounted. The United States continued to be a hotbed of entrepreneurial enthusiasm. New companies (Wal-Mart, Microsoft, Apple Computer) thrived. And by standard economic indicators, the United States performed as well as or better than its main rivals, and the gap would widen. From 1992 to 2000, U.S. economic growth averaged 3.7 percent annually compared with 1.8 percent for Germany and 1.2 percent for Japan.[18]

Falling inflation also promoted globalization through the dollar. The world economy, like all successful economic systems, requires reliable money. For centuries, gold and silver coins served this role. In the late nineteenth century, the British pound—readily convertible into gold—also provided global money. After World War II, the dollar did. No other large country had a trusted currency, and gold was too scarce and unevenly distributed (in the late 1940s, the United States had 70 percent of the world supply) to restart the gold standard. It's not just the United States that uses dollars. More than half of Japan's exports are still priced in dollars, as are about 70 percent of its imports. For South Korea and Thailand, four-fifths of exports and imports involve dollars. Even for France and Germany—where the euro dominates—a third of exports are priced in dollars. But continuation of the dollar's central role was not inevitable. Recall why confidence in the currency ebbed in the late 1970s: Inflation cut its purchasing power; U.S. interest rates remained near or below inflation; U.S. stock prices lagged inflation. Why use unstable dollars for trade? Why hold them as a reserve or store of value?[19]

By reviving confidence in the dollar, Volcker and Reagan unconsciously transformed the global trading system. From 1980 to 1985, the dollar rose 62 percent against the deutsche mark, 5 percent against the yen and 112 percent against the French franc (France was having inflation problems of its own). The "strong" dollar thrust America's trade balances into a rising and almost continuous deficit—creating in the process a huge export subsidy for other countries to embrace globalization. At these levels, the dollar encouraged U.S. imports and discouraged U.S. exports. Although the dollar's value fluctuated in later years, the basic changes endured for about two decades. The dollar stayed strong, and large U.S. trade deficits persisted. In 1980, U.S. trade was virtually balanced. By 1987, the deficit was $145 billion, or 3 percent of GDP. By 2005, it was $717 billion, or nearly 6 percent of GDP.*[20]

Though overlooked, this change powerfully promoted globalization. Because exports create jobs—a popular objective—the stronger dollar represented a bonanza for other countries. It improved the competitiveness of their exports, spurred economic growth and reduced the threat of imports, particularly American imports, to local jobs. As a result, it became easier for countries to endorse expanded trade even if that meant reducing their own trade barriers. From the jobs perspective, the game seemed fixed in their favor. As long as Americans didn't respond by adopting protectionist measures, the arrangement would encourage both trade and trade liberalization. That's generally what happened.† Americans toler-

---

* A popular, but mistaken, view in the 1980s held that the trade deficits resulted from Reagan's budget deficits. Higher U.S. interest rates— allegedly caused by the budget deficits—attracted foreign money into the United States, lifting the dollar's exchange rate as foreigners sold their currencies and bought dollars. Later events discredited this theory. In the late 1990s, despite U.S. budget *surpluses,* the trade deficits widened. Foreign money flowed into the United States in the 1980s and 1990s because foreigners found American investments attractive. As for U.S. interest rates, a budget deficit or surplus is only one influence on them. Others include inflation, the stage of the business cycle, the supply and demand for credit, and investors' psychology.

† To be sure, there were contrary pressures. U.S. firms protested the high dollar in the early 1980s. The Reagan administration responded by persuading foreign exporters to adopt "voluntary" limits on auto, steel and machine-tool shipments. Later, the Reagan administration promoted a

ated deficits, because a strong economy kept unemployment low and cheap imports satisfied consumers and helped restrain inflation. Global trade growth accelerated. Hurt by the U.S. recession, world exports grew only 11 percent from 1980 to 1985. From 1990 to 2000, they increased 85 percent.[21]

The restored dollar similarly transformed international finance by encouraging a breakdown of barriers to cross-border flows of money into stocks, bonds and bank loans. This was a fundamental change. In the late nineteenth century, large money flows between countries were common. But after World War II, most countries imposed capital controls—restrictions on inflows and outflows. Of course, capital flows never ceased completely. The Marshall Plan supplied Europe with $13.3 billion from 1948 to 1951 (today's value: more than $600 billion).* In general, the United States didn't impose capital controls, and dollars went abroad as foreign aid, military aid and the investments of U.S. multinationals. In the 1950s, these flows were regarded as essential to provide Europe and Japan with the dollars they needed to buy imports and rebuild war-torn industries. Other channels for global capital included the "Eurodollar" market—dollars held outside the United States. The Soviet Union started the market in 1954. The Soviets had earned dollars by selling gold, but they didn't want to deposit the dollars in the United States. So the dollars were deposited in London.[22]

---

depreciation of the dollar, notably at a September 1985 meeting of major countries at the Plaza hotel in New York. However, the dollar was already declining.

* It was named after the wartime army chief of staff and Truman's Secretary of State, General George C. Marshall.

Still, the strong prejudice against international capital flows was rooted in history. In the 1930s, capital movements aggravated the Great Depression. Investors had withdrawn bank deposits or sold securities, then converted paper currencies (say, British pounds or Austrian schillings) into gold that was shipped abroad. These outflows fed banking crises, as banks lost deposits and cut lending. After the war, these stinging memories discouraged free capital flows. Some countries accepted investments of multinational firms in factories or offices—so-called foreign direct investment (FDI)—because they created jobs. But FDI was a spotty exception to pervasive restrictions on cross-border money flows. In general, people saved and invested at home. Outside the United States, many countries' stock and bond markets were reserved for their citizens, and most people and companies couldn't easily move money abroad. If you were French, you saved in francs, which were invested in France.

No more. Capital controls have been widely dismantled (a major exception: China). In 1980, individuals and firms held $3.2 trillion worth of assets—stocks, bonds, bank deposits—outside their home countries, equal to about 27 percent of the world economy (global GDP). By 2003, that had increased to $47 trillion, equal to 130 percent of world GDP. In part, capital controls broke down because firms had greater needs to transfer funds across borders. But the strong dollar and mushrooming U.S. trade deficits were catalysts. Countries with large trade surpluses had to dispose of the excess dollars they earned. In Europe and Japan, the most appealing choice was often for dollars to be reinvested abroad, mostly in the United States. That would keep dollars off foreign exchange markets and mean that their own currencies remained undervalued for trade.

Governments in some countries (Japan, China) deliberately rein- vested dollars in U.S. Treasury securities; other governments recy- cled dollars by allowing private investors (individuals, banks, insurance companies) to invest them abroad. Exporters earned dol- lars; investors bought them on foreign exchange markets and sent most of them to the United States.[23]

In these decades, the United States received a flood tide of foreign funds to acquire U.S. stocks, bonds, real estate and entire companies. This made it harder for other countries not to relax their controls: If Japanese could invest in America, why couldn't Americans invest in Japan? There were other pressures. Developing countries increas- ingly sought foreign investment, especially FDI in factories. Dis- mantling controls was tedious and technical. The changes occurred slowly, but the cumulative effect was massive. One survey of 10 ad- vanced and 24 "middle income" countries (including Brazil, Singa- pore and Indonesia) found that 8 of the advanced countries and 19 of the middle-income countries significantly reduced controls from 1973 to 1996. In 1986, the European Union adopted the Single Eu- ropean Act, which committed members to removing controls by June 1990. From 1980 to 1990, annual FDI flows to developing countries went from $6 billion to $135 billion. As late as 1987, no private company from a developing country had sold bonds on in- ternational markets. In 2003, they floated almost $14 billion.[24]

So globalization did *not* result just from better technology and the end of the Cold War. Having a trustworthy global currency was also crucial. It promoted trade, cross-border money flows and confi- dence. In effect, the United States provided a service to the world in the form of global money, and the dollar's high exchange rate (reflecting demand for the currency) enabled other countries to pay for the service. They sent us goods; we sent them dollars. That largely explained the huge U.S. trade deficits. If you try to visualize a hypothetical and alternate history—one with continued U.S. inflation and economic instability—the whole structure of global trade and finance would have evolved differently and more slowly. Higher inflation would have meant a weaker economy and depreciating dollar. American exports might have increased and imports diminished. But this would have reduced other countries' exports and dulled their appetite for trade. Instead of attracting huge foreign investments, the United States might have experienced outflows. Then, the government might have restricted how many dollars U.S. citizens and companies could take abroad. "If the dollar had continued to fall—as it had in the Carter years—we would have used capital controls to bottle up the pressures," said economist Barry Eichengreen of the University of California at Berkeley.* Other countries might have erected new controls.[25]

What kind of globalization would have resulted with an inflationary and wobbling United States is impossible to say. But trade and finance might have become politicized and regionalized, as

---

* The aim would have been to limit dollar sales on foreign exchange markets. In the 1960s, President Johnson restricted what U.S. banks and multinational firms could invest abroad in an effort to limit foreign government demand for gold at $35 an ounce. These controls, largely ineffective, were rescinded in the early 1970s after the dollar was devalued. In 1964, Congress also imposed an "interest equalization tax" on foreign bonds that paid higher rates than U.S. bonds. It aimed to deter purchases of foreign bonds and was ultimately repealed.

occurred in the 1930s. Most countries then faced a dilemma: Not being self-sufficient, they had to trade, but they feared that trade would aggravate unemployment. To resolve the dilemma, countries retreated into preferential trade blocs that provided essential imports while limiting other imports. To some extent, the strong dominated the weak. By the spring of 1938, Germany had bilateral trade agreements with twenty-five countries, including many of its close neighbors. These agreements often compelled its trading partners to accept terms generous to Germany (high prices for Germany's exports, low prices for their own exports). England favored trade with its empire and discriminated against others. A weak dollar and America might have similarly caused the world to splinter into regional blocs. But none of this happened. Instead, global capitalism spread, and American companies and workers now compete in a world in which technology, labor and capital are highly mobile. The pressures to maximize profits and minimize costs now play out on a global stage.[26]

IV

It would be preposterous to argue that inflation alone refashioned the American economy. Regardless of inflation, technology would have advanced. Personal computers and the Internet would have spread. Regardless of inflation, some verson of a global economy would have evolved. Recovered from World War II, Europe and Japan would have inevitably become our economic rivals. The notion that America could excel in every aspect of every industry—

a common view in the 1950s and 1960—was a patriotic fantasy. Still, inflation assumed a pivotal role in a transformation that transcended economics and also affected politics and popular culture. In a wise essay nearly twenty years ago, the late economist Herbert Stein cautioned against defining capitalism by a narrow list of economic characteristics. Capitalism, he noted, had to adapt to social realities. It had survived the political threat of the Great Depression and "had gone on to great successes" precisely because it could change.

> [T]he capitalism that survived and succeeded was not the capitalism of 1929. The capitalism that will succeed in the next sixty years may not be the capitalism of the late twentieth century. Capitalism succeeded in large part because it adapted. Capitalism is not a blank slate upon which anything can be written; it has a central core that must be preserved if it is to remain capitalism. But the large penumbra around that core can change without ending capitalism, and it has to change from time to time if capitalism is to survive. The central core of capitalism, without which a society would not be capitalist, is freedom. But absolute freedom is impossible, and no one has satisfactorily defined the amount and kind of freedom that is essential to qualify as capitalism.[27]

Against Stein's elastic standard, the resurrected capitalism since the 1980s has permeated popular culture as well as the economy. It has altered mass beliefs, values and interests. Writing in 2004, journalist Roger Lowenstein noted that, in the 1970s, most newspapers "carried at most a single account of the previous day's action on Wall Street, and television barely covered it at all." What happened to the stock market simply did not concern most Americans. "Today, at my daughter's middle school in New Jersey, an investing club is busily educating future market wizards, but in the '70s, through four years on an Ivy League campus, I didn't hear a mention of the stock market." Colleges and universities now offer courses in entrepreneurship, and successful business founders—say, Larry Page and Sergey Brin, Google's founders—are celebrated as heroes. Wealth creation is seen as a vital, risky and, to some extent, romantic undertaking; it is not, as in the 1960s and early 1970s, taken as the inevitable outcome of corporate investment and management (this effortless quality is why Lowenstein, the college student, heard so little of it). Popular culture and ideas have shifted in ways not discernible in economic statistics.[28]

The intellectual godfathers of the old order, Keynes and Galbraith, argued that technocrats could control the economic system for the greater social good. Economists would conquer the business cycle; modern managers would produce technological advances. By contrast, the new order's leading economic philosophers, Milton Friedman and Austrian-born Joseph Schumpeter (1883–1950), thought that economic progress originates in free markets. Schumpeter coined the evocative phrase "creative destruction": Capitalism advances on waves of innovation that, though initially disruptive, ultimately make people better off. The most powerful competition involved "the new commodity [product], the new technology, the new source of supply, the new type of organization." Under the old order, growing national wealth and stability were assumed to be assured and—properly managed—would solve pressing social problems, from poverty to pollution. Under the new order, economic growth was chancy. Because it depended on a willingness to invest and take risks, government had to maintain a supportive climate through its tax and regulatory policies.[29]

The shift was social as well as intellectual. It coincided with a generational transition in American business that reinforced new attitudes. The Depression and World War II wave of executives was retiring. Someone who was twenty-five in 1945 turned sixty in 1980. The new business leaders were not so politically defensive as their predecessors. They worried less about avoiding the class warfare of the 1930s and more about safeguarding the future of their companies in a hostile climate. They also saw themselves as more individualistic. To simplify slightly: The early postwar executives cast themselves as enlightened business engineers who smoothed capitalism's rough edges without crippling its productive capacity. They drew their identity from the group affiliation with their companies: U.S. Steel, IBM, General Motors. Their successors imagined themselves more as warriors and free agents, whose success depended on defeating their business rivals and scoring high on capitalism's standard achievement tests: market share, stock prices, return on investment and (not coincidentally) personal wealth. Jack Welch, Jr., appointed as CEO of General Electric in 1981, became the poster boy for the new type of manager. He focused singlemindedly on improving profits and GE's stock price; he showed no reluctance to fire workers or jettison underperforming businesses.

The contrasts emerge in two landmark business books of the past half century: *My Years with General Motors,* published in 1963 and written by Alfred P. Sloan, Jr., president and then chairman of GM from 1923 to 1946; and *Only the Paranoid Survive,* published in 1996 and written by Andrew Grove, president and then CEO of Intel from 1979 to 1998. Each headed the dominant company in a dominant industry—cars through the 1960s; computer chips now. The contrasts are dramatic. In Sloan's era, big enterprises seemed suited to serve mass markets through economies of scale in production and distribution. But they might founder if their size spawned chaos and waste. In the early 1920s, General Motors—the result of many mergers—was highly disorganized. Suffused throughout Sloan's account is confidence that competent management could overcome size's drawbacks and exploit its advantages. Here are some chapter titles: "The Concept of the Organization," "Co-ordination by Committee," "The Development of Financial Controls." These subjects now strike us as dull, but they were real challenges in creating suitable business methods. Sloan wrote:

I do not regard [GM's size] as a barrier. To me it is only a problem of management. My thoughts on that have always revolved around one concept . . . the concept that goes by the oversimplified name of decentralization. The General Motors type of organization—co-ordinated in policy and decentralized in administration—not only has worked for us, but also has become the standard practice in a large part of American industry.[30]

Grove exuded none of Sloan's confidence. Instead, he saw threats everywhere, and even when he couldn't see them, he feared they were there. "[W]hen it comes to business, I believe in the value of paranoia," he wrote. "The more successful you are, the more people want a chunk of your business and then another . . . until there is nothing left." Companies could not flourish just by producing quality products at low cost, or by excelling in research and development, or by expanding into new markets. Firms also had to overcome what Grove called "strategic inflection points"—a new label for "creative destruction." Strategic inflection points are new products, technologies or management methods that alter "the way business is conducted." Personal computers had dethroned IBM. Containerization had harmed some ports (New York, San Francisco) and helped others (Seattle, Singapore) that adapted faster. People always resisted change. In 1927, *The Jazz Singer*—the first successful sound movie—debuted. Yet, even in 1931, Charlie Chaplin, the famous silent-movie star, declared, "I give talkies six months more."[31]

Different life experiences separated Sloan and Grove. When Sloan's book appeared, the postwar boom was still in full swing, and U.S. companies seemed invincible. Grove, on the other hand, had witnessed successful challenges to many U.S. industries (steel, autos, televisions), and his own industry—on the cutting edge of technology—was in constant competitive turmoil. Sloan wasn't naïve (as was perhaps Galbraith) about competition. Too much success for a firm, he warned about GM, "may bring self satisfaction. . . . In that event, the urge for competitive survival, the strongest of all economic incentives, is dulled. The spirit of venture is lost in the inertia." That, indeed, helped explain GM's later distress. But for Grove, fierce competition was an everyday reality. It prevented complacency. A company might not sacrifice just a few points of market share. It might disappear. Old-style capitalism no longer seemed dated. "[N]obody owes you a career," Grove warned. That was the implicit promise of the old economic order; it wasn't of the new.[32]

Contrary to much commentary, government's size did not shrink in the new economic order. Government regulation remains pervasive. But there was a shift in its role and in perceptions and emphasis. Government became less ambitious, because people lost faith that new programs could solve all social and economic problems. That was a major political legacy of inflation and the failure to end the business cycle. Ideas changed. This was particularly true of economic policy. At the Fed, Friedman's view that money creation is at the core of inflation became conventional wisdom.*

"Central bankers over the past several decades have absorbed an important principle," wrote Alan Greenspan, Volcker's successor as Federal Reserve Board chairman. "Price stability is the path to maximum sustainable [economic] growth." Serving from August 1987 until January 2006, Greenspan was determined not to squander Volcker's gains:

---

* Not all of Friedman's ideas triumphed. His view that inflation is a monetary phenomenon was widely accepted. But he also wanted the Fed to follow a simple monetary rule, increasing the money supply by a given amount (say, 3 percent) a year. This, Friedman argued, would create just enough money to permit economic growth without kindling inflation. Though some recessions would occur, the Fed didn't know enough to do better. But a money rule wasn't permanently adopted, and most economists regard it as impractical, because devising a precise statistical definition of money is so difficult.

When I arrived, a very large part of the price inflation had
been defused. Volcker's actions in October of 1979 and following on into the 1980s essentially broke the back of inflation's
acceleration. When I came, the real problem was that, as is often
the case when you come from 12 percent—or whatever it
was—down to four percent, then you get a bounce [back]. . . .
I did not want to be involved in losing the significant progress
that Volcker had achieved, which meant that there was a defi-
nite bias towards tightness.[33]

Four times, the Greenspan Fed raised interest rates to prevent
higher inflation (1988–90, 1994–95, 1999–2000 and 2004–06). In
July 1996, the FOMC debated the nature of price stability. It concluded that, given the technical difficulties of measuring price
changes (higher prices for higher-quality goods—say a longer-
lasting tire—should not count as inflation) and potential dangers of
deflation (falling prices), an inflation up to 2 percent would be acceptable. Fifteen years earlier, the debate would have been impossible. High inflation seemed too intractable. By 2004, Greenspan
declared victory: "Our goal of price stability was achieved by most
analysts' definition by mid-2003. Unstinting and largely preemptive
efforts over two decades have finally paid off."[34]

To be sure, the Fed had help. In the 1990s, productivity growth
was high, oil prices were low, the spread of "managed care" held
health costs—for a while at least—down, and stiff competition from
imports, reflecting the strong dollar, helped restrain the prices of
manufactured goods. One study estimated that all these factors, plus
some technical revisions of the Consumer Price Index, might have

shaved nearly one percentage point annually from inflation from 1994 to 1999. Good luck and good policy reinforced each other, but the two were connected. The good luck stemmed partly from good policy. If the Fed had tolerated higher inflation, oil prices would have been higher, the dollar would have been lower (and imports competition weaker) and the advent of "managed care" less effective.[35]

Subsiding inflation that eventually led to a crude sort of price stability was both cause and consequence of America's restored capitalism. But the new economic order also has manifest shortcomings, and just how it might—as Stein suggested—evolve and adapt in the future remains an open question partly dependent on how the American public weighs its relative strengths and weaknesses. Understandably, these issues have become the focus of fierce debate.

6

PRECARIOUS PROSPERITY

Thousands of American companies traveled the path from the old order to the new. Stanley Works, a leading manufacturer of hand tools, including hammers, socket wrenches and pliers, was one. Well into the 1970s, its success seemed secure. Most production was located in the United States. If business softened, factory workers were furloughed by seniority. When sales revived, most workers were recalled. White-collar workers—managers, salesmen, secretaries—were rarely even furloughed. But in the late 1970s, the company suddenly faced Asian imports priced at a 40 percent discount. Costs had to be cut. The first CEOs made changes slowly. Having spent long careers at the company, they were torn between new pressures and old norms. White-collar jobs initially dropped by attrition. Factories were automated, leaving some (if fewer) jobs. Some work moved abroad. But in 1997, the firm's directors, dissatisfied with the company's lackluster stock price, hired an outsider as CEO. He closed forty-three of the remaining eighty-three plants—concentrated in the United States—and shifted more work abroad. "Layoffs and plant closings," he told the journalist Louis Uchitelle, "are not such rare events anymore that one generally makes a big deal out of them."[1]

Although the new economic order was superior to the old, it often didn't seem that way. As the experiences of Stanley Works and other companies suggested, it delivered a perplexing prosperity with manifest imperfections. Jobs were more plentiful—but less secure. Living standards were higher—but incomes were more unequal and less predictable. Business cycles were milder—but financial markets became more erratic and unstable. Competition inspired new technologies and products—but also threatened companies and industries wedded to old technologies and products. The economic adaptability that we admire—the ability to make the most of change—imposed the very insecurity that we deplore. "Hardly any company is too successful nowadays to consider a large-scale cutback in jobs," social critic James Lardner has written. Consider Intel, he said. Though consistently profitable, the giant computer-chip maker announced job cuts in early 2007 of 10,500, about 10 percent of its worldwide workforce, to make the company "more agile and efficient."[2]

It is easy to caricature the new order as the triumph of profit maximization, CEO enrichment and the culture of efficiency, and as such, it often seems a step backward. What good are higher incomes if, at any moment, they can be abruptly withdrawn? Economic progress, as the term was widely understood in the first decades after World War II, did not refer exclusively to more and more material possessions. It also meant enhanced economic security—mainly job security, but also protection against impoverishment from sickness, disability and old age. Peace of mind was part of the postwar living standard, and the new order seemed to relegate it to a lowly place, if not ignore it altogether. The new order often seemed obsessed with money to the exclusion of all other values. The old order, with its more protective corporations and greater emphasis on "fairness," seemed more humane and morally superior.

As with many caricatures, this one rings true up to a point, but it is also artificial and contrived. It treats the evolution of our economic system as a conscious choice, controlled by a selfish elite of investment managers and corporate executives who manipulated the system to increase profits and their own wealth. In this, their natural allies and fellow travelers were conservative politicians who idolized "the market" and were obsessed with lowering taxes and shrinking government. The reality was different. Government didn't shrink, and the rise of the new economic order was an unplanned and protracted process, largely a reaction to the crippling shortcomings of the old order. People now forget that in the 1970s the economy was becoming more inflation-prone, unstable and subject to rising unemployment. These developments were wildly unpopular. American firms were also less capable of generating higher living standards, even as they were losing markets to German, Japanese and other foreign companies. The old order was not, as popular lore now holds, deliberately discarded. Instead, it slowly succumbed under the weight of its own failures.

Its economic illusion—which explains its powerful, nostalgic appeal—was that we could create a virtually utopian system that would marry all the advantages of an expanding economy (more jobs, technological advances, new products, higher living standards, and more personal choices) with all the advantages of a static economy (greater job security, more certainty, familiar technologies and business methods), without suffering the disadvantages of either. The central contradiction was that an economic system premised on change could simultaneously banish change. We would enjoy the gains and avoid the pain. The fact that the ideal seemed to have been realized briefly in the late 1960s, when American companies dominated the world and the U.S. economy was in the midst of a fabulous boom, created the myth—still cherished by some—that the old order was a practical possibility. In fact, this temporary triumph was mostly the result of the first intoxicating phase of inflationary economic policies (which created the initial boom) and the lingering aftereffects of World War II (which eliminated most international competition). In the 1970s, both these props collapsed.

The new economic order was indeed inferior to the *imagined and romanticized* version of the old order. But it was superior to the old order *as it actually operated*. Still, the new order's defining characteristics consisted of a series of paradoxes. Consider:

First: Although the economy became more stable—with fewer and milder recessions—individual workers and companies faced more insecurities and uncertainties about jobs, wages, fringe benefits and the very survival of firms.

Business cycles became gentler. The two brief recessions between

1982 and 2007 (those of 1990–91 and 2001) lasted only sixteen months combined.★ Otherwise, the economy generally expanded. Economists called this smoothing of the business cycle "the Great Moderation." Its causes are still unclear, but some of the improvement surely came from disinflation. Lower inflation meant that efforts to control it were less disruptive. But the benefits for individual workers often seemed illusory. Because companies resorted more quickly to layoffs and dismissals, career jobs became less reliable. In 1983, the median job tenure of men age forty-five to fifty-four was nearly thirteen years, meaning that half of these men had been with the same employer for at least thirteen years. By 2006, that figure had dropped to eight years.†3

Moreover, job insecurity moved up the income scale. In the early post–World War II decades, layoffs afflicted mostly blue-collar factory, construction and service workers. White-collar middle managers and professionals (accountants, engineers, analysts) now became almost equally vulnerable. From 1981 to 1983, the share of high school graduates losing their jobs (14 percent) was double the rate for college graduates (7 percent). By 2001–03, the figures were virtually identical, 12 percent and 10 percent. Older workers were also increasingly affected, and once people lost their jobs, finding new ones was harder, according to studies by Robert G. Valletta of the Federal Reserve Bank of San Francisco. In 2004, about a fifth of

---

★ As noted, the U.S. economy entered a deep recession in late 2007.

† In theory, declining job tenure might reflect more voluntary decisions by workers to quit and get something better. There is little evidence of that.

the jobless had been unemployed for more than half a year—about the same proportion as in 1983 even though the unemployment rate then (9.6 percent) was much higher than in 2004 (5.5 percent).

Second: Although the economy became more productive—and Americans much wealthier—economic inequality increased dramatically. The economic pie got larger, but those at the top received much bigger pieces.

It is not true (though often asserted) that only the very wealthy advanced materially. Since 1980, most households have experienced substantial income gains. Vast numbers of Americans enjoy gadgets and conveniences that didn't exist then or barely existed (computers, cell phones, flat-screen TVs). Homes got larger. Poverty rates fell. In the 1970s and 1980s, a third or more of blacks routinely had incomes beneath the government's official poverty line. By 2001, that had dropped to 22.7 percent (by 2005, it had risen to 24.7 percent). The idea that typical living standards stagnated over any meaningful period (say, ten to fifteen years) is preposterous. But the broad advance was also skewed. It wasn't just that corporate chief executives, investment bankers, sports stars and celebrities benefited more than most. The gap between college and high school graduates widened. In 1979, college graduates earned on average 21 percent more than high school graduates; by 2002, the difference was 44 percent.[4]

Pay systems increasingly emphasized greater skills. In 1980, full-time male workers at the ninetieth percentile of earnings (those with wages and salaries higher than nine-tenths of all workers) made more than four times the earnings of workers at the tenth percentile; by 2005, the advantage was six to one. Weaker unions and eroding manufacturing employment hurt those in the middle. More immigration, feeding the supply of both poorly and highly skilled workers, widened the polarization of wages and salaries. So did mushrooming of "winner-take-all" contests: These are competitions whose victors—whether top executives, lawyers, athletes or doctors—reaped fabulous rewards, far greater than the runners-up.[5]

Third: The expansion of domestic and international finance—the greater availability of credit and investment funds from stocks, bonds and other securities—invigorated economic growth. But it also became a large source of actual and potential economic instability.

Finance loomed large in any economic history of the past quarter century. The greater availability of credit and investment money promoted economic expansion. Venture capital and the rising stock market lubricated the tech boom of the 1990s. The great real estate boom of the early twenty-first century derived largely from easier housing credit provided by the widespread "securitization" of home mortgages. For twenty-five years, greater stock market and real estate wealth prompted households to spend more of their income and borrow more. Developing countries benefited from the mushrooming of cross-border money flows. But financial collapses also loomed larger, starting with the 1987 stock market crash, when the Dow Jones Industrial Average dropped 508 points, or 22.6 percent, in a single day. Then came the 1997–98 Asian financial crisis, when many developing countries defaulted—or came close—on international credits. In 2000, the "tech bubble" burst, and the economy went into recession. In 2007 and 2008, the "real estate bubble" burst.

On reflection, these three paradoxes are less puzzling. Greater insecurity for individual workers and firms often contributed to overall economic stability. As we've seen, competition and uncertainty restrained price and wage increases, helping to muffle inflation and, thereby, promoting longer expansions and milder recessions. Economists Diego Comin and Thomas Philippon contend there was another connection: Intensified competition desynchronized the cycles of individual industries from the overall business cycle. Driven by separate competitive pressures, the ups of some industries (say, computers and autos) cancelled the downs of others (say, airlines and housing). Because layoffs and business closings were not all bunched together during recessions—they were spread across the business cycle—the recessions became less brutal but the expansions involved more angst. This change, though it may have partly explained the Great Moderation, did not apply to the 2007–09 recession.[6]

Similarly, greater inequality may partly explain higher productivity. Companies altered pay practices to get better results. Compensation systems deemphasized "fairness" and seniority and directed rewards to workers considered the most productive or valuable— those who had special knowledge or who had mastered new technologies. Gaps widened between the less and the more skilled, between jobs that seemed more and less crucial. Companies resorted more to commissions, bonuses and incentives to motivate workers. A survey of 1,056 large firms by Hewitt Associates, a consulting company, found that in 2005 almost 11 percent of payroll was distributed by these various incentives, up from 4 percent in 1990. These changes contributed to widening wage inequality and also made year-to-year incomes less stable and predictable. By one study, about a quarter of the increase in wage inequality between the late 1970s and early 1990s stemmed from the growing use of individual incentives. Whether they always achieved their intended results is unclear, but they reflected a new moral code. In the old order, inequality existed, but it was rarely applauded and advertised. In the new, it was often flaunted as a badge of success.[7]

That explains the new order's moral ambiguity. Were its most visible rewards justified by superior performance? Or did they merely rationalize greed and self-interest? The questions clustered most conspicuously around CEO pay, which soared. In the old order, unspoken inhibitions imposed self-restraint. If all in a corporation benefited from the organization's performance and owed a basic allegiance to it, then CEOs could justify higher pay (they had greater responsibilities) but not disproportionately larger gains. If those at the bottom got 5 percent increases, so would those at the top. And that's what happened. From the late 1940s to the 1970s, pay for a typical CEO at a major firm went from about $900,000 (in inflation-adjusted 2000 dollars) to $1.17 million—an increase proportional to what lower-paid workers received. But in the new order, CEOs were awarded lavish stock options that supposedly "aligned" their interests with shareholder interests. The CEO's job was to get the stock price up. By 2000–05, average CEO pay in similar firms had exploded to $9 million. Management may have improved, but much of the gain was a disinflation windfall, as lower inflation and interest rates boosted stock prices. Some observers (including me) believe that many CEOs manipulated the compensation process in their favor and were richly rewarded for, at best, adequate performance. Their personal bonanzas reflected privileged positions in the corporate hierarchy more than exceptional leadership.[8]

II

S till, the new economic order had not completely abolished the old; it had often grafted itself onto the old. Institutions, beliefs and behaviors evolved over time. Familiar practices were modified to meet changed circumstances, and the result was a confusing mosaic. True, corporate allegiance no longer counted for much. Even in the 1980s, senior executives at 56 percent of major companies believed that "employees who are loyal to the company and further its business goals deserve assurance of continued employment." By the 1990s, only 6 percent agreed. But that did not mean that career jobs had vanished. Many workers still formed long-lasting employment relationships. The labor market had not shattered into a merciless free-for-all, with most people regularly pitched out and constantly needing new jobs. Persistent headlines announcing layoffs and "downsizings" depicted wrenching change, but they also exaggerated the change and disguised the continuity. Among workers fifty-five to sixty-four in 2006, about a quarter had been with their current employer for twenty years or more (29 percent for men, 22 percent for women) and almost 70 percent had been with the same employer for at least five years (69 percent for men, 70 percent for women).[9]

Long-term job relationships endured partly because workers and firms had some shared interests. As people age, they generally want more stability in their lives to raise families, repay mortgages and build savings. For companies, their most important economic resource is often their workers' accumulated knowledge, experience and contacts. It's expensive to rehire and retrain workers. In the past, companies deliberately embraced employment practices intended to produce loyalty and long-term stability. In a well-known paper in 1979, economist Edward Lazear of Stanford argued that many companies underpaid younger workers and overpaid older workers relative to their worth. The reason, he said, was to induce workers to remain with the firm during their most productive middle years. Because rewards were skewed toward the final years of their careers, workers had strong incentives to stay. The big payoffs came at the end. Pension benefits typically increased with workers' tenure. Health insurance became more valuable as workers aged, because medical bills rose for their children and for themselves.

It's true that all these traditional bonding mechanisms have weakened. The Lazear-style implicit contracts are less powerful and widespread.* Job security remains strong, but—as Lardner observed—it isn't absolute even at highly successful firms. Many companies have also moved from "defined benefit" pensions to "defined contribution" plans. The first guaranteed workers monthly payments for as long as they lived, with amounts usually based on workers' salaries and years of service. Under the second, employers make contributions to an investment pool (the most common: the 401(k) plan) that becomes available to each worker on retirement. Retirees

---

* Ironically, the advent of age-discrimination laws may also be to blame. Lazear argued that outlawing mandatory retirement might doom seniority arrangements by forcing companies to pay older workers more than they were worth for many years. This partly explains early-retirement "buyouts" for older workers. Prohibited from cutting older workers' wages, firms in effect bribe them to retire. Workers are offered one-time payments to leave.

can tap their personalized investment pools, but when the funds are gone, retirees are on their own. In 1979, 62 percent of workers with pensions were covered by defined benefit plans, only 16 percent by defined contribution and 22 percent by a combination of both; by 2005, the figures were reversed—63 percent had defined contribution plans, 10 percent defined benefit and 27 percent some combination. There was also some erosion of employer-sponsored health insurance.[10]

What occurred, contends Yale political scientist Jacob Hacker, was a "great risk shift." The web of formal and informal guarantees that protected many workers from joblessness, steep health-care costs and poverty in old age had unraveled. The major corporations that once bore these risks had transferred them to the workers themselves, pensions being a clear example. Writes Hacker:

> [E]conomic security strikes at the very heart of the American Dream. It is a fixed American belief that people who work hard, make good choices, and do right by their families can buy themselves permanent membership in the middle class. The rising tide of economic risk swamps these expectations, leaving individuals who have worked hard to reach their present heights facing uncertainty about whether they can keep from falling. . . . [T]he prospect of economic insecurity—of being laid off, or losing health coverage, or having a serious illness befall a family member—stirs up anxiety.[11]

The changes depicted by Hacker, though undeniable, were less dramatic and sensational than he suggests. They might be better labeled "the moderate risk shift," because the old order never achieved universal protections and the new order had not entirely abandoned collective protections. Most companies still made sizable pension contributions: In 1987, 58.4 percent of full-time workers participated in employer-based retirement plans; in 2004, the comparable figure was 56.6 percent. Similarly, most medium-sized and large firms still offer health insurance: In 2006, 92 percent of firms with 50 to 199 workers and 98 percent of firms with 200 or more workers did. It was true that workers' premiums had risen sharply, but that mainly reflected rapidly escalating health-care costs, not proportionately smaller company contributions.[12]

Peter Gosselin, a former reporter at the *Los Angeles Times* who has done the most thorough examination of these trends, found a mixed picture. Families' chances of experiencing a financial setback from common life experiences—unemployment, divorce, a major illness, the birth of a child, retirement or disability—actually decreased slightly between the 1970s and early 1980s and the early 2000s. This was particularly true of unemployment. But the consequences of setbacks had increased. A bit more than a quarter of the families suffering unemployment experienced a drop of 50 percent or more of their income; in the 1970s, the similar figure was 17 percent. Indeed, Gosselin found that large income swings—up and down—had become much more pronounced. "High school graduate families, families headed by those with some college but no degree, and those headed by college graduates have all seen their chances for big fluctuations in their incomes rise," he wrote in *High Wire: The Precarious Financial Lives of American Families.* Economic uncertainty was not just a headline; it was an everyday affair.[13]

Still, it's worth remembering that not all change is unwanted. Many people don't like feeling that they're chained to their jobs. For some, weaker Lazear-style contracts are preferable. Many quit for better wages. Others leave because they want more congenial or challenging work. Still others move because their personal circumstances have changed: They get married or divorced; they relocate; they graduate from school. A flexible labor market accommodates these changes. One recent study estimated that almost 30 percent of job changes in a typical three-month period, equal to roughly 4 percent of employment, were voluntary moves—workers leaving one job and starting another almost immediately. By this study, typical wage increases averaged from 5 percent to 10 percent. Defined contribution as opposed to defined benefit pensions also makes changing jobs easier; the retirement account can simply be moved to the new firm. Finally, the possibility that workers may quit is also a check on employers. It forces them to improve wages, fringe benefits and working conditions to maintain a qualified workforce.[14]

After insecurity, inequality was the other great indictment of the new economic order. Only a tiny elite was said to benefit. The rich got richer, the poor got poorer and the middle class ran in place. Here, too, the caricature is partly true. Look at the table below. It reminds us of the dramatic widening of income differences, especially since 1980. The table shows the average pretax incomes of the poorest fifth of households, the richest fifth and the median household income (the median household is precisely in the middle). Employer-paid fringe benefits are not included; nor are noncash government transfers such as food stamps, or cash raised by borrowing. All figures are in inflation-adjusted 2006 dollars.

HOUSEHOLD INCOMES, 1970–2006

(In 2006 Inflation-Adjusted Dollars)

	POOREST FIFTH	RICHEST FIFTH	MEDIAN INCOME
1970	$9,032	$98,322	$39,604
1980	$10,041	$108,322	$41,258
1990	$10,716	$130,309	$44,778
2000	$11,892	$166,571	$49,163
2006	$11,352	$168,170	$48,201

CHANGE			
1970–2006	+26 percent	+71 percent	+22 percent
1980–2006	+13 percent	+55 percent	+17 percent
1990–2006	+6 percent	+29 percent	+8 percent
2000–2006	−5 percent	+1 percent	−2 percent

Source: Tables A-1 and A-3, *Income, Poverty, and Health Insurance Coverage in the United States: 2006* (Washington, D.C.: U.S. Census Bureau, August 2007).

On their face, these figures are shocking. In 1970, the incomes of the richest fifth were about eleven times those of the poorest fifth; by 2006, they were almost fifteen times higher. If the median household income is taken as the "typical household"—a standard convention, though a misleading one—then income gains for middle Americans since 1970 have averaged less than 1 percent annually; between 2000 and 2006, there was a slight decline. Moreover, these figures miss huge gains for the top 1 or 2 percent. The Census Bureau surveys, on which these figures are based, have sample sizes too small to capture the very rich. Estimates by economists Emmanuel Saez and Thomas Piketty, based on tax returns, suggest that the share of the nation's income going to the top 1 percent nearly doubled from 1980 to 2005, increasing from 7.5 percent to 14.4 percent. The rich seem to squeeze everyone else. Case closed? Not exactly. Here, again, the standard numbers conceal as much as they reveal.[15]

Just because the rich did best doesn't mean that no one else did well. By 2006, almost one-fifth of U.S. households had pretax incomes of $100,000 or more: a once-exclusive threshold that, after adjustment for inflation, is exceeded more often than in 1980 (8.6 percent) and 1995 (14.2 percent). Moreover, "median household income" is no longer a good indicator of middle-class fortunes. Over the years, the nature of households has changed. There are more elderly, divorced couples, single parents and singles. There are more two-earner couples. These trends depress median incomes and increase inequality. If a $100,000 couple with two equal earners divorce, the result is two $50,000 households.* When households are examined by size—that is, by the way people actually live—income gains are larger. From 1990 to 2005, the median household income rose 6.8 percent. But median income rose 10.6 percent for households with three people, 15.8 percent for those with four people and 16.9 percent for those with five people.[16]

Lifestyle changes such as these—well-educated people marrying one another, people living longer or divorcing—explained at least as

---

* A "household" is a single person or two or more people living together, whether related or not; a "family" is two or more related people living together.

much about widening income inequality as wage differences did. In one study, economist Chulhee Lee attributed three-quarters of the increase of inequality from 1968 to 2000 to broad social changes. Married couples, most with two earners, dominated the richest fifth of families; in the poorest fifth, less than half were married and a third of heads—presumably old, disabled, unskilled or unmotivated—had no job. Studying the shorter period of 1979 to 2004, economist Gary Burtless of the Brookings Institution came to a similar conclusion, though he attributed only half the increase of inequality to social trends. To some extent, income gains were also understated, because more and more of pay was diverted to employer-paid health insurance. By one estimate 35 percent of the increase in average compensation for full-time workers from 2000 to 2005 went to health benefits.[17]

Finally, immigration also reduced median incomes and worsened inequality. In effect, America imported people at both the top and the bottom of the income distribution, widening the gap between the two. Huge numbers of low-skilled Hispanics, both legal and illegal, clustered near the bottom. They lowered the median income (the midpoint) and increased the number of people below the government's poverty line ($20,164 for a family of four in 2006). The effect grew over time, because Hispanics' share of all households increased from 4.7 percent in 1980 to 11.2 percent in 2006. Meanwhile, smaller numbers of Asian immigrants and their descendants were concentrated closer to the top.[18]

The picture, then, was more complicated than the rich getting richer at everyone else's expense. The on-the-ground reality contradicts the rhetoric. Drive around most metropolitan areas: What you see is a broad-based prosperity. In some unmeasured ways, the social distance between the middle class and the rich has narrowed, because the gap between luxury items and their mass market equivalents is much smaller than the gap between something and nothing. The difference between a Chevrolet and a Ferrari is mostly status, especially if both drivers are stuck in traffic. Some causes of growing income disparities are perverse. Although new immigrants are mostly better off, their presence depresses reported U.S. incomes. The fact that people live longer is regarded as progress, but elderly households typically have less money in retirement than in their peak earning years (expenses are also usually much lower—child, work and housing costs are reduced or eliminated). Finally, it's worth noting that most of the poor aren't poor because the rich are rich. Family breakdown, low skills, bad work habits, poor health and bad luck are more likely causes. If the rich were poorer—and the market redistributed some of their income—the likely gainers would be the near-rich, today's upper-middle class.

None of this means that the frustrations and anxieties felt by countless Americans aren't genuine. But some are unavoidable. The very process of economic advance creates new "necessities," wants and desires. Being middle class is a moving target. What was ample yesterday no longer suffices today. Before 1920, a car was a luxury; after 1950, it was—for most Americans—a necessity. Before World War II, going to college was a privilege of the well-to-do or an honor for the gifted; after World War II, it became a middle-class staple. In 1985, a mobile phone was an expensive business accessory or personal indulgence; now almost everyone has one. In 2008, 70 percent of households had satellite or cable TV, 66 percent had high-speed Internet and 42 percent had flat-screen TVs.[19] Twenty-five years earlier, the comparable figures would have been negligible or zero. The trouble is that our "needs" and wants often outrun our incomes, creating a sense of failure and of falling behind. This is one aspect of the new economic order that is no different from the old.

III

If the new order represented an improvement, its most appealing feature was the Great Moderation, or the taming of the business cycle. After the 1981–82 recession, the economy expanded most of the time. It created jobs most of the time. It fostered higher living standards most of the time. All this acted as a social shock absorber, lessening discontent from greater inequality and shakier job security. The new order was in part hostage to the Great Moderation. A resurgent business cycle—harsher and more frequent slumps—could fan hostility toward business and heighten pressures for government intervention. What caused the Great Moderation? We do not lack for theories.

Business cycles stem from shifts in spending. Higher spending (on, say, housing or cars) promotes expansion. Weaker spending threatens recession. As already noted, inflation's decline abetted the Great Moderation by minimizing stop-go economic policies. But the Great Moderation probably had other causes as well. The historic shift away from manufacturing and farming, both susceptible to dramatic swings rooted in inventory and investment cycles as well as harvest conditions, may have promoted stability (the effects may also have occurred in the 1950s and 1960s before being overwhelmed by inflation). Bigger government may stabilize overall spending; except for war, its disbursements are not prone to dramatic fluctuations. Moreover, it provides "automatic stabilizers" (in recessions, unemployment insurance increases and the bite of progressive taxes moderates; the opposite occurs in expansions). Computerized inventory controls to match sales and orders, widely adopted in the 1980s and 1990s, may have prevented businesses from overstocking. The greater availability of consumer credit may have helped families smooth their spending.

The trouble, of course, was that although the economy had been fairly stable for a quarter century, this did not mean that it would remain stable—a lesson that became painfully obvious in 2008. A capitalist system that constantly reinvents itself can also breed new sources of disorder. The unexpected source of disorder was the financial system. Some people and companies save; others invest—in homes, factories, new products. Banks and financial markets (for stocks, bonds and other securities) connect the two. Anyone who took introductory college economics in the 1960s (as I did) and for many years thereafter was barely exposed to finance. It was considered a backwater. The standard approach to business cycles was to decompose the economy's spending into four broad categories. Private consumption—everything from furniture to fast food—was the biggest; investment by businesses and in housing, government spending and net exports (a trade surplus or deficit) were the other three. Significant shifts in any of these four spending streams could induce economic expansions and recessions.

Professors with a historic bent might have recalled that there had once been bank panics—depositors demanding their money—that, by causing contractions of bank lending, had influenced business cycles. But those were the bad old days before the creation of deposit insurance in the 1930s prevented bank panics. (Federal deposit insurance, now generally $250,000 per account, protects individuals against loss even if the bank fails.) The role of finance was portrayed as passive. Finance responded to events. It didn't initiate them. If consumers or companies needed to borrow, they went to banks or sold bonds. Similarly, the stock market was mainly a barometer of how well or poorly companies were doing. Few firms raised capital by selling new shares.

But it turned out that what I and many others were taught was wrong or, at least, has become dated and incomplete. In the past quarter century, finance has been a driver of events—causing both expansions and, through "bubbles," recessions. High stock and home values persuaded millions of Americans to spend more of their incomes, borrow more money, or both. People felt wealthier and so they spent more; economists called this "the wealth effect." Consumer spending rose from 63 percent of GDP in 1980 to 70 percent in 2004, and that steady gain buttressed living standards and the economy's growth. Then the same run-up in stock prices and home values reversed and brought the economy down. The greater availability of venture capital (from $18 billion in 1997 to $107 billion in 2000) initially fed the boom in Internet and computer start-ups, many of which subsequently collapsed along with sky-high stock prices in the "tech bubble." The pattern was similar in real estate. Greater availability of mortgage loans pushed up home prices, which made anxious buyers more frantic to purchase homes; that led to more lending, buying and higher prices. The boom fed on itself until the "bubble" popped and home prices—no longer supported by credulous credit—dropped. In both cases, the initial rise in prices—triggered by falling inflation and interest rates— fostered a false belief in the inevitability of ascending values.

The crucial point is that these rhythms of spending were dictated by the financial system, which had changed dramatically from the bank and S&L dominance of thirty years earlier. Their losses in the 1980s—many S&Ls and banks failed, and others had their lending limited by depleted capital—left a void that was filled by "securitization": the packaging of mortgages, auto loans, credit card debt and other loans into bondlike securities that were sold to institutional investors (insurance companies, pension funds, college endowments, mutual funds). Computerization led to faster trading and more complex investment strategies. Even in the early 1970s, as writer Martin Mayer has recalled, most major securities firms had "cages" that handled the physical transfer of stock certificates and cash that settled daily trading. Now, virtually all transfers occur electronically. From 1980 to 2006, average daily trading on the New York Stock Exchange rose from 45 million shares to 1.8 billion. Many investment banks went from small, clubby partnerships to massive publicly owned firms. At the end of the 1950s, Morgan Stanley had one office and about one hundred employees; in 2007 it operated in thirty-three countries and had 47,000 employees. The breakdown of global capital controls meant that money also moved increasingly among different countries.[20]

Mainstream economics needs to be revised to incorporate the benefits and dangers of a complex financial system that is highly interconnected internationally. Finance seems susceptible, notes Josh Lerner of the Harvard Business School, to regular cycles of productive invention and reckless speculation. The cycle usually starts with some worthwhile innovation, say "securitization," venture capital or LBOs. This leads to imitation, which is generally good because it creates competition and improvement. Finally, there's a speculative binge. Crowd psychology takes charge; the quest for quick profits overwhelms underlying economics. Prices get stretched, dubious deals and trades multiply, and the process ends with a "crash" of artificial values. If the "crashes" only made some rich people poorer, they wouldn't matter much. But the consequence can also include widespread wealth losses, depressed confidence and constricted credit.[21]

We simply do not know whether the economy is self-stabilizing—and, if not, whether government can always stabilize it. This is a great unsettled issue in economics and will probably stay unsettled. For years, recent history had suggested optimism. Since the Great Depression, only a few recessions had been exceptionally harsh.* In theory, economic downturns could feed on themselves. Slumping sales could lead to higher joblessness, which could lead to lower sales, more joblessness and so on. But in practice, the economy

---

* See Appendix 2 for details.

had many self-correcting mechanisms. Interest rates and prices abated; surplus inventories were sold. Government also had tools (tax cuts, spending increases, interest-rate changes) to promote stability. But the severe 2008–2009 slump and its worldwide nature cast a cloud over this optimism.

In a weird way, optimism was actually vindicated. The Federal Reserve and other government central banks apparently defused a financial crisis that might have cascaded into a global depression. The classic response to bank panics, as conceptualized by Walter Bagehot (1826–1877), editor of *The Economist,* was for central banks to lend cash to solvent banks suffering depositor runs. But by 2008, much lending occurred outside of banks (aka "securitization"), and losses on "subprime" mortgages mounted. Financial institutions grew leery of lending to one another, because no one knew which institutions had suffered losses. To offset this credit stinginess, the Fed lent liberally to both banks and nonbanks. Its actions may have averted a depression, but the long-run consequences for both the economy's stability and the nature of the economic system remain unclear.

What Americans generally want from their economic system are higher incomes and ample security in their everyday lives. A healthy economy is not an end in itself but a means to an end—the realization of what we expansively and vaguely call "the American Dream." Alan Greenspan often argued approvingly that "flexibility" was one of the chief strengths of the U.S. economy. By that he presumably meant its ability to respond to change and move people and capital to the areas of greatest opportunity. This is surely true. But it's also true that there's another side to "flexibility": declining industries, bankrupt companies and lost jobs. By and large, Americans dislike and fear the potential precariousness and capriciousness of their economic system, though they crave the abundance it produces.

The new economic order maintained an uneasy standoff between our conflicting wants. It provided the opportunity that most Americans expect, a yearning that goes back to the republic's earliest days, even if the gains were distributed increasingly unevenly. It also created a fair amount of order and security for most Americans, but that order and security were much less than many had come to expect almost as a birthright. The Great Moderation was the glue that has held this shaky arrangement together. Unfortunately, it has shown itself to be a passing phase and not a permanent blessing.

7

THE FUTURE
OF AFFLUENCE

I

I t is part of American folklore that every generation shall live
better than its predecessor—and history is littered with the discredited prophecies of those who have said otherwise. Technological gains have been unending, raising living standards, if often
haphazardly. Things that are now routinely available to most Americans (personal computers, cheap air travel, knee replacements, mi-
crowave ovens, cell phones, air conditioning—and air-conditioned
cars) would surprise the Americans of 1950 and completely astonish
the Americans of 1900. Still, it is hard not to wonder whether in recent years we have not crossed some unmarked threshold that heralds

a new era of disappointment. We may suffer from what might be called, for lack of a better term, "affluent deprivation."

The prognosis is not that we become poor. We are already a wealthy society, and, quite probably, we will become wealthier. Technological advances will not suddenly halt. What will be commonplaces twenty-five or fifty years from now would no doubt astound us just as our commonplaces would dazzle our ancestors. In a statistical sense—dividing our production by our population—the future will be richer than the past. But we may feel poorer ("deprived") because our accumulating affluence can't meet all Americans' expectations of prosperity—mainly, a greater sense of security and more discretionary income. The future may be less secure than the recent past, and higher taxes, health costs and energy prices may squeeze discretionary income.

As we have seen, the economic crisis that burst on the world in 2007 and 2008 was a last legacy of the inflationary experience. The crisis shattered the promise of the Great Moderation. It is no longer possible to believe that the business cycle, if not completely conquered (as economists hoped in the 1960s), has been at least permanently tamed. The notion was that greater economic knowledge, which gave economists the tools to limit downturns, and the self-correcting characteristics of a low-inflation economy would lead to long expansions and short recessions. Seemingly validated by a quarter century's experience (from about 1982 to 2007), this seductive vision has vaporized. We vastly overestimated our understanding of the economy and our capacity to control it. Its behavior constantly changes as a result of new technologies, trading patterns, markets, laws, international conditions—and much more.

Financial panics, for example, were supposedly abolished. The creation of bank deposit insurance in 1933 and the Fed's power as "lender of last resort" rendered panics impossible. So it was thought. Worried depositors wouldn't pull their money, because their funds were protected. The Fed could preempt any generalized panic. We now know this was wishful thinking. As Yale economist Gary Gorton has shown, the financial crisis of 2007–08 resembled an old-fashioned panic, only with details changed: individual depositors were replaced by large institutional investors (insurance companies, corporations), and deposits by short-term "repo" loans to banks and investment firms. But the effect was the same: when the "repo" loans were withdrawn or reduced—because institutional lenders feared they wouldn't be repaid—borrowing institutions either failed or had to get emergency credit elsewhere. Regulators, bankers, investors and scholars all played catch-up to financial changes whose full implications were poorly understood.*[1]

Slower economic growth may accompany less stable growth. In some ways, this seems inevitable. America is an aging society. The impending retirement of baby boom workers will depress growth by stunting labor force increases. Arithmetically, economic growth equals the percentage change in the labor force (measured typically by the number of hours worked) plus the percentage change in pro-

---

* "Repo" is financial shorthand for "repurchase agreement" loan. Under a standard "repo," the borrower receives cash and, in return, provides collateral (usually securities such as Treasury bills or bonds) to the lender as insurance against nonpayment. The credit stipulates that the securities shall be "repurchased," meaning the loan will be repaid in a given period of time. Most "repo" loans are short-term, days or weeks.

ductivity (measured by output per hour worked). By this math, slower economic growth seems unavoidable. From 1960 to 2005, the annual growth of the economy (Gross Domestic Product) averaged 3.4 percent, with contributions from labor force and productivity growth varying in different periods. Averaged over the entire span, productivity rose 1.9 percent annually and working hours 1.5 percent. By the mid-2020s, the Social Security Administration expects economic growth to slow to about 2 percent annually. Labor force growth would be scant (about 0.3 percent annually), as new workers barely offset retirees; productivity growth (1.7 percent annually) is assumed to remain close to its recent average.[2]

What we don't know is how economic, social and political developments might alter these plausible projections, for better or worse. So many factors (technology, management, competition, workers' skills, government policies) influence productivity that predicting its future is impossible. But should productivity gains decline, economic growth would come almost to a standstill. The implications are sobering. If a slowing economy collides with rising popular expectations—for higher living standards, more government spending—the frustrations might then spawn greater political, social and class conflict. To invoke an old cliché: instead of sharing ever-larger pieces of an expanding economic pie, Americans would fight for larger shares of a stagnant pie.

The resulting contentiousness would depart from recent history. A remarkable fact about the post–World War II era is that, with the exception of double-digit inflation, economic problems have not caused great political and social strife. At first blush, this claim seems absurd. Economic issues dominate politics and the news. Most

Americans have always worried about their jobs, wages, debts, home values and savings. Nevertheless, these are *not* the issues that have truly frightened or divided Americans since World War II. By and large, these lie elsewhere: the Cold War; Vietnam; civil rights; the "sexual revolution"; abortion; the role of religion in politics; immigration; terrorism; and the 2003 Iraq war.

The seemingly endless discontent over the economy qualifies mostly as low-level grumbling and not pervasive rage. Americans have worried about the economy in the same way that most parents worry about their children. There's constant anxiety, but it's usually not paralyzing. On the whole, the years since World War II have been economically kind to Americans. Postwar recessions, excluding those of 1957–58, 1973–75, 1981–82 and 2007–09, have generally been brief and mild. Americans have enjoyed unprecedented material well-being, while expanded government programs—for education, health care, old-age assistance, unemployment and disability benefits—have mitigated poverty, insecurity and inequality. Economic growth has been a political tranquilizer, calming social and class tensions.

All that could change. The old and the young, cities and suburbs, the middle-class and poor, the rich and everyone else—potential struggles are endless. Between now and 2050, the population is expected to grow from just over 300 million to almost 440 million. Of the increase, about four-fifths are reckoned to represent new immigrants, their children and grandchildren. By 2050, Hispanics, the largest immigrant group, are projected to be 29 percent of the population, up from 14 percent in 2005. As now, many will be poor and low-skilled. Their assimilation has been slow. We can anticipate greater pressures for government aid from opposite ends of the age spectrum: for schools, hospitals and housing from younger and poorer immigrants; and for health care and income transfers from retirees. Meanwhile, the middle-class children of baby boomers will want more take-home income to raise their families. But pretax gains could be eroded by higher taxes, energy prices and health-care costs driven by new legislation and large amounts of government debt incurred to fight the recession.[3]

So we are at a critical juncture. The 2007–09 economic crisis was not just a jarring interlude to prosperity. Combined with the aging of America, it represents a break from the recent past. The foundations for economic expansion established in the 1980s have weakened and crumbled. New foundations will have to be constructed, and it's uncertain whether the new economic edifice will support all the competing claims and expectations heaped on it.

II

Just how we got here cannot be understood (again) without reference to the inflationary cycle. The 2007–09 crisis was its final act. To recapitulate briefly: The long disinflation that began in the early 1980s induced a virtuous circle that, in the end, turned vicious. As lower inflation fed into lower interest rates, stock prices and housing values rose. Feeling richer, many Americans skimped on saving or borrowed more. Powerful consumer spending favored job creation, greater globalization, higher profits and faster productivity growth. But this engine of prosperity could not run forever, because people ultimately exhaust their ability to borrow or spend ever-larger shares of their income. Borrowers become overburdened, and lenders—fearing default—tighten loan standards. Overconfidence in the inexorability of rising stock prices and home values caused dangerous "bubbles," first in stocks in 2000 and then in houses in 2007.

As the crisis unfolded, various theories were offered to explain it. Mortgage bankers were vilified for making poor loans. Investment bankers were blamed for "securitizing" these loans—and also borrowing too much money themselves (aka "leverage") to carry risky investments. More broadly, "deregulation" and "free market ideology" were assailed for creating an unsupervised financial system prone to greed and shortsightedness. Former Federal Reserve chairman Alan Greenspan, who had been lavishly praised when he retired from the Fed in early 2006, was criticized for having lowered interest rates too much in 2003 and 2004. The resulting cheap credit allegedly encouraged lax lending. China was blamed for having amassed huge trade surpluses in dollars that, reinvested in U.S. securities, depressed interest rates on Treasury bonds and mortgages. To some extent, all the theories were correct. But what was unsaid was also important: all were also connected to inflation and disinflation.

It's true that Greenspan's Fed reduced the Fed funds rate from 6.5 percent in early 2001 to 1 percent in 2003 and kept it there for a year in order to blunt recession and spur recovery (the economy was then suffering from both the collapse of stock prices in 2000 and the fallout from the terrorist attacks of September 11, 2001). At the time, Greenspan's policy was praised as deft economic management; after the housing bubble, it was harshly condemned. Either way, it was a byproduct of disinflation. If the Fed hadn't crushed inflation—and inflationary expectations—a 1 percent interest rate would have been impossible. It would have been seen as wildly inflationary. Similarly, the Chinese would never have accumulated their mountains of dollars, earned from trade surpluses, if globalization hadn't been encouraged by the 1980s' restoration of confidence in the dollar.

Many of the risky mortgages could be (and, at the time, were) justified by the steady upward march of housing prices in the 1980s and 1990s, which was a prominent feature of disinflation. From 1990 to 2000, the median price of an existing home rose about 50 percent to $147,000; by 2004, it was up another 33 percent to $195,000. This was a bonanza, even for weaker borrowers. Ever-higher home prices meant that they could refinance their mortgages in two or three years at more advantageous terms (that is, lower interest rates), because lenders would have more protection against default. Rising home prices seemed to guarantee that even if borrowers didn't repay, their homes could be sold at a profit to cover the loan. Where was the risk? Lax loan standards were rationalized.[4]

The investment banks and banks that took on more "leverage" and created complex mortgage-backed securities could also point to the decline in risk. The economic and financial world seemed calmer and more resilient. The modest recession that had occurred in 2001, and the Federal Reserve's capacity to combat it with sharp cuts in interest rates, indicated greater stability. Financial markets were also less erratic. The key concept here was "volatility," the routine swings in the prices of financial assets (stocks, bonds, currencies). By 2004, volatility had declined in most financial markets. Everyone was aware of this. One regulatory report speculated that the change reflected "sustained [economic] expansion and low inflation," as well as more sophisticated financial practices. Facing less risk—smaller swings in prices reduced the odds of losing money—investment banks and others could defend borrowing more money to enhance profits.[5]

This belief in a calmer and more stable world, a consequence of disinflation, was the chief catalyst in the destructive risk-taking that culminated in the financial and economic crisis. The central cause was not, as is often asserted, "deregulation" or poor regulation. The old financial system was not (as, again, is often asserted) consciously replaced by a new, unregulated system. Much of the old system collapsed or was reshaped under the weight of inflation, the S&Ls' demise being a prime example. Many changes were isolated and driven by circumstances: The rise of "securitization" was initially intended to offset the loss of lending power by banks and S&Ls. Regulation hardly disappeared; banks, at the center of the subsequent crisis, remained heavily regulated. But many regulators were as lulled as everyone else by the buoyancy and adaptability of markets.

People are conditioned by their own experiences. With hindsight, we know that investors, traders, and bankers engaged in reckless risk-taking that created financial and economic havoc. We also know that regulators turned a blind eye to practices that, in retrospect, were ruinous, unethical and sometimes criminal. But while dangerous speculation and complacency flourished, the prevailing belief was that the economy and financial system had become safer. In early 2003, Greenspan gave a speech debunking the notion of a national housing "bubble." Homes weren't like stocks. People couldn't just sell; they had to move out. Markets were local, not national. "[A]ny bubbles that might emerge would tend to be local, not national," he argued.[6]

At the time, Greenspan seemed vindicated. With low interest rates, housing flourished. "By 2005, with unemployment declining and housing prices surging, delinquencies and defaults had dropped to record lows," the economist Mark Zandi has written. "Regulators would have had great difficulty making the case to lenders that their lending standards were out of whack." In 2005, only 3 percent of subprime mortgages were in default (by late 2008, the figure was 13 percent). Borrowers were happy, lenders were happy, politicians were happy. Home ownership, a symbol of the American Dream, was near a record 70 percent of U.S. households. The paradox is that, thinking the world less risky, people took actions that made it more risky. Ironically, the mistakes and blunders that led to the crisis were ultimately rooted in the benefits of disinflation—and the conviction that those benefits would endure no matter what.[7]

III

If slower economic growth awaits us, it's worth asking whether this is actually so threatening. I have argued that it is, and many Americans would agree. But the conclusion is not self-evident, and a case can be made that our obsession with growth has outlived its usefulness. Even if average U.S. incomes froze at current levels—an unlikely outcome—most Americans would still enjoy living standards, including free time, inconceivable in most of history. As we have seen, recent economic growth has been purchased partly at the cost of rising individual insecurity and economic inequality. To sacrifice some growth for other goals—added security, less inequality, diminished global warming, more stability—might seem a good bargain. If economic growth is no longer a useful yardstick of social progress, then its weakening would be less cause for concern.

The question of how to use our prosperity, as opposed to merely getting more of it, dates at least to *The Affluent Society,* John Kenneth Galbraith's 1958 bestseller. In it, Galbraith correctly observed that modern societies (of which the United States was then the preeminent example) had passed a historic milestone in the twentieth century. In these societies, Galbraith noted, most people had been liberated from age-old fears and deprivations.

> [P]overty has always been man's normal lot, and any other state was in degree unimaginable. This poverty was not the elegant torture of the spirit that comes from contemplating another man's more spacious possessions. It was the unedifying mortification of the flesh—from hunger, sickness, cold. Those who might be freed temporarily from such a burden could not know when it would strike again. . . . It is improbable that the poverty of the masses of people was made greatly more bearable by the fact that a very few—those upon whose movements nearly all recorded history centers—were very rich.[8]

Galbraith himself did not see much conflict between achieving high rates of economic growth and reallocating more of the benefits to the public sector. Society needed to spend more on education, the arts, the environment and health care. Because growth depended (in his view) mainly on corporate planning, diverting more of growth's fruits into government spending was a political choice, not an economic sacrifice.

Perhaps Galbraith's most thoughtful and eloquent successor is economist Robert Frank of Cornell University. Galbraith argued that much of modern consumption was unsatisfying and artificially stimulated by advertising. Frank goes further. The obsessive nature of modern consumption, he contends, actually spawns discontent while starving the public sector. Middle-class Americans are caught up in self-defeating consumption wars. If you buy a bigger grill, then I have to buy a bigger grill. The bigger grills don't make us happier; all the striving mostly makes us anxious. If only grills and shoes were involved, these status struggles wouldn't matter much. But, Frank says, the same logic applies to costlier purchases: homes, cars, flat-screen TVs. If everyone had smaller homes, Frank says, everyone would be just as happy. He's almost certainly correct. Considerable research has confirmed the folk wisdom: Beyond a certain point, money doesn't buy happiness.*[9]

---

* To discourage what he regards as needless consumption, Frank proposes a progressive consumption tax. At very high consumption levels, the tax would be 200 percent. This would, he asserts, raise economic growth by increasing total saving. People would save more of their incomes, because saving would be untaxed. My own view—aside from believing such a tax would never be enacted—is that it would discourage risk taking (why bother if you can't enjoy most of the rewards?) and stimulate a massive flight of money and ambitious people out of the country.

In very poor societies, economic growth does increase happiness, as traditional afflictions—hunger, homelessness, punishing physical labor—recede. This was Galbraith's point. But after rising from poverty, societies don't become happier as they become wealthier, a relationship first pointed out by economist Richard Easterlin in 1974. In 1977, 36 percent of Americans said they were "very happy," 53 percent said "pretty happy," and 11 percent "not too happy," reports the National Opinion Research Center at the University of Chicago. In 2004, when the country was much wealthier—most Americans had bigger homes, more health care and more gadgets (computers, cell phones)—the comparable figures were 34 percent, 55 percent and 12 percent. Among households, reported happiness improves between the very poor and the middle class; people don't like being on the bottom. For the middle class and beyond, it's not especially sensitive to income. It depends more on personal relationships (married people report higher happiness than singles or divorcees), satisfying work, spiritual peace and personal temperament. Some people have a sunny disposition and stay hopeful through stress and tragedy; others are resolutely grim despite good fortune. Interestingly, higher government spending also seems ineffective at generating happiness; since Galbraith's time, social spending has increased enormously without elevating reported happiness.[10]

But just because economic growth doesn't expand statistical happiness does not mean it's useless. In wealthy societies, its social role goes beyond the material improvement of people's lives, which is what it had been throughout most of history. Its central contribution now is to foster social peace and political cohesion. Growth mutes the collision between private and public wants—between personal selfishness and the larger social good. As early as 1976, the sociologist Daniel Bell observed that economic growth "has become the secular religion of advanced societies: the source of individual motivation, the basis of political solidarity, the ground for mobilization of society for a common purpose."[11]

More recently, Harvard economist Benjamin Friedman★ has argued, in *The Moral Consequences of Economic Growth,* that in most societies at most times, economic growth has encouraged praiseworthy qualities such as "tolerance of diversity, social mobility, commitment to fairness and a dedication to democracy." The relationship is not entirely coincidental, Friedman argues. Economic growth breeds optimism. People believe that their lives will improve in the future. They're more inclined to be generous. By creating a new business elite and, more important, an expanded middle class, economic growth also assaults entrenched tribal, aristocratic and dictatorial bastions of power and authority. A social system that rewards economic success tends to become more open in its political and social relationships because it is more open in its economic relationships. The connections are not mechanical and automatic; but there are strong tendencies.[12] People grow used to making market choices, not being dictated to by government. They grow accustomed to the idea that they can advance through their own efforts. Freedom becomes an experience, not just an abstraction.

Friedman's perspective offers a counterpoint to the stereotype of

★ No relation to economist Milton Friedman.

a selfish, obsessively materialistic culture that is irrationally driven to crave what it does not need. There is a moral case for economic growth that transcends the mere relief of human misery. All this implies that a future of much slower growth—or stagnation—would produce a more contentious and grumpier society. As individuals and groups felt frustrated in their hopes and goals, they would vent their disappointments on others. Contrary to Marx, who envisioned economic growth as creating political and social conflict, we have learned that economic growth often mutes conflict. In particular, economic disputes are easier to settle than religious, ethnic or tribal disputes. When all that's at stake is money, it's easier to split the difference than when the argument is over whose god is to be worshipped or whose ethnic group is to be privileged or persecuted.

So, economic growth matters. The idea that rearranging the existing prosperity—through income redistribution and more government services and protections—will satisfy most people is a false promise. Though this might help, it will not suffice. It is impossible not to notice an impending collision between rising private wants (for homes, furniture, vacations, college tuitions) and demands for government services and transfers: for retirees; for refurbishing roads, sewer systems, schools; for environmental protection; for poorer immigrants and their children; and for military spending and homeland security. There is probably no plausible rate of economic growth that could satisfy all these demands. But slower growth would intensify conflict and compound disappointment.

Against that backdrop, threats to growth are worth considering. Our predicament is this: Developments that, on the whole, have contributed to American economic growth and well-being may now do the opposite. There are three prime candidates—the welfare state, the "democratization" of credit (more Americans can borrow in more ways than ever before), and globalization. Since World War II, the expansion of the welfare state has provided psychological and economic security for the unemployed, the poor, the disabled and the elderly. The growth of credit has allowed millions of Americans to benefit from purchases (of a home, a car, a college education) before fully saving for them. Globalization has significantly raised living standards. But each of these beneficial changes might now boomerang.

IV

Start with the welfare state. It's overcommitted; that is, it's made more promises than we can easily or sensibly afford. To say that we have a welfare state in the same sense as France or Germany means that the government taxes some people (mainly workers and investors) and transfers their income to others to improve their welfare. Perhaps half of U.S. families receive some sort of federal benefit, from college grants to farm subsidies. But the welfare state's mainstays are programs for older people: Social Security, Medicare (health insurance for those sixty-five and over) and Medicaid (mostly nursing home and care for the elderly poor). Already, these three programs constitute about 45 percent of federal spending. From 2000 to 2030, the sixty-five-and-over population will double, from 35 million to 72 million and from 12 percent of the total to almost 20 percent. Along with rapidly rising health-care spending, this balloons the cost of Social Security, Medicare and Medicaid. By 2030, they could easily reach 70 percent of today's budget, posing the question of how much we will allow spending on retirees to crowd out the rest of government or the economy.[13]

If other government programs claim the same share of national income (GDP) as today—and there are no expensive new programs—the federal budget would rise from about 20 percent of GDP to 27 percent. To balance the budget could easily require a tax increase of 50 percent from today's levels. In present dollars, the amount would exceed $1 trillion annually. Even in wartime, we have never before experienced such tax burdens, so it is impossible to know the full consequences. None of the alternatives to higher taxes is appealing. There are only three: (1) deep cuts in other governmental programs—the FBI, defense, scientific research, environmental regulation, college aid, highways and everything else the federal government does; (2) implausibly large government budget deficits; and (3) sizable cuts in Social Security, Medicare and Medicaid by raising eligibility ages and reducing benefits.[14]

Health care makes the welfare state's future seem especially intractable. If the "aging problem" involved only Social Security, it would be less daunting. About three-quarters of the projected increase in federal spending for those sixty-five and over by 2030 involves Medicare and Medicaid. As a society, we haven't learned how to control health-care spending. Americans generally regard access to health care as a moral "right." It thus evades the two mechanisms by which we usually control spending: income and politics. We allocate most "private goods" by income. If you can't afford a big car, you get a little car—or none at all. Through elections and legislation, we decide how much to spend on "public goods"—roads, police, parks, defense—with presumed collective benefits. But health care, through the provision of public and private insurance, stays mainly on automatic pilot. We view it as an "ethical good": People should get it when they need it. Medicare and Medicaid spending have consequently risen largely unchecked. Spending controls have been highly ineffective and purposely so. Americans don't want to ration care.

Uncontrolled health spending and steady increases in social security threaten to create an oversized welfare state that may weaken the economy in three ways. As already noted, higher taxes may penalize work effort, risk taking and investment. People might slacken if the rewards of success are taxed too heavily. The welfare state and economy could then go into a death spiral. Higher taxes reduce economic growth, making it harder to pay welfare benefits without even higher taxes—which would further depress economic growth. A second danger arises from bigger federal budget deficits, which would (in theory) raise interest rates and "crowd out" private investment in plants, equipment and new technologies.

Finally, rising health-care spending could divert more of society's resources—people, buildings, machines—into unproductive spending. Health-care spending was already 16 percent of GDP in 2006, up from 5 percent in 1960. Projections suggest it could hit 20 percent by 2015 and 30 percent by midcentury. Some scholars see this as natural. In an ever-wealthier society, people spend more to stay fit.

Maybe. But added spending may not always make people healthier. It may simply be waste. One study by Jack Weinberg of the Dartmouth Medical College examined 4.7 million Medicare patients with twelve chronic diseases (including heart disease and cancer) who died from 2000 to 2003. In New York, hospitalization rates were twice as high as at the Mayo Clinic in Rochester, Minnesota, but patients fared no better.[15] Wildly expensive and often futile care goes to those with terminal illnesses or who are at the near-certain end of their lives. But how to control this spending has proven an impossible political and moral problem.

Like the Great Inflation, the welfare state has fallen victim to good intentions. Though it still serves the essential needs of many, its expansion now threatens the very economy that supports it. There is an irony here. As initially imagined by Franklin Roosevelt, the welfare state was an appendage of the "free enterprise" system. Its aim was not to replace capitalism but to strengthen it by making it more acceptable to the public. Roosevelt was explicit about this. In 1934, he told Congress: "Fear and worry based on unknown danger contribute to social unrest and economic demoralization." His proposed programs of unemployment assistance, aid to widows and the elderly aimed to subdue that fear. "We have not opposed the incentive of reasonable and legitimate profit," Roosevelt continued. "We have sought rather to enable certain aspects of business to regain the confidence of the public."[16] If an expansive welfare state now depresses economic growth, it will have become the opposite of what Roosevelt envisioned and intended.

The second force threatening economic growth is the debt burden of ordinary households. Just as the welfare state is overcommitted, consumers—as a group—are overborrowed. Consider what's happened. In 1946, personal debt was 23 percent of household income. In a year, a typical family then earned more than four times all of its debts. By 2006, debt was 134 percent of annual income; typical families had borrowed more than they earned. This couldn't continue indefinitely, because debt levels can't grow faster than incomes forever. The "subprime" mortgage crisis marked the tipping point. Americans are borrowing less because they're uneasy with high debt burdens and because lenders have tightened credit standards. The retrenchment will, at least temporarily, retard rises in living standards and economic growth. With hindsight, we can liken the increase of debt—especially since 1980—to an economic afterburner. Metaphorically, the economy flew faster. Now the afterburner is sputtering out.[17]

We're told that this is the unavoidable reckoning, the hangover after the spree. We'd become a nation of credit junkies, addicted to another credit card, a bigger mortgage. Now we'll pay the price. Despite the compelling imagery, the reality is more complicated. For starters, the rise in debt has been on the whole a good thing. It reflects the "democratization of credit." Like fast food and cars, consumer borrowing has become a mass market, ordinary and respectable. By 2003, Americans held 1.5 billion credit cards, an average of seven for every adult. People have more flexibility in their spending. They don't have to save in advance to buy every appliance, car or home. Because about three-quarters of personal debt consists of housing mortgages, the liberalization of credit has boosted home ownership, which stood at about 68 percent of households in 2007, up from 44 percent in 1940.

A century ago, the situation was much different. Borrowing was a sign of shame, indicating that families were short of cash. Shop owners provided "store credit" to regular customers, according to economic historian Martha Olney of the University of California, Berkeley. Desperate families relied on pawnbrokers. "The city can no more dispense with pawnbrokers," wrote one journalist in 1894, "than it can with the banker or milkman."* Home mortgages were hard to get, usually requiring big down payments of up to 50 percent and lasting only five to ten years. Modern consumer credit dates to the 1920s, when installment lending mushroomed for cars and other big-ticket items (refrigerators, stoves, radios). Manufacturers decided it was in their interest to provide loans to customers. Borrowing slowly became more socially acceptable. After World War II, consumer lending increased with the spread of "credit bureaus" and, later, "credit scoring" that helped lenders evaluate potential borrowers. Businesses now buy more than 10 billion FICO scores—the most common credit rating—a year. Loan terms were liberalized. Auto loans, which had maturities of one to two years in the 1920s, gradually lengthened to five years or more. Home mortgages required progressively smaller down payments, and maturities stretched to thirty years.[18]

Nor is it true that taking on debt is simply a sign of irresponsible impatience. As the historian Lendol Calder has noted, the decision

---

* Pawnshops advanced cash against collateral, expecting to be repaid with interest—and if they weren't, they could sell the collateral.

to borrow often constitutes a commitment to conventional lifestyles and economic values.

Once consumers step onto the treadmill of regular monthly payments, it becomes clear that consumer credit is about much more than instant gratification. It is also about discipline, hard work, and the channeling of one's productivity [toward repaying the debt]. The nature of installment credit ensures that if there is hedonism in consumer culture, it is disciplined hedonism.[19]

But all the forces that fed the post–World War II credit expansion are now waning: the "democratization" of credit, the borrowing needs of the baby-boom generation, and the wealth effects of higher stock and home values. The "democratization" went as far as it could go—indeed, too far, as the collapse of "subprime" mortgage lending showed: Borrowers who weren't creditworthy got credit. Next, the huge baby-boom generation is passing its peak years of borrowing. There's a life cycle for credit. People borrow heavily in their thirties and forties as they become home owners, have children and pay for college tuitions; then they reduce debt as mortgages mature and children leave home. Almost 90 percent of families headed by someone 35 to 54 have debt. By contrast, only about 60 percent of families headed by someone 65 to 74 have debt. The amounts also shrink. Finally, the effect of disinflation via higher stock and home prices has weakened. The upshot is that credit expansion, once a robust force for economic growth, is already less so.[20]

A last threat to economic growth arises from globalization. The problem is not that it will directly lower living standards—that, for example, all "good jobs" will flow abroad. The danger is that globalization may breed economic instability. The huge cross-border flows of trade and investment may contain the seeds of their own destruction, leading to periodic financial crises, violent business cycles, trade wars or the interruption of crucial supplies (most obviously, oil). Barring this sort of disorder, globalization seems mostly beneficial. The extra competition and choice of international trade and investment have raised U.S. incomes by an estimated 10 percent over the past half century. Gains for other countries have been even larger. Countless millions have escaped poverty. Since 1950, average incomes have increased eleven times in Japan, sixteen times in South Korea and six times in Spain. Globalization contributed heavily through trade and the transfer of technology and management. But all the upbeat statistics conceal a hazardous contradiction: Economics has raced ahead of politics and culture. Countries that trade and invest with one another don't always share the same values and interests. The global economy is hostage to this contradiction.[21]

We are now at the twilight of Pax Americana: a global economic system dominated and largely constructed by the United States after World War II. Security threats were held at bay by U.S. troops—stationed in Europe, Japan, South Korea—and American nuclear deterrent. In addition, the United States provided economic services to the rest of the world: a) it encouraged trade by keeping its own market open to imports; b) it maintained a global currency, the dollar, that made trade and many cross-border investments easier; and

c) it engaged in "crisis management" to minimize economic and political threats.★

Unfortunately, this system is breaking down, in part because what we called "the world economy" in the 1960s and 1970s really wasn't. It excluded, mostly by their own choice, more than half the world's population: China, which pursued self-sufficiency; the Soviet Union, which ran its own trading system (COMECON) with its Eastern European satellites; and India, which maintained a regulated, protectionist economy.† The "old" world economy had political coherence. The major trading nations—the United States, Western European countries, Japan—shared democratic values and were military allies. Their economic system was shaped by a common purpose (winning the Cold War) and a common memory (the Great Depression, which was aggravated by protectionism). The "new" world economy lacks this cohesion. It has more power centers (adding China, India, Russia, Saudi Arabia, Brazil). They are not joined by common alliances or shared political values. China, a one-party police state, differs radically from Western democracies. There are also other threats. In 2007, about a quarter of the world's oil came from the Persian Gulf, where supplies are vulnerable to

---

★ Of course, the United States did not always play these roles perfectly. High inflation temporarily reduced the dollar's usefulness as a global currency. Various presidents adopted protectionist measures. But it's unlikely another major country would have tolerated huge trade deficits or would have intervened militarily to reverse Saddam Hussein's invasion of Kuwait in 1990, which threatened world oil supplies. Similarly, the United States took the lead in combating the 1997–98 Asian financial crisis.

† In 1972, all these countries plus an impoverished Africa—which was

terrorism, war or political embargoes. Some major oil producers (Venezuela, Iran) are openly hostile to a U.S.-led world economy.[22]

Globalization has also occurred so rapidly—particularly in finance—that we no longer fully understand how it works. Economies achieve stability by balancing supply and demand. In a self-contained national economy (a "closed economy," in the jargon), the balancing occurs through both the market and the government. Prices balance production and consumption; wages balance workers and jobs; interest rates balance savings and investment. If the process goes awry, government intervenes. It changes taxes, spending or interest rates. Or its central bank combats financial panic by acting as a lender of last resort. When international trade and investment were modest, economic theory could assume that most countries—especially big ones like the United States—had largely closed economies. Domestic conditions and policies largely determined employment, inflation, wages, profits, investment and productivity. Globalization alters this presumption. Though domestic influences still dominate, international pressures loom ever larger; the convenient separations between what's local and what's global are breaking down.

There are already flash points: trade imbalances, most obviously. These stem partly from the dollar's role as a global currency. Foreigners accumulated dollars earned from exports and, rather than spend them on imports, used them as reserves against economic setbacks or as vehicles for foreign investment. The biggest imbalances reflect deliberate policies by Asian nations—first Japan and now

---

also effectively outside the global economy—had 2 billion people out of a total of 3.7 billion.

China—to enhance their export competitiveness by holding down the value of their currencies. They send us cars, toys, steel, cell phones and TVs; we send them dollars, which they reinvest in our financial markets. Americans have high consumption rates and low savings rates; Asians have the opposite. The whole arrangement rests on a set of exchange rates that must change but, if too rapidly altered, would disrupt the economies of all involved. Production cannot instantly shift. A firm that exports tractors today won't make toasters for domestic consumption tomorrow. The high oil prices of 2006-08 have compounded the strains by enlarging the trade surpluses of oil-exporting countries.

Because all these surpluses are heavily invested abroad, the world's stock and bond markets are increasingly interconnected. We have already learned from the 1997–98 Asian financial crisis that sudden reversals of global money flows can be hugely disruptive. Initially, large flows into Thailand, Indonesia and South Korea promoted local booms. Converted into local currencies, foreign funds were then lent out by banks and other financial institutions to which they had been entrusted. But when foreign lenders realized that the resulting investments—in shopping malls and condominiums in Thailand, in industrial conglomerates in Korea—were going bad, they abruptly withdrew the money. As credit evaporated, speculative booms became speculative busts. A rescue effort, organized by the International Monetary Fund and the U.S. government, provided new credit and avoided a global recession.

Sometimes the global economy needs governmental supervision. The question is whether it will be there in the future. The United

States is less able to perform the stabilizing role—its trading position is diminished, its currency is less preeminent, its military power is less effective against terrorist threats—but there is no obvious substitute. At present, the world economy is somewhat rudderless, as more countries come under its influence. Global markets, shaped both by impersonal forces and by governments' political decisions, are poorly understood. Yet most nations are tempted to pursue their own narrow interests on the assumption that some other country—or group of countries—will watch out for everyone's collective interests. There is no iron law that says that this system must come to grief. After all, most of the participating nations have an interest in its stability. Still, there's a conspicuous vacuum of power, both in politics and ideas, about how to protect the system. Its stability is hardly a foregone conclusion.

V

What can be done? The future of affluence depends in part on how we cope with these various challenges and at least one other, global warming. Some of these problems will resolve themselves. Americans' high debt burdens will subside spontaneously, following the dictates of tighter credit standards, borrowers' realistic capacity to pay and an aging society. Elsewhere, our actions (or inactions) matter. Until now, this book has been mainly descriptive. In the following pages, I shift gears and become prescriptive by offering suggestions about how we might improve our economic prospects.

First, an observation. It's sometimes said that the continuation of reasonable productivity gains will make future Americans so wealthy that they will have little trouble attaining higher living standards and addressing large national problems. This is too glib. So far as I know, no one has attempted a complete accounting of all the claims that will be made against future productivity gains. But the list is impressive. It's not just Social Security, Medicare and Medicaid for retiring baby boomers, but also the refurbishing of aging public investments—roads, sewers, ports—and the future health and pension costs of state and local government workers. One partial accounting done by Sylvester J. Schieber, a well-known employee benefits consultant, has estimated that already four-fifths of typical workers' plausible income gains may be consumed by higher taxes, health costs and their own pension savings. As this rudimentary analysis makes clear, working families cannot take palpable increases in living standards for granted.[23]

With that as background, here are a few common sense ideas about safeguarding future prosperity.

We start, naturally enough, with the necessity of controlling inflation. The Federal Reserve has informally defined price stability as consumer price inflation of zero to 2 percent annually. This modest range is a reasonable accommodation to the practical difficulties of hitting zero on a consistent basis and of measuring price changes. Studies suggest price changes are often overstated, because they do not adequately account for new goods and quality improvements of existing products: A car that lasts 20 percent longer and costs 10 percent more actually has a price decline. But letting inflation permanently slip above this range would invite trouble. As we have learned, once inflationary psychology takes hold, it can propel wages, prices and interest rates up with surprising momentum that would ultimately damage the economy.

The Fed's task is an art, not a science. One part of the art is knowing when to do nothing. Another is knowing when to act decisively. Historically, the Fed has erred on both counts. In the 1930s, when it failed to provide ample money and credit, the banking system collapsed. In the 1970s, overreaction to economic weakness fostered the Great Inflation. These episodes capture the Fed's two traditional roles: guardian of the currency and lender of last resort. Unfortunately, there's a tension between them. As lender of last resort, the Fed must make credit freely available in time of crisis; the idea is to prevent a financial panic from feeding on itself because banks don't have the cash to pay frightened depositors, or sellers of securities can't find buyers at any price. As guardian of the currency, it must be stingy; too much money will degrade the currency.

The 2007–09 crisis highlighted the tension. As losses on "subprime" mortgages and other loans rose, banks and investment banks became reluctant to deal with each other, because no one knew what the others' losses might be. To prevent a complete credit collapse, the Fed—now under chairman Ben Bernanke—used its own credit to replace private credit. It lent money to banks, investment banks, money market funds; it bought a bewildering array of securities, including mortgage bonds, long-term Treasury bonds (not usually part of Fed purchases) and bonds issued by the mortgage agencies Fannie Mae and Freddie Mac. By these means, the Fed pumped out more than $1 trillion of extra credit between mid-2007 and early 2009. While the economy remained depressed, the extra credit posed little inflationary risk. Much of it substituted for frightened private credit, and high unemployment and idle factory capacity held down wages and prices.

But economic recovery would confront the Fed with a classic dilemma, magnified by both the magnitude of its outstanding credit and the severity of the recession: If it reversed policy too quickly (that is, raised interest rates and drained credit from the economy), it might abort the recovery; but if it acted too slowly, it could kindle inflation. Moreover, if it appeared too reluctant to tighten credit, it might inspire inflationary expectations—that is, a belief that it would tolerate high inflation. Once inflationary expectations take hold, they can become self-fulfilling. Wages and prices move up; the dollar depreciates. Once the immediate crisis has passed, the Fed may also face increased pressure to "monetize" the federal debt by buying large quantities of Treasury bonds. That would lighten the debt burden but only by inducing inflation. From 2009 to 2019, the federal debt could grow by more than $10 trillion, reflecting in part spending to stimulate a recovery, according to projections by the Congressional Budget Office.

Controlling inflation is not just the job of the Fed; Congress and the president also have a role. As economist Paul London argues, competitive markets matter. They promote higher productivity and suppress monopolistic wage and price increases. Measures shielding specific industries or workers from competition—trade barriers, preferential regulations—abet inflation. The same is true of policies that mandate higher wages and prices. Subsidies to biofuels, particularly ethanol from corn, helped raise food prices in 2008. Government restrictions on drilling increased oil prices by reducing supplies. By legislating inflation, these policies hamper the Fed.[24]

Second, we need to stem the welfare state's mounting costs. This means curbing the spending for older Americans. If we don't, the great danger is—as already noted—that the economy and welfare state will go into a death spiral. Higher taxes or budget deficits would lead to lower economic growth—which would make promised benefits harder to pay and threaten yet higher taxes or budget deficits. Social Security, Medicare and Medicaid are essential parts of the nation's social fabric, but that does not mean that every benefit must be perpetuated forever. I have proposed elsewhere★ that the normal eligibility ages for Social Security and Medicare should gradually be raised to seventy by, say, 2025 or 2030. Between sixty-five and the new eligibility age, most people would be required to pay for Medicare or demonstrate that they had equivalent private coverage. (The poor would continue to receive the present large subsidies.) Social Security benefits should also be trimmed for more affluent retirees; and even when people go on full Medicare, most should pay more—through higher premiums, deductibles and co-payments—than they do now.

★ The reference is to my columns in *Newsweek* and *The Washington Post*.

The basic problem is that we have not modernized these programs to reflect changed economic and social conditions. When Congress enacted Social Security and Medicare in 1935 and 1965, respectively, many older Americans were poorer than the rest of the population. In the Great Depression, from 30 percent to 50 percent of the sixty-five-and-over population was thrown onto the mercy of children, relatives and friends for food, shelter and care. In 1965, perhaps three-quarters of the elderly had no health insurance. But now many older Americans are reasonably healthy and wealthy; they've had time to save for retirement. Social Security and Medicare have moved beyond their original purpose of protecting people from destitution and have become retirement subsidies—welfare payments to enable people to enjoy their "golden years."[25]

If the subsidies were less generous and started later, we'd find (no surprise) that people worked longer. That would be desirable, because life expectancy has increased (at birth, it was sixty-two in 1936 and is now seventy-seven), and work—having moved to offices from factories and farms—has become less physically grueling. The fact that we haven't made these and other changes says a lot about the welfare state. It is a profoundly conservative institution. It favors the past over the future. For recipients, the very fact of receiving— or being promised—benefits creates a moral right to receive them, even if the original circumstances that justified them have vanished. Not by accident do we call these benefits "entitlements" as opposed to the more straightforward term "welfare." Many recipients think they've "earned" their benefits through the previous payment of taxes, which were saved and are simply being returned. This is a myth. Both Social Security and Medicare are mainly pay-as-you-go programs. Yesterday's taxes paid yesterday's benefits; today's taxes pay today's benefits. But the self-serving vocabulary avoids the pejorative stigma of "welfare," which in America signifies charity or a handout.[26]

The result is that the welfare state has in part created a reverse Robin Hood effect: It sometimes transfers income from the struggling young to the relaxed old. Even if this did not threaten economic growth, it would pose a moral issue: Is it fair? Is it fair to force younger people to transfer so much of their incomes to older people who may be richer? But having long avoided these contentious issues, there is now no easy way to resolve them. If we cut benefits for baby boomers—as we should, because they're the source of rising costs—many retirees will feel mistreated and will complain that they were not given adequate notice. They'd be correct. But if we don't cut benefits, younger workers may soon feel that their rising taxes are oppressively high and that other government programs (education, defense, the environment) are being unwisely squeezed to pay retirees. They'd also be correct.

Turning to health care, the central issue is how to refashion the system to control spending without sacrificing essential care. There are two broad approaches. One would mandate universal insurance coverage either through private plans (again: subsidies for the poor) or something like universal Medicare. Through regulation or legislated budget limits, government would control spending. Rationing might result. The other approach would focus more on cost control than universal coverage. Medicare beneficiaries would receive "vouchers" to buy a basic package of benefits. For those under 65, the government would provide limited tax credits for people to shop for insurance coverage. The basic idea is to stimulate competition, as health insurance plans compete for policyholders on the basis of coverage cost and quality. Facing competitive pressures, the health industry would restructure itself. Doctors' practices, hospitals and clinics would form networks to create efficiencies and curb wasteful medical care by adopting effective treatment protocols. Philosophically, I prefer the second approach. But I'm skeptical of both, because the record on cost control—by either government or the private sector—has been bleak.

An aging society poses one final, daunting reality: Even if we act sensibly—that is, do everything I suggest—and somehow deal with health care, we will still face higher taxes. Plausible cuts in individual benefits will only temper the increases in government spending. We ought to ask what kind of taxes would least harm the economy. My preference is for a tax on consumption—probably an energy tax—rather than higher taxes on labor and investment income. Indeed, by also curbing some existing tax breaks, we might construct an income tax system with only four rates: 10 percent, 15 percent, 25 percent and 30 percent. In return for a lower top rate (the top now: 35 percent), higher income taxpayers would lose many tax breaks (mortgage interest rate deductions, low rates for capital gains and dividends, the exclusion of health insurance) that favor them. Tax gamesmanship among the rich (for instance: converting ordinary income into capital gains) would subside. Strong incentives for work and investment would remain.

Next, we need to come to terms with globalization. This means embracing two apparently contradictory propositions. First: Globalization is not the cause of every economic problem and shouldn't be cast as an all-purpose scapegoat. Second: Far more powerful than it was two decades ago, globalization could become a dangerous source of international strife unless we find ways to police its potential instabilities and conflicts. Globalization isn't going away; we need to find ways to deal with it.

For starters, we should keep its ill effects in perspective. It's been indicted for almost everything that Americans dislike: job loss, increased economic insecurity and inequality. Blame foreigners. Blame multinational companies. The allegations are exaggerated, and the danger is that they might inspire a nationalistic backlash against globalization that would be self-defeating—feeding protectionism here and abroad that would end up denying us overseas markets, worsening inflation and creating new uncertainties for global financial markets.

Let's examine some common allegations. Start with jobs. It's true that competition from imports can destroy jobs. But these effects are overstated. Although manufacturing employment has been declining for more than two decades, the main cause is improved productivity. Factories can produce more with fewer workers. In 1980, manufacturing employment of 18.7 million workers represented 21 percent of all payroll jobs. By 2006, manufacturing output had more than doubled, but employment had dropped to 14.2 million, only 11 percent of payroll employment. Trade's effects on this decline were modest. By one estimate, imports reduced manufacturing jobs by 1.3 million from 2000 to 2005—a period when, despite the 2001 recession, all U.S. jobs grew by 4.8 million and ended at 142 million. Domestic influences still dominate the labor market. After the high-tech and housing "bubbles," job losses soared among Internet and telecommunications workers and (later) construction workers and real estate agents. These losses had nothing to do with trade.*[27]

Nor is globalization the main source of rising economic inequality. Superficially, it can be made to seem so. Competition from imports, it's said, depresses blue-collar wages; meanwhile, companies boost profits and executives' salaries by sending jobs offshore to cheap labor markets. Workers lose, bosses win. But again, the effects are modest. Economist Robert Lawrence of Harvard has estimated that from 1980 to 2006, trade reduced the wages of blue-collar workers (factory workers, construction workers, manual laborers) by only 1.4 percent. Again, the major influences on wages are domestic, because most jobs satisfy domestic markets. Corporate profits as a share of national income did rise after 1999. But as Lawrence also notes, the big increase occurred in the financial sector—banks, brokers, investment banks—and not manufacturing. Gains came from making loans, trading securities, offering advice. These activities were largely domestic.[28]

Globalization is not destiny—not yet anyway. Countries' economic fates still depend decisively on national policies and cultures. The United States is not identical to Japan or even Canada; Ireland

---

* It's true that some service work—call centers, software programming, back office operations—has also been moved offshore. But so far, these job losses are even a smaller share of the total than manufacturing. One recent study of the drain of service jobs to India and China found the net loss to be negligible. (See "Much Ado About Nothing," Working Paper 14061, National Bureau of Economic Research.)

is not identical to Portugal; Singapore is not identical to Thailand. People, values, institutions and political systems differ, and the differences have consequences. Blaming globalization reflexively for our problem distracts attention from our own responsibility or culpability.

The more relevant question about globalization is whether it can be protected from itself. Or will it become a source of conflict? All successful economic systems require trust and confidence, some agreement on common rules (whether by custom or law) and ways of resolving conflicts and handling political or financial crises. People, firms and nations need a framework to cooperate. In the global economy, this framework is increasingly weak. After communism's collapse, it was assumed that the United States would continue to maintain the framework. This assumption now seems naïve, because it didn't anticipate dramatic shifts in economic geography and power. America is not getting weaker and poorer so much as other countries are getting stronger and richer.

As the global economy expands, they loom larger in trade and the demand for raw materials. America's importance shrinks. The same is true of finance. If China's economy continues growing 8 percent to 10 percent annually—a possibility—its total size will overtake the U.S. economy within a few decades, though American per capita incomes would remain much higher. The reinvestment of huge trade and oil surpluses has created new financial powers. In 2007, Persian Gulf nations had $1.8 trillion in foreign financial assets (stocks, bonds, real estate, entire companies). By 2020, the total could exceed $10 trillion.[29]

Economic nationalism is rising along with economic interdependence. The newly powerful countries have their own interests and distrust American motives, power and competence. China seems intent on refashioning the global economic order to meet its own needs, including access to raw materials (oil, minerals, grains). Regional economic blocs are already assuming added importance. Economic warfare is not inconceivable, with some countries pursuing their interests at the expense of others. As the Cold War alliance of the United States, Europe and Japan frays, the small group of nations that dominated the post–World War II global economic institutions—the International Monetary Fund, the World Bank, the General Agreement on Tariffs and Trade—has splintered. Consensus is harder to achieve, because more nations, including China, India and Brazil, must usually agree.

Somehow, accommodations must be reached. From America's perspective, it's important that currency rates change so that the major trade imbalances diminish, if not disappear. That would reduce one large potential source of instability. But there are others: access to raw materials; agreement on common rules for trade, finance and banking supervision; protection of patents and copyrights; cooperation in times of financial crisis. No country can be expected to abandon its national interests. But major countries need to acknowledge that their national interests include maintaining a viable global economy. Highly nationalistic policies—trade protectionism, restrictions on financial flows—may be emotionally satisfying and politically appealing, but aside from risking retaliation, they could also make cooperation difficult or impossible. The challenge is safeguarding our sovereignty without compromising global economic stability.

Finally, we need to be candid about controlling global warming.
With present technologies—which can change—not much can be
done. This is the harsh, perhaps even tragic, reality. The great prospective
increases in energy use and greenhouse gas emissions will come
from poorer countries, led by China and India. Understandably, they
show little interest in sacrificing their economic growth, aimed at reducing
mass poverty, to mitigate long-term global warming. Plausible
reductions in greenhouse gases by advanced countries, including
the United States, aren't large enough to offset increases elsewhere.
Ambitious U.S. programs to curb greenhouse gases might make
Americans feel virtuous, but they might also be a fool's errand:
costly to our prosperity but barely affecting global warming.

Many Americans seem to imagine that greenhouse gases can be
cut painlessly by fiat, without much cost to the public. Just order
companies to do it. This is a fantasy. If coal-fired power plants don't
get built—because regulations are restrictive or uncertain—then
there may be brownouts or blackouts. It's doubtful that solar, wind
or nuclear will fill the gap. If solar power costs more than coal-generated
electricity (as it now does), Americans will pay higher
prices; that will depress their real incomes. Under a "cap and trade"
system, a favorite anti–global warming approach, the government
would limit the volume of permitted greenhouse gases. Companies
would receive—or buy—quotas. Companies that needed to exceed
their limit (the "cap") would buy quotas (the "trade") from other

firms. But the costs would add to prices, which would reduce real incomes. If the "cap" were lax, the effects—on both economic growth and gas emissions—would be slight; if the "cap" were restrictive, the economic effects would be greater but, without big cuts by developing countries, the impact on global warming would still be slight.★

Consider some basic energy arithmetic. From 2005 to 2030, the world's population is projected to grow about 28 percent, from 6.4 billion to 8.2 billion. If energy use per person remained constant, total energy consumption would rise by 28 percent. But energy use per person will increase, as poor nations grow richer and buy more cars and trucks and construct more power plants to run factories, offices and appliances. By 2030, total global energy use may increase 55 percent from 2005 levels, projects the International Energy Agency (IEA) in Paris. China and India alone would account for almost half the increase and other developing countries another quarter. In India alone, about 400 million peo-

★ Some environmental groups have argued, based on computer-driven models, that the costs of sharply reducing greenhouse gases for the United States would be negligible. The argument is that, faced with higher prices for fossil fuels, businesses and consumers would invest in new energy-saving or nonfossil fuel technologies whose lifetime costs would be little higher than today's fossil fuels. These self-serving conclusions should be treated skeptically. First, the models assume that the shift from fossil fuels occurs smoothly: The alternate energy sources needed by the economy are always there. But in the real world, the energy may not be there. If coal-fired plants aren't built, it is not automatic that wind mills or solar plants will be approved to replace them. Energy is a pivotal commodity. If it's scarce, other activities will suffer; energy prices will

ple still lack access to electricity. Even if (implausibly) our reductions offset their increases, total global energy use would remain constant.[30]

So, too, would greenhouse gas emissions. About four-fifths of the world's energy now comes from fossil fuels, mainly oil (35 percent), coal (25 percent) and natural gas (20 percent). Can't we switch to nonfossil fuels (solar, wind, nuclear) and dampen energy use through more efficiency ("greener" lightbulbs and cars)? Well, yes—but only partially. The IEA performed a simulation that optimistically assumed widespread adoption and improvement of available alternative and energy-saving technologies. By 2030, solar energy was assumed to expand a hundredfold; wind grew by a factor of sixteen. Still, they provided only 7 percent of the world's electricity in 2030. Even with these favorable assumptions, annual greenhouse gas emissions would rise 27 percent by 2030. Economic growth would overwhelm new efficiencies and alternative fuels. In China, for example, the number of vehicles is projected to increase from 35 million in 2005 to 269 million in 2030.

Based on what we now know, global warming is a fairly intractable problem. The stated goal is to stabilize or reverse the rising

---

soar. Second, models actually have a poor track record in predicting many basic economic phenomena, including inflation, business-cycle turning points, productivity and interest rates. If the models can't predict these (for which there's much historic experience and data), why should they do better predicting something unprecedented: a shift from fossil fuels? Unsurprisingly, the models didn't predict the $145-a-barrel oil that occurred in 2008 or the jump in food prices that resulted in part from diverting corn into the production of biofuels.

concentration levels of greenhouse gases (the biggest: carbon dioxide) that trap heat close to the earth's surface. Since the early 1800s, concentration levels of carbon dioxide have increased from 280 parts per million to 380 parts in 2006. Because gases linger in the atmosphere for many decades, even reducing annual emissions would—if the theory is correct—not prevent global warming, because concentration levels would still be rising. This means that, for the United States alone, many anti–global warming proposals are a bad bargain: They penalize U.S. economic growth but achieve little else. The potential for unintended consequences is enormous: In 2008, the diversion of American corn for "biofuels" (ethanol) helped push up food prices.

Does that mean we can't do anything? Well, no.

The first thing is to undertake a large-scale program of research and development. The only real hope for significantly curbing greenhouse gases involves new technologies that would produce, at acceptable costs, the energy needed for economic growth without adding to greenhouse gases. Offered these technologies, poorer countries would find it attractive to curb their emissions. If "carbon capture and storage" technology (channeling carbon dioxide emissions from coal-fired power plants back into the ground) could be done cheaply, it would be a major breakthrough. Coal-fired plants, which now supply more than 40 percent of the world's electricity, would remain viable in a carbon-hostile world. Battery-powered cars would dramatically cut oil use, though raising the demand for electricity. On balance, there would probably be large net savings of fossil fuels.[31]

The second thing is to adopt policies, desirable on other grounds, that would also limit greenhouse gas emissions, if only slightly. For example, we should increase the fuel efficiency of cars and trucks because our dependence on unreliable foreign oil represents an obvious security problem. In 2007, Congress passed legislation requiring automakers to raise the average fuel efficiency of new vehicles from twenty-five miles per gallon (including cars, SUVs and light trucks) to thirty-five miles per gallon by 2020. They should go higher. We should also enact a fuel tax to favor more fuel-efficient vehicles as well as to discourage some driving. We might even enact a carbon tax to take some of the pressure off income taxes. Finally, we could also permit drilling for natural gas in offshore areas and parts of Alaska that are now prohibited. Natural gas used for electricity generation has lower carbon dioxide emissions than coal.

But we should not delude ourselves: Global warming—whatever its possible hazards—poses a stubborn dilemma: For now, anything that would sharply reduce greenhouse gases requires shutting down large parts of the global economy that produce those gases. Measures short of that may be economically costly as well as ineffective. Only major technological advances can break the dilemma. Will we admit this? It seems doubtful. Our politics seem predisposed toward denial. We won't admit the inconsistence, conflicts and simplicities of many appealing goals. We strive for the impossible and ignore the obvious.

Indeed, this condition characterizes most of the problems I have discussed. It's hard to be optimistic that we will genuinely tackle any of them. There's a political bias for avoidance and immediate gratification. What succeeds and would be popular in the long run is often unpopular in the short run. What's popular in the short run often fails in the long run.★

Here, we encounter a powerful parallel with double-digit inflation. It took hold because the policies that produced it were initially so appealing—the first effect was a boom—and the policies to reverse it were so unappealing. What was remarkable about the Volcker-Reagan policies is that they defied the standard political logic. All the adverse consequences (high unemployment, lost profits) were up front. All the benefits were indeterminate and lay in the hazy future. Their actions constituted the single most beneficial act of economic policy in the past half century. But at the time, what they were doing was highly unpopular, even if most Americans deplored inflation and wanted government to get rid of it.

VI

Viewed in this way, our economic future resembles a treacherous obstacle course. If we're not confounded by an oversized welfare state, then it may be globalization or a futile fight against global warming. "Affluent deprivation" hardly seems impossible. Still, we also need to keep perspective. We're peering into the

★ As this paperback edition goes to press, the Obama administration is moving in directions opposite from the suggestions here. It has done nothing to limit spending on the elderly, while it has proposed more health spending and a pervasive "cap and trade" program to regulate greenhouse gases.

dark—and most prophetic exercises end in embarrassment. The grim picture that I've sketched recalls the theory of "secular stagnation," proposed in 1939 by Harvard economist Alvin Hansen, who sought to explain the persistence of the Great Depression. After a decade, double-digit unemployment remained. The basic problem, he argued, was an exhaustion of investment opportunities. Birthrates were low, so markets weren't expanding. Technology was reaching its limits, so there were few new companies or giant projects. The "frontier," meaning the West, had been settled. The resulting scarcity of investments caused "sick recoveries that die in their infancy and depressions which feed on themselves."[32]

All this was plausible, but we also know that it was completely wrong. After World War II—and partly because of wartime production and victory—birthrates exploded (resulting in the baby boom), new technologies (television, commercial aviation) flourished, and Americans settled a new frontier: suburbia. There was no dearth of investment opportunities, and an economy that had seemed semi-permanently disabled demonstrated unmistakable vitality. History intruded in unexpected ways that contradicted forecasts from well-informed and sophisticated observers. So it may be now. Despite somber omens, our economic future may be bright. This case, too, can be made.

The global economy may now be experiencing the greatest boom in history, with the 2007–09 crisis merely a temporary interruption that marked a shift away from lopsided growth led by the United States—and the ravenous buying of American shoppers—and toward more balanced growth based in the emerging economies of China, India, Brazil and others. Big trade imbalances may shrink spontaneously; currency rates may realign to more realistic and stable levels. As for the United States, culture is often destiny, and America's is steeped in striving, ambition, inventiveness and risk-taking. There are underlying reservoirs of vitality that may defy demographic trends or dubious government policies. The "next big thing" might soon emerge, unleashing a new wave of economic expansion and prosperity.

It's also possible that the burdens of the welfare state may turn out to be more bearable than I've implied. After extensive studies, economist Peter Lindert of the University of California, Davis, concluded counter-intuitively that Europe's big welfare states had not hampered economic growth. Europe had minimized the deadening effects of higher taxes by relying heavily on consumption taxes that didn't dampen the rewards for work and investment. Europe's low growth, Lindert argued, resulted from overregulation—"worker protection laws, high minimum wages, import barriers, hours restrictions [on store openings] or government ownership of industry."[33]

The point is not to settle all these arguments. It is simply to acknowledge the uncertainties that limit our ability to imagine the future. By contrast, we can draw some reliable lessons from the past. Looking back on the last half century, we can reach some sensible conclusions about the nature of the contemporary political economy.

Modern, advanced democracies are dedicated in part to delivering as much prosperity as possible to as many people as possible for as long as possible. One lesson is that this promise itself may be a source of economic instability. The quest for ever-more and ever-better subverts itself. Twice since World War II, this has happened. The first episode resulted in the Great Inflation and all its associated ills, when academic economists convinced political leaders and the public that the generally satisfactory economic expansion of the 1950s could be improved and enhanced. The second episode culminated in the 2007–09 financial crisis, when the widespread benefits of disinflation created a false sense of security and optimism in private markets and public policy alike. As these assumptions spread, ordinary Americans, businesses and investors acted increasingly in ways that made the assumptions false; and the Federal Reserve moved aggressively—perhaps too aggressively in hindsight—to limit recessions.

Prolonged prosperity itself seems an underlying cause of instability; we are not so far removed from the nineteenth century's booms and busts as was once thought. People—opinion leaders, government officials, investors, managers, workers—are not content to leave well enough alone. Prosperity breeds pressures to make it better and to have it last longer that, in the end, prove self-defeating. Government policies and private behavior become careless. Behind the promise of ever-improving performance lies the presumption that economic and financial knowledge have improved sufficiently to allow governments to supervise and manage the financial system and the larger economy. The advance in knowledge meant that governments could be held accountable for economic outcomes. But the innate human tendency to overdo things suggests that the very striving for a perpetual, ever-improving prosperity creates its own undoing.

This news is sobering for ideologues of all varieties. For those who believe in the virtues of government intervention, the lesson is that too much intervention to produce "sustained growth" achieves at best Pyrrhic victories: temporary gains from lengthy expansions that are followed by deeper, longer, more punishing slumps. For those who place great faith in "markets," the lesson of the 2007–09 crisis is that they are sometimes given to destructive instability. Though they may ultimately self-correct, the wild swings may involve such huge social costs that no democratically elected government could watch passively while they played out.

There is, it seems, no self-evident "happy medium," no utopian mix of market power and government power that will achieve unending expansion. It might be better to tolerate more frequent, milder recessions and financial setbacks than to strive for some superficially more appealing but unattainable ideal. But this objective, if stated and acknowledged publicly, would almost certainly be highly unpopular and roundly criticized. Nor is there much scholarly research suggesting just how much instability might be beneficially accepted. What's clear is that the promise of modern economics (or, more precisely, "macroeconomics"—the study of the overall economy's behavior) that it understood and could limit economic instability is vastly overstated. Economic institutions and behavior change more rapidly than our understanding of them.[34]

So the future of American affluence cannot be definitively delineated. Whatever happens, it will be a state of mind as much as a state of production. It is human nature to generate new needs and wants. There can never be a terminal point of output and satisfaction—and this is especially true of Americans, who believe it is their birthright to get ahead and compulsively compare themselves to friends, neighbors and relatives. Enough will never be enough, and even in a prosperous economy, many things will seem amiss. Because our expectations are shaped by experience, our national moods follow a perverse pattern. Periods of poor performance dampen expectations—make us fearful of the future—and give rise to an exaggerated sense of relief when, as often happens, the economy defies the prevailing pessimism. Similarly, economic booms often breed disappointment, because they create euphoric expectations that are subsequently dashed.

We have experienced these cycles repeatedly since World War II. The 1950s boom was especially enjoyable because it confounded widespread fears that the Great Depression would resume. The Great Inflation of the 1970s was so disheartening in part because it shattered the glistening visions of "full employment" proffered in the 1960s. The expansions of the 1980s and (especially) the 1990s were intoxicating because they contrasted so starkly with the previous stagflation. Now we are again in the cycle's dispiriting phase: Today's economy disappoints next to the powerful expectations incubated during the late stages of the 1990s boom.

Traveling in the United States in the early 1830s, Alexis de Tocqueville was struck by Americans' faith in "the indefinite perfectibility of man"—a belief that society and its institutions could be constantly improved. In some ways, U.S. history is a chronicle of applying this impossible standard to market capitalism. A century ago, the struggle was to come to terms with new industrial enterprises—railroads, steel mills, slaughterhouses, oil refineries—whose very size seemed to contradict the premises of our democracy, because they represented the sort of concentrated power that Americans instinctively abhorred and opposed. In time, antitrust laws and social regulations seemed to check some of the raw power of massive corporations.[35]

The Great Depression signaled the next significant adjustment. No longer was the focus mainly on the large business firm itself. Now the complaint was against the system as a whole. If it was given to great spasms of instability, could government intervene to limit these lurches and provide protections against unavoidable hardships? The result was the welfare state and the idea of economic management, which would minimize the most destructive swings of the business cycle. As before, the underlying motive was not to repudiate capitalism but to make it more socially useful. But the initial and modest success of this approach bred the overconfidence that led to the Great Inflation. The ensuing failure ultimately stemmed from the futile effort to attain de Tocqueville's "indefinite perfectibility." Capitalism could be improved; but there were limits. After the 2007–09 crisis, we are embarked on yet another reappraisal.

We are, it seems, condemned to imperfectability. Most capitalist systems, and certainly ours, mix private and government power in ways intended to promote growth, stability and "fairness." The trouble is that the essence of capitalism is change and upheaval. It is a massive system of trial and error that creates new technologies, products and forms of organization and markets. So our efforts to pacify and control its energies—to channel them to make the system more humane and to advance larger social goals—pose a dilemma. If these efforts are too constricting, they will compromise or cripple capitalism's capacity to increase wealth. But if we tolerate the system's shifts without limit or succor for its victims, then we ordain constant and undesirable disruption. Our relentless search for some sensible balance can never reach a permanent resting place. The practices, technologies and customs of one era may be unsuited for the next. Some economic turmoil is always inevitable, and the very effort to suppress it may bring it about. If prosperity is too placid for too long, it will inspire the careless or reckless behavior—in private spending, investing and borrowing or government policies—that with time will create the very reverses that people sought to avoid. The Great Inflation and its aftermath was but one episode. Doubtless, there will be others.

GLOSSARY

This glossary is intended as a reader's aid. In the text, I have tried to define terms as I used them, but I have not redefined them as I repeated them. The list below aims to help readers who, on encountering an unfamiliar phrase or concept, won't have to leaf backward in the book to find the original reference.

In constructing this glossary, I have relied slightly on similar glossaries in the Congressional Budget Office's annual *Economic and Budget Outlook* and in N. Gregory Mankiw, *Principles of Economics,* 4th ed. (Mason, Ohio: Thomson Higher Education, 2007).

bank panic (or bank run). A situation when many depositors suddenly want to withdraw their money. Because banks have lent out most of their deposits, a run threatens to make the bank insolvent: It won't have the funds to pay depositors. A successful "run" at one bank may trigger runs on other banks, resulting in a full-scale panic. The creation of federal deposit insurance in the 1930s ended most traditional bank panics. The ability of the Federal Reserve to lend money to besieged banks—to act as a lender of last resort—has also mitigated financial panics. See also "financial panic," "deposit insurance" and "lender of last resort."

bank reserves. Cash held by banks to meet withdrawal demands from depositors or to cover losses. Although some reserves are held as vault cash, most are now held at one of the twelve regional Federal Reserve banks. The Federal Reserve sets reserve requirements: the proportion of deposits that must be held as reserves. Before the Fed began operations in 1914, most bank reserves were held either as vault cash or, in the case of smaller banks, as deposits at larger banks in major cities, such as New York and Chicago.

capital controls. Restrictions imposed by a government on the movement of money in and out of the country. Controls can affect both inflows (the ability of foreigners to buy a country's stocks and bonds or to make investments in local businesses and to buy real estate) and outflows (the ability of a country's citizens to invest abroad). The United States has few capital controls, and since 1980, many countries have dismantled controls that were widespread in the first decades after World War II. See also "capital flows."

capital flows. Money flows between countries. Often, these flows require one country's currency to be converted into another's on foreign exchange markets. For example, Americans wanting to invest in Japan would have to buy yen by selling dollars. Capital flows can take different forms. "Foreign direct investment" refers to investment in physical property, whether factories, real estate or an interest in (or control of) local businesses. "Portfolio investment" refers to the purchase of securities, such as stocks and bonds. Foreign funds can also be deposited in local banks. The dismantling of capital controls since 1980 has resulted in a huge increase of capital flows. See also "capital controls."

central bank. A bank created by the government to regulate money and credit conditions and to oversee a nation's financial system. The Federal Reserve is the United States' central bank. Other major central banks include the European Central Bank, the Bank of Japan and the Bank of England.

Consumer Price Index (CPI). The government's best-known inflation indicator. It is published monthly and reflects price changes in a market basket of goods and services judged to be typical of urban consumers. In 2004, food (including meals in restaurants) represented 15 percent of the index's weight, housing (including utilities) 42 percent, transportation (including gasoline) 17 percent and clothes 4 percent. The remainder included health care, recreation, education, communications (including television and phone service), personal care and other goods and services. Some economists prefer the "personal consumption expenditure (PCE)" price index to the CPI. See also "PCE Price Index."

core inflation. A measure of inflation that excludes energy and food prices. The argument for omitting them is that they are volatile—increases in one period may be offset by decreases in the next. Thus, the argument goes, policy makers should pay attention to the enduring sources of price changes and not be distracted by temporary ups and downs. The argument weakens if food and energy price changes are permanent, as they may have been in recent years. In 2008, food and energy represented about 24 percent of the CPI, meaning that "core inflation" reflected the remaining 76 percent of prices.

Cost-of-Living Adjustment (COLA). An automatic adjustment, usually annual, of payments for inflation. The best-known COLA today involves Social Security payments, which are increased for changes in the CPI. In the 1970s, many wage agreements had COLAs. Payments that are automatically adjusted for inflation are said to be "indexed" to inflation.

Council of Economic Advisers (CEA). A panel of three economists that provides analysis of economic conditions and makes recommendations on economic policy to the president. The CEA was created by the Employment Act of 1946.

current account. A broad measure of a country's international transactions but one that excludes "capital flows." The main component of the current account is the nation's trade balance in goods and services—food, fuel, manufactured products and services such as airfares, insurance or freight (air or sea). In addition, the current account includes other "current" payments, such as foreign aid, remittances from immigrants to their home countries, interest and dividends earned on foreign investments and other foreign government payments (for example, Social Security payments made to recipients abroad). See also "capital flows."

deflation. A general fall of prices—the opposite of inflation. In the late nineteenth century, American prices underwent deflation. The term sometimes refers to falling prices for particular products or assets. Falling home prices would constitute a real estate deflation.

deposit insurance. Government-provided protection against losses from failures of banks and savings and loan associations. Created in 1933, the Federal Deposit Insurance Corporation now protects deposits up to $100,000 and, for some retirement accounts, up to $250,000. All told, the FDIC insures more than $3 trillion of deposits.

discount rate. The interest rate at which commercial banks and some other financial institutions can borrow from the Federal Reserve. Banks present collateral (usually government and high-grade corporate bonds) to the Fed, and the Fed makes loans based on the collateral. In its early years, this was the main way in which the Fed was supposed to prevent bank panics. Decisions on the discount rate are made by the seven-member board of governors, not the FOMC. See also "Federal Open Market Committee." Under Chairman Ben Bernanke, the Fed has liberalized access to the discount window, accepting a greater variety of securities and allowing some investment banks (such as Goldman Sachs and Morgan Stanley) to borrow along with commercial banks.

Depression, the United States effectively abandoned the gold standard, though some limited and technical connections remained until 1971. See also "fiat currency."

Great Depression. The period roughly from late 1929 to late 1939 when the economy experienced large declines in output and persistently high unemployment. Unemployment peaked at 25 percent in 1933 but was in double digits for most of the decade.

Great Inflation. The period between the mid-1960s and the early 1980s when the United States experienced its worst peacetime inflation. Measured by the CPI, inflation rose from about 1 percent in 1960 on an annual basis to a peak of about 13 percent in 1979 and 1980.

Gross Domestic Product (GDP). The total value of all the final goods and services produced in the nation's formal economy (excluded from GDP, for example, are the value of a family's child-rearing or housekeeping services). GDP is the national income. It is now about $14 trillion and has four major components: consumption spending; investment spending by businesses and households (mainly in homes); government spending; and net exports (a trade surplus or deficit).

inflation. The general rise of prices. Inflation usually refers to an increase in the overall price level and not just the increase in a few prices, which may be caused by circumstances peculiar to that product. Higher oil prices, for example, might result from an unexpected surge in demand or a prolonged underinvestment in new supplies. See also "deflation" and "disinflation."

lender of last resort. Traditional role of government central banks, dating back to the mid-nineteenth century, to loan money to solvent banks that suddenly face a depositors' run. The theory is that if a bank is fundamentally sound, it should not be put out of business by a panic. In these circumstances, the central bank makes emergency loans of cash so that the besieged bank can pay enough depositors to reassure the rest that their money is safe. In today's financial markets, the lender of last resort role has become more elastic, and central banks sometimes buy securities to create a safety net for a falling market.

monetary policy. Government policies—determined mainly by the Federal Reserve—to influence interest rates, credit conditions and the money supply. See also "Federal Reserve," "Federal Open Market Committee," "Fed funds," "Fed funds rate" and "money supply."

money multiplier. The relationship between the amount of bank reserves and the amount of measured money. The money multiplier in effect estimates how far the addition (or subtraction) of reserves from the banking system translates into more (or less) money through the process of borrowing and lending. The money multiplier is highly technical. See also "open market operations" and "bank reserves."

money supply. The measurement of what people use to buy and sell. In the United States, there are two basic definitions of money: M1 consists of currency, checking deposits, NOW accounts and traveler's checks; M2 consists of M1 plus savings deposits, savings certificates of less than $100,000 (not including retirement accounts) and money market mutual funds (again, not including retirement accounts).

money velocity. The turnover of money. To take a simple example: If an economy had a money supply of $100 and a GDP of $1,000, the velocity of money would be 10. Various technical innovations (checks, credit cards, electronic transfers) have increased the velocity of money. See also "money supply."

natural rate of unemployment. The rate of unemployment at which inflation stabilizes. The name is misleading, because this "natural" rate is thought to vary between countries and, even within the same country, to shift over time. It reflects laws (minimum wage and unemployment insurance, for example) and the age of workers, among other things. If unemployment is kept persistently below the "natural rate," inflation will continually worsen, according to the theory. If it is above the natural rate, inflation will decline. See also "Non-Accelerating Inflation Rate of Unemployment."

nominal values. Measurements of economic values (of output, wages, incomes, spending) without any adjustment for inflation. See also "real values."

Non-Accelerating Inflation Rate of Unemployment (NAIRU). Economists' most recent terminology for the "natural rate." See "natural rate of unemployment."

open market operations. The means by which the Federal Reserve adds to—or subtracts from—bank reserves and, thereby, influences the Fed funds rate and money supply. When the Fed buys U.S. Treasury securities, the money it provides to the banking system tends to lower the Fed funds rate and increase the money supply. When the Fed sells Treasury securities, the money paid to it goes out of circulation, tightens credit and tends to raise interest rates and decrease the money supply. See also "Federal Open Market Committee," "Fed funds" and "Fed funds rate."

PCE Price Index. Another index of consumer prices—one preferred by the Federal Reserve as more comprehensive and accurate than the Consumer Price Index (CPI). The big difference between the two indexes is that the PCE index includes health-care spending paid for by insurance and government, whereas the CPI covers only consumers' out-of-pocket health-care spending. In the PCE, medical care is about 20 percent of the total compared with only 6 percent for the CPI. Other components are smaller. Housing is 23 percent in the PCE and 42 percent in the CPI. In the past, the PCE had tended to rise slightly more slowly than the CPI; but this might not be true in the future. See also "Consumer Price Index."★

Phillips Curve. The purported relationship between unemployment and inflation. It's named after the economist A. W. Phillips, who showed in a 1958 paper that historically there had been a fairly fixed relationship between wages—a proxy for inflation—and unemployment in Britain. This suggested that countries could choose between how much inflation or unemployment they wanted. But the relationship broke down when government aggressively tried to increase economic growth and reduce unemployment. See also "natural rate of unemployment."

quantity theory of money. The general idea that all high inflations result from too much money chasing too few goods. By this theory, if money consistently increases faster than real production of goods and services, inflation will result or get worse.

real values. Measurement of economic values (of output, wages, incomes, spending) after an adjustment for inflation. See also "nominal values."

★ For details, see Brian C. Moyer, "Comparing Price Measures—The CPI and the PCE Price Index," available at the Bureau of Economic Analysis's website, www.bea.gov.

APPENDIX 1

The American Economy Since 1950

For those who like numbers, the table below provides an overview of the American economy since 1950. The first column shows Gross Domestic Product—the annual output of goods and services, which is also our national income. The second column adjusts GDP for price changes and indicates, in so-called "constant" 2005 dollars (prices as they were in the year 2005), "real" GDP. The third column indicates annual increases in real GDP, which is usually called the economy's growth rate. Productivity, the next column, is what most people would call efficiency; it's measured in "output per hour worked" and applies to the economy's "non-farm business sector," which represents about three-quarters of GDP (the rest is agriculture, government and nonprofit organizations, for which productivity is difficult to measure). The next two columns show inflation—price increases—as recorded by the Consumer Price Index (CPI), with the second CPI column excluding changes in energy and food prices (which account for about one-quarter of the

CPI index). The changes in the CPI are measured from December of one year to December of the next and are not annual averages. The final three columns show average annual unemployment rates, average annual interest rates on 10-year Treasury bonds and the year-end close of the Standard & Poor's index of 500 stocks.

YEAR	GDP (IN CURRENT $, BILLIONS)	REAL GDP (IN CONSTANT 2005 $, BILLIONS)	ANNUAL % CHANGE IN REAL GDP	ANNUAL % CHANGE IN PRODUCTIVITY	ANNUAL % CHANGE IN CPI (DEC.–DEC.)	ANNUAL % CHANGE IN CPI MINUS FOOD AND ENERGY (DEC.–DEC.)	AVERAGE UNEMPLOY-MENT RATE (%)	INTEREST RATE ON 10-YEAR TREASURY BOND (%)	STANDARD & POOR'S 500 STOCK INDEX, YEAR–END CLOSE
1950	$293.7	$2,006.0	+8.7	+6.6	+5.9	NA	5.3	NA	20.41
1951	$339.3	$2,161.2	+7.7	+2.7	+6.0	NA	3.3	NA	23.77
1952	$358.3	$2,243.9	+3.8	+1.8	+0.8	NA	3.0	NA	26.57
1953	$379.4	$2,347.2	+4.6	+2.3	+0.7	NA	2.9	2.85	24.81
1954	$380.4	$2,332.4	−0.6	+1.9	−0.7	NA	5.5	2.40	35.98
1955	$414.7	$2,500.3	+7.2	+4.3	+0.4	NA	4.4	2.82	45.48
1956	$437.5	$2,549.8	+2.0	−0.7	+3.0	NA	4.1	3.18	46.67
1957	$461.1	$2,601.1	+2.0	+2.6	+2.9	NA	4.3	3.65	39.99
1958	$467.2	$2,577.6	−0.9	+2.2	+1.8	+1.7	6.8	3.32	55.21
1959	$506.6	$2,762.5	+7.2	+3.9	+1.7	+2.0	5.5	4.33	59.89
1960	$526.5	$2,830.9	+2.5	+1.2	+1.4	+1.0	5.5	4.12	58.11
1961	$544.8	$2,896.9	+2.3	+3.1	+0.7	+1.3	6.7	3.88	71.55
1962	$585.7	$3,072.4	+6.1	+4.5	+1.3	+1.3	5.5	3.95	63.10

YEAR	GDP (IN CURRENT $, BILLIONS)	REAL GDP (IN CONSTANT 2005 $, BILLIONS)	ANNUAL % CHANGE IN REAL GDP	ANNUAL % CHANGE IN PRODUCTIVITY	ANNUAL % CHANGE IN CPI (DEC.–DEC.)	ANNUAL % CHANGE IN CPI MINUS FOOD AND ENERGY (DEC.–DEC.)	AVERAGE UNEMPLOYMENT RATE (%)	INTEREST RATE ON 10-YEAR TREASURY BOND (%)	STANDARD & POOR'S 500 STOCK INDEX, YEAR-END CLOSE
1963	$617.8	$3,206.7	+4.4	+3.5	+1.6	+1.6	5.7	4.00	75.02
1964	$663.7	$3,392.3	+5.8	+2.9	+1.0	+1.2	5.2	4.19	84.75
1965	$719.1	$3,610.2	+6.4	+3.1	+1.9	+1.5	4.5	4.28	92.43
1966	$787.7	$3,845.3	+6.5	+3.6	+3.5	+3.3	3.8	4.92	80.33
1967	$832.5	$3,942.5	+2.5	+1.7	+3.0	+3.8	3.8	5.07	96.47
1968	$909.9	$4,133.4	+4.8	+3.4	+4.7	+5.1	3.6	5.65	103.86
1969	$984.5	$4,261.8	+3.1	+0.2	+6.2	+6.2	3.5	6.67	92.06
1970	$1,038.4	$4,270.0	+0.2	+1.5	+5.6	+6.6	4.9	7.35	92.15
1971	$1,126.9	$4,413.3	+3.4	+4.0	+3.3	+3.1	5.9	6.16	102.09
1972	$1,237.9	$4,647.7	+5.3	+3.3	+3.4	+3.0	5.6	6.21	118.05
1973	$1,382.3	$4,917.1	+5.8	+3.2	+8.7	+4.7	4.9	6.84	97.55
1974	$1,499.5	$4,889.9	−0.6	−1.6	+12.3	+11.1	5.6	7.56	68.56
1975	$1,637.7	$4,879.5	−0.2	+2.8	+6.9	+6.7	8.5	7.99	90.19

YEAR	GDP (IN CURRENT $, BILLIONS)	REAL GDP (IN CONSTANT 2005 $, BILLIONS)	ANNUAL % CHANGE IN REAL GDP	ANNUAL % CHANGE IN PRODUCTIVITY	ANNUAL % CHANGE IN CPI (DEC.-DEC.)	ANNUAL % CHANGE IN CPI MINUS FOOD AND ENERGY (DEC.-DEC.)	AVERAGE UNEMPLOYMENT RATE (%)	INTEREST RATE ON 10-YEAR TREASURY BOND (%)	STANDARD & POOR's 500 STOCK INDEX, YEAR-END CLOSE
1976	$1,824.6	$5,141.3	+5.4	+3.3	+4.9	+6.1	7.7	7.61	107.46
1977	$2,030.1	$5,377.7	+4.6	+1.6	+6.7	+6.5	7.1	7.42	95.10
1978	$2,293.8	$5,677.6	+5.6	+1.3	+9.0	+8.5	6.1	8.41	96.11
1979	$2,562.2	$5,855.0	+3.1	−0.4	+13.3	+11.3	5.8	9.44	107.94
1980	$2,788.2	$5,839.0	−0.3	−0.3	+12.5	+12.2	7.1	11.46	135.76
1981	$3,126.9	$5,987.2	+2.5	+1.4	+8.9	+9.5	7.6	13.91	122.55
1982	$3,253.2	$5,871.0	−1.9	−1.1	+3.8	+4.5	9.7	13.00	140.64
1983	$3,534.6	$6,136.2	+4.5	+4.4	+3.8	+4.8	9.6	11.10	164.93
1984	$3,930.9	$6,577.1	+7.2	+2.0	+3.9	+4.7	7.5	12.44	167.24
1985	$4,217.5	$6,849.3	+4.1	+1.6	+3.8	+4.3	7.2	10.62	211.28
1986	$4,460.1	$7,086.6	+3.5	+3.1	+1.1	+3.8	7.0	7.68	242.17
1987	$4,736.4	$7,313.3	+3.2	+0.3	+4.4	+4.2	6.2	8.39	247.08
1988	$5,100.4	$7,613.9	+4.1	+1.7	+4.4	+4.7	5.5	8.85	277.72
1989	$5,482.1	$7,885.9	+3.6	+0.8	+4.6	+4.4	5.3	8.49	353.40

YEAR	GDP (IN CURRENT $, BILLIONS)	REAL GDP (IN CONSTANT 2005 $, BILLIONS)	ANNUAL % CHANGE IN REAL GDP	ANNUAL % CHANGE IN PRODUCTIVITY	ANNUAL % CHANGE IN CPI (DEC.–DEC.)	ANNUAL % CHANGE IN CPI MINUS FOOD AND ENERGY (DEC.–DEC.)	AVERAGE UNEMPLOYMENT RATE (%)	INTEREST RATE ON 10-YEAR TREASURY BOND (%)	STANDARD & POOR'S 500 STOCK INDEX, YEAR-END CLOSE
1990	$5,800.5	$8,033.9	+1.9	+1.8	+6.1	+5.2	5.6	8.55	330.22
1991	$5,992.1	$8,015.1	–0.2	+1.5	+3.1	+4.4	6.8	7.86	417.09
1992	$6,342.3	$8,287.1	+3.4	+4.0	+2.9	+3.3	7.5	7.01	435.71
1993	$6,667.3	$8,523.5	+2.9	+0.6	+2.7	+3.2	6.9	5.87	466.45
1994	$7,085.2	$8,870.7	+4.1	+1.0	+2.7	+2.6	6.1	7.09	459.27
1995	$7,414.6	$9,093.8	+2.5	+0.4	+2.5	+3.0	5.6	6.57	615.93
1996	$7,838.5	$9,433.9	+3.7	+2.6	+3.3	+2.6	5.4	6.44	740.74
1997	$8,332.4	$9,854.4	+4.5	+1.5	+1.7	+2.2	4.9	6.35	970.43
1998	$8,793.5	$10,283.5	+4.4	+2.9	+1.6	+2.4	4.5	5.26	1,229.23
1999	$9,353.5	$10,779.9	+4.8	+3.3	+2.7	+1.9	4.2	5.65	1,469.25
2000	$9,951.5	$11,226.0	+4.1	+3.3	+3.4	+2.6	4.0	6.03	1,320.28
2001	$10,286.2	$11,347.2	+1.1	+3.0	+1.6	+2.7	4.7	5.02	1,148.08
2002	$10,642.3	$11,553.0	+1.8	+4.5	+2.4	+1.9	5.8	4.61	879.82
2003	$11,142.2	$11,840.7	+2.5	+3.7	+1.9	+1.1	6.0	4.01	1,111.92

YEAR	GDP (IN CURRENT $, BILLIONS)	REAL GDP (IN CONSTANT 2005 $, BILLIONS)	ANNUAL % CHANGE IN REAL GDP	ANNUAL % CHANGE IN PRODUCTIVITY	ANNUAL % CHANGE IN CPI (DEC.–DEC.)	ANNUAL % CHANGE IN CPI MINUS FOOD AND ENERGY (DEC.–DEC.)	AVERAGE UNEMPLOY-MENT RATE (%)	INTEREST RATE ON 10-YEAR TREASURY BOND (%)	STANDARD & POOR'S 500 STOCK INDEX, YEAR-END CLOSE
2004	$11,867.8	$12,263.8	+3.6	+2.8	+3.3	+2.2	5.5	4.27	1,211.92
2005	$12,638.4	$12,638.4	+3.1	+1.7	+3.4	+2.2	5.1	4.29	1,248.29
2006	$13,398.9	$12,976.3	+2.7	+1.0	+2.5	+2.6	4.6	4.80	1,418.30
2007	$14,077.7	$13,254.1	+2.1	+1.9	+4.1	+2.4	4.6	4.63	1,468.36
2008	$14,441.4	$13,312.2	+0.4	+1.8	+0.1	+1.8	5.8	3.66	903.25

APPENDIX 2

Post–World War II U.S. Business Cycles

Business cycles are fluctuations in economic activity. Since World War II, there have been eleven economic expansions—when output, employment and incomes are generally increasing—and ten recessions, when output, employment and incomes are usually falling. A committee of the National Bureau of Economic Research, a group of academic economists, determines the precise dates. A popular definition of a recession is at least two quarters of declining Gross Domestic Product (GDP), but the committee defines a recession in broad terms as "a signficant decline in economic activity spread across the economy, lasting more than a few months." It dates changes in business cycles on a monthly basis and consults a variety of statistics, including changes in employment, industrial production, personal income and wholesale and retail sales. The table below shows the changes in GDP, industrial production, employment and inflation associated with the post–World War II expansions and recessions. The longest expansion in U.S. history occurred in the 1990s and lasted exactly ten years; the second longest was in the 1960s and lasted almost nine years.

EXPANSIONS

TROUGH	PEAK	DURATION (IN MONTHS)	INCREASE IN REAL GDP (%)	INCREASE IN INDUSTRIAL PRODUCTION (%)	GROWTH IN NONFARM JOBS (%)	UNEMPLOYMENT RATE (LOWEST) (%)	INFLATION RATE (CPI) (HIGHEST)%
Oct. 1945	Nov. 1948	37	NA	24.7	17.1	3.4	19.7
Oct. 1949	July 1953	45	27.9	50.2	17.7	2.5	9.4
May 1954	Aug. 1957	39	13.3	21.9	8.5	3.7	3.7
April 1958	April 1960	24	11.7	22.9	7.4	4.8	1.7
Feb. 1961	Dec. 1969	106	51.2	74.9	33.0	3.4	6.2
Nov. 1970	Nov. 1973	36	16.3	26.2	10.7	4.6	12.3
March 1975	Jan. 1980	58	23.2	29.9	18.5	5.6	14.8
July 1980	July 1981	12	4.4	6.5	2.0	7.2	10.8
Nov. 1982	July 1990	92	37.4	32.7	23.7	5.0	6.3
March 1991	March 2001	120	40.3	50.9	22.1	3.8	3.8
Nov. 2001	Dec. 2007	73	17.7	14.7	5.5	4.4	5.4
Average		58	24.3	32.3	15.1	4.4	8.6

Appendix 2

RECESSIONS

PEAK	TROUGH	DURATION (IN MONTHS)	DECREASE IN REAL GDP (%)	DECLINE IN INDUSTRIAL PRODUCTION (%)	DECLINE IN NONFARM JOBS (%)	UNEMPLOYMENT RATE (HIGHEST) (%)	INFLATION RATE (CPI) (LOWEST) (%)
Nov. 1948	Oct. 1949	11	−1.6	−8.6	−5.0	7.9	−2.9
July 1953	May 1954	10	−1.9	−9.0	−3.0	6.1	−0.7
Aug. 1957	April 1958	8	−3.2	−12.7	−4.0	7.4	0.3
April 1960	Feb. 1961	10	−0.5	−6.2	−2.3	7.1	0.7
Dec. 1969	Nov. 1970	11	−0.2	−5.8	−1.2	6.1	2.7
Nov. 1973	March 1975	16	−3.4	−14.8	−1.8	9.0	4.9
Jan. 1980	July 1980	6	−2.2	−6.2	−1.2	7.8	9.6
July 1981	Nov. 1982	16	−2.8	−9.5	−3.2	10.8	2.5
July 1990	March 1991	8	−1.5	−4.3	−1.3	7.8	2.6
March 2001	Nov. 2001	8	−0.4	−6.3	−1.2	6.3	1.1
Dec. 2007	NA	NA	NA	NA	NA	NA	NA
Average		10.4	−1.8	−8.3	−2.4	7.6	2.1

SOURCES: National Bureau of Economic Research; Moody's Economy.com based on data from Bureau of Economic Analysis, Bureau of Labor Statistics and Federal Reserve Board.

NOTES: Unemployment data begin in 1948. High and low points for inflation are measured monthly—the year-over-year change in the CPI. Peaks and troughs in inflation (as well as unemployment) may occur outside the precise dates of the associated expansions and recessions.

NOTES AND FURTHER READING

What follow are detailed endnotes. I found a number of sources particularly useful, and I would recommend them highly to those interested in greater detail on various subjects covered in the book. For a compelling narrative of the Federal Reserve through the late 1980s, William Greider's *Secrets of the Temple* is wonderfully detailed and beautifully written. *Nixon's Economy: Booms, Busts, Dollars and Votes* by Rice University historian Allen J. Matusow is a clear and comprehensive account of how economic policy was made during these crucial years. For those interested in the Fed's critical policy change in October 1979, a special issue of the *Federal Reserve Bank of St. Louis Review* 87, no. 2, part 2 (March/April 2005), provides many fascinating details and is generally understandable by nonexperts. Particularly interesting are papers by David E. Lindsey, Athanasios Orphanides and Robert Rasche and by Allan Meltzer. (The *Review* is available at http://www.stlouisfed.org. Click on "publications.") Those wanting a better feel for the insecurities faced by American workers might read two first-rate journalistic accounts: *The Diposable American: Layoffs and Their Consequences* by Louis Uchitelle and *High Wire: The Precarious Financial Lives of American Families* by Peter Gosselin.

1: THE LOST HISTORY

1. For all CPI figures, see various issues of the *Economic Report of the President*. All quotes from 1960 to 2007 can be found in table B-63 of the 2008 report.

2. Lyndon Baines Johnson, *The Vantage Point: Perspective of the Presidency, 1963–1969* (New York: Holt, Rinehart & Winston, 1971), 325–26. A good summary of the budget politics of this episode is found in Robert P. Bremner, *Chairman of the Fed: William McChesney Martin Jr. and the Creation of the American Financial System* (New Haven, Conn.: Yale University Press, 2004), 219–30.

3. For inflation figures with and without energy, see table B-63, *Economic Report of the President, 2008*. A case for the modest effect of oil prices on inflation is made in Robert Barsky and Lutz Killian, "Oil and the Macroeconomy Since the 1970s," *Journal of Economic Perspectives* 18, no. 4 (Fall 2004): 115–34. A similar point is made in many other studies. See Federal Reserve Bank of San Francisco, "Oil Price Shock and Inflation" (Economic Letter, October 28, 2005); Benjamin Hunt, "Oil Price Shocks: Can They Account for the Stagflation of the 1970s?" (Working Paper 5/215, International Monetary Fund, Washington, D.C., 2005); and J. Bradford DeLong, "America's Peacetime Inflation: The 1970s," in *Reducing Inflation, Motivation and Strategy*, ed. Christina D. Romer and David H. Romer (Chicago: University of Chicago Press, 1997).

4. Daniel Yergin, *The Prize: The Epic Quest for Oil, Money and Power* (New York: Simon & Schuster, 1991), 598–632 (616–17). Gasoline and crude oil prices from the Energy Information Administration's website, www.eia.doe.gov.

5. For details on gasoline lines, see Allen J. Matusow, *Nixon's Economy:*

Booms, Busts, Dollars, and Votes (Lawrence: University of Kansas Press, 1998), 267.

6. Price changes cited in Burton G. Malkiel, *A Random Walk Down Wall Street* (New York: W. W. Norton, 1996), 27.

7. For poll data, see Pew Study Global Attitudes Project, Spring 2007.

8. Daniel Yankelovich, "The Noneconomic Side of Inflation," in *Inflation and National Survival,* ed. Clarence C. Walton (New York: Academy of Political Science, 1979), 20.

9. Peter Bernholz, *Monetary Regimes and Inflation: History, Economic and Political Relationships* (Northampton, Mass.: Edward Elgar Publishing, 2003), 2, 8; Eric D. Weitz, *Weimar Germany: Promise and Tragedy* (Princeton, N.J.: Princeton University Press, 2007), 145.

10. John Maynard Keynes, *A Tract on Monetary Reform* (London: Macmillan, 1923), 1.

11. Hourly wage data from table B-47, *Economic Report of the President, 2006.* Details of the meat shortage in Mastusow, *Nixon's Economy,* 229. Information on inflation indexing from Stanley Fischer, "Adapting to Inflation in the United States Economy," in *Inflation: Causes and Consequences,* ed. Robert E. Hall, National Bureau of Economic Research (Chicago: University of Chicago Press, 1982), 181–82. The quote from the Harvard economist is in Peter T. Kilborn, "Consumer, Resigned to Inflation, Is Learning New Ways to Hedge," *New York Times,* April 22, 1979, A-1.

12. I am indebted to Karlyn Bowman of the American Enterprise Institute for providing the public opinion data. As a young reporter, I tried to

trace the origins of the word "stagflation." I failed. See Robert J. Samuelson, " 'Stagflation' and Other Jargon," *Washington Post,* September 19, 1971, 89. Kraft quote from *Washington Post,* February 25, 1971, A-21.

13. Edward M. Gramlich, "Monetary and Fiscal Policies," in Walton, *Inflation and National Survival,* 141.

14. James Tobin, *Politics for Prosperity: Essays in a Keynesian Mode,* ed. Peter M. Jackson (Cambridge, Mass.: MIT Press, 1987), 318. Kahn quoted in Theodore H. White, *America in Search of Itself: The Making of the President 1956–1980* (New York: Harper & Row, 1982), 149.

15. *Public Papers of the Presidents of the United States: Jimmy Carter, 1979, Book 2—June 23, 1979, to Dec. 31, 1979* (Washington, D.C.: U.S. Government Printing Office, 1980), 1225–41.

16. White, *America in Search of Itself,* 155 (White quote), 416 (exit polls), 417 (Carter's judgment about inflation).

17. Seymour Martin Lipset and William Schneider, *The Confidence Gap: Business, Labor, and Government in the Public Mind* (New York: Free Press, 1983), 156, 142.

18. *The Budget and Economic Outlook: Fiscal Years 2008 to 2018* (Washington, D.C.: Congressional Budget Office, 2008), 42.

19. Robert J. Samuelson, *The Good Life and Its Discontents: The American Dream in the Age of Entitlement, 1945–1995* (New York: Crown, 1995), 114.

20. Profit figures for 1964–74 from table B-28 of *Economic Report of the President, 2007.* General Motors figures from Joseph E. Connor, "Recognizing the Cost of Inflation," speech and pamphlet, Commonwealth

Club of California, April 1979. Pretax profit margins provided by Mark Zandi of Moody's Economy.com, based on data from the Bureau of Economic Analysis. Margins reflect pretax profits of domestic nonfinancial corporations divided by the output of the nonfinancial corporate sector. The nonfinancial sector excludes banks and other financial service firms. *Wall Street Journal* editorial cited in Financial Standards Accounting Board, "Financial Reporting and Changing Prices: The Conference Proceedings" (Stamford, Conn.: Financial Accounting Standards Board, 1979). *BusinessWeek* quote, May 4, 1981, 81.

21. Interest rates from table B-73, *Economic Report of the President, 2008*.

22. Data on S&Ls and commercial banks comes from the websites of the Office of Thrift Supervision and the Federal Deposit Insurance Corporation. Much of the other data in this and the subsequent paragraph comes from Lawrence J. White, *The S&L Debacle: Public Policy Lessons for Banks and Thrift Regulation* (New York: Oxford University Press, 1991). The number of thrifts comes from table 4-2, p. 58. The quote is from p. 59.

23. The $160 billion figure comes from the Government Accountability Office and is cited in *History of the Eighties—Lessons for the Future, Volume 1: An Examination of the Banking Crises of the 1980s and Early 1990s* (Washington, D.C.: Federal Deposit Insurance Corporation, 1997), 169.

24. For Greider quote, see William Greider, *Secrets of the Temple: How the Federal Reserve Runs the Country* (New York: Simon & Schuster, 1987), 83–84. Grain prices from Economic Research Service of U.S. Department of Agriculture. Land prices from "Banking and the Agricultural Problems of the 1980s" in FDIC, *History of the Eighties*, vol. 1, 259–90.

25. For background on the Latin debt crisis, see "The LDC Debt Crisis," in FDIC, *History of the Eighties*, vol. 1.

26. James E. Buck, ed., *The New York Stock Exchange: Another Century* (Lyme, Conn.: Greenwich Publishing, 1999), 178–79; "The Death of Equities," *BusinessWeek,* August 13, 1979, 54. The source is the same for much of the information in the following paragraph.

27. See, for example, Robert J. Shiller, "Low Interest Rates and High Asset Prices: An Interpretation in Terms of Changing Popular Economic Models" (Working Paper 13558, National Bureau of Economic Research, Cambridge, Mass., October 2007).

28. Share of households owning stock is from table 6 of "Recent Changes in Family Finances: Results from the 1998 Survey of Consumer Finances," Federal Reserve Bulletin, January 2000. For Yahoo! price/ earnings ratio, see John Cassidy, *Dot.con: The Greatest Story Ever Sold* (New York: HarperCollins, 2002), 262, appendix. For study of the length of the "bubble," see J. Bradford DeLong and Konstantin Magin, "A Short Note on the Size of the Dot-Com Bubble" (Working Paper 12011, National Bureau of Economic Research, Cambridge, Mass., January 2006).

29. See historical data from the Federal Reserve's "Flow of Fund Accounts of the United States" at http://www.federalreserve.gov/releases/z1.

30. Jimmy Carter, *Keeping Faith: Memoirs of a President* (Fayetteville: University of Arkansas Press, 1995), 535–39.

31. Kenneth S. Rogoff, "Globalization and Global Disinflation," in *Monetary Policy and Uncertainty: Adapting to a Changing Economy,* symposium sponsored by the Federal Reserve Bank of Kansas City in Jackson Hole, Wyoming, August 2003, and published by the Federal Reserve Bank of Kansas City. For individual countries, "early twenty-first century" refers to averages from 2000 to 2003. Updated statistics for the larger groups of countries for 2005 and 2006 were provided by Rogoff.

2: THE "FULL EMPLOYMENT" OBSESSION

1. Nixon quote from Matusow, *Nixon's Economy*, 17. Eizenstat quote from "Economists and White House Decisions," *Journal of Economic Perspectives* 6, no. 3 (Summer 1992): 67–68.

2. "Get America moving again" quote from Herbert Stein, *Presidential Economics: The Making of Economic Policy from Roosevelt to Reagan and Beyond*, 2nd rev. ed. (Washington, D.C.: American Enterprise Institute for Public Policy Research, 1988); Kennedy quote from Theodore H. White, *The Making of the President, 1960* (New York: Pocket Books, 1961), 308.

3. Walter W. Heller, *The New Dimensions of Political Economy* (Cambridge, Mass.: Harvard University Press, 1966), 1–2.

4. Poll for 1946 and quote from Truman in Samuelson, *The Good Life and Its Discontents*, 31. The quote on suburbanization is from White, *The Making of the President, 1960*, 259.

5. For per capita incomes see Susan B. Carter, et al., *Historical Statistics of the United States*, millennial ed., vol. 3 (New York: Cambridge University Press, 2006), tables Ca 1–8 and Ca 9–19. Monthly unemployment data from the website of the Bureau of Labor Statistics, http://data.bls.gov/PDQ/servlet/SurveyOutputServlet. Stein quote from Stein, *Presidential Economics*, 77.

6. Yale economist James Tobin was one complainer. See James Tobin, *The New Economics, One Decade Older* (Princeton, N.J.: Princeton University Press, 1974), 36–37. Johnson and Okun quotes from Arthur Okun, *The Political Economy of Prosperity* (Washington, D.C.: Brookings Institution, 1970), 33; the book is based on lectures given in 1969. The final two quotes are from Stein, *Presidential Economics*, 29–30.

7. Tobin, *New Economics,* 57.

8. The Samuelson-Solow discussion is drawn from DeLong, "America's Peacetime Inflation" in Romer and Romer, *Reducing Inflation,* 252–53. The original Samuelson-Solow article was "Analytical Aspects of Anti-Inflation Policy," *American Economic Review* (May 1960): 185–97.

9. Heller, *New Dimensions of Political Economy,* 27.

10. Tobin, *New Economics,* 38.

11. For Kennedy's view, see Theodore C. Sorensen, *Kennedy* (New York: Bantam Books, 1966), 454.

12. For Sidey quote and background, see Seymour E. Harris, *Economics of the Kennedy Years and a Look Ahead* (New York: Harper & Row, 1964), 4–5. For Kennedy quote, see Sorensen, *Kennedy,* 483. Unemployment dropped from 6 percent in December 1961 to 5.4 percent in July 1962. After that, it fluctuated between 5.4 percent and 5.7 percent. In December 1962, it was 5.5 percent.

13. For the "biggest gamble in history," see Sorensen, *Kennedy,* 484. Low approval rating for fiscal responsibility cited in Johnson, *Vantage Point,* 39. Figures for GDP and unemployment from House Budget Committee, *Chronology of Major Fiscal and Monetary Policies (1960–1977)* (Washington, D.C.: U.S. Government Printing Office, 1978), 6–7.

14. *Time* magazine, December 31, 1965.

15. Stein, *Presidential Economics,* 135.

16. Schultze quote, personal interview with the author, January 5, 2005.

DeLong observation from DeLong, "America's Peacetime Inflation," in Romer and Romer, *Reducing Inflation*, 266.

17. Vietnam troop levels from James T. Patterson, *Grand Expectations: The United States, 1945–1974* (New York: Oxford University Press, 1996), 595. LBJ quote from ibid., 597–98.

18. Matusow, *Nixon's Economy*, 1.

19. Nixon's quote to Haldeman in ibid., 83. The history of the Democrats' authorization of wage-price controls in ibid., 67.

20. Matusow quote in ibid., 116. This paragraph relies heavily on Matusow. Poll results in ibid., 114, 156. Nixon's World War II experience in ibid., 266.

21. This and the following paragraph rely heavily on W. Carl Biven, *Jimmy Carter's Economy: Policy in an Age of Limits* (Chapel Hill: University of North Carolina Press, 2002). See particularly pages 86–88. The CBO report is dated January 11, 1977.

22. Eckstein predictions from transcript of the White House meeting, 11.

3: THE MONEY CONNECTION

1. Friedman quote in Milton Friedman, *Money Mischief: Episodes in Monetary History* (New York: Harcourt Brace Jovanovich, 1992), 49. Data for money-supply growth for the 1950s and 1960s is from table B-52 of the *Economic Report of the President, 1972*. For the 1970s, it is from table B-69 of the *Economic Report of the President, 2007*. Data for the first two

decades is measured from December to December. For the 1970s, the figures are annual averages.

2. Burns's lecture was the 1979 Per Jacobsson Lecture, available at http://www.perjacobsson.org/lectures/1979.pdf.

3. Allan Meltzer, "From Inflation to More Inflation, Disinflation and Low Inflation" (keynote address, Conference on Price Stability, Federal Reserve Bank of Chicago, November 3, 2005), 4. See page 1 for Martin's dislike of forecasts.

4. Personal interview, Athanasios Orphanides.

5. Faulty estimates of full employment and potential output in this paragraph and the preceding paragraph provided by Athanasios Orphanides to the author. See also Athanasios Orphanides and John C. Williams, "The Decline of Activist Stabilization Policy: Natural Rate Misperceptions, Learning and Expectations" (International Finance Discussion Papers, no. 804, Board of Governors of the Federal Reserve, April 2004).

6. Orphanides and Williams, "Decline of Activist Stabilization Policy."

7. Walter T. K. Nugent, *The Money Question During Reconstruction* (New York: W. W. Norton, 1967), 56–57.

8. Jeremy Atack and Peter Passell, *A New Economic View of American History: From Colonial Times to 1940,* 2nd ed. (New York: W. W. Norton, 1994), 496.

9. Farley Grubb, "Benjamin Franklin and the Birth of a Paper Money Economy" (essay based on a lecture given at the Federal Reserve Bank of Philadelphia, March 30, 2006).

10. Carter et al., *Historical Statistics of the United States,* table Cc 205–266.

11. Ernest L. Bogart and Charles M. Thompson, *Readings in the Economic History of the United States* (New York: Longmans, Green, 1929), 722–25.

12. For list of panics, see Milton Friedman and Anna Jacobson Schwartz, *A Monetary History of the United States, 1867–1960* (Princeton, N.J.: Princeton University Press, 1963), 821.

13. Details on gold from David Tripp, *Illegal Tender: Gold, Greed and the Mystery of the Lost 1933 Double Eagle* (New York: Free Press, 2004); and Friedman and Schwartz, *Monetary History of the United States,* 462–70.

14. Much of this and following paragraphs rely on Hugh Rockoff, *Drastic Measures: A History of Wage and Price Controls in the United States* (New York: Cambridge University Press, 1984).

15. Rockoff, *Drastic Measures,* 40–41, 147.

16. Heller, *New Dimensions of Political Economy,* 45.

17. Joseph A. Califano, *The Triumph and Tragedy of Lyndon Johnson: The White House Years* (New York: Simon & Schuster, 1991), 94.

18. Ibid., 102, 137.

19. Ibid., 140–46.

20. Burns's initial speech warming to incomes policy occurred at the Annual Monetary Conference of the American Bankers Association in Hot Springs, Virginia, on May 18, 1970. Some quotes in the text are from "The Problem of Inflation," a speech to the American Economics Association, December 29, 1972, in Toronto, Canada, which is clearer in

its explanation. Both are reprinted in Arthur Burns, *Reflections of an Economic Policy Maker* (Washington, D.C.: American Enterprise Institute, 1978), 91–102, 143–154.

21. See Joanne Gowa, *Closing the Gold Window: Domestic Politics and the End of Bretton Woods* (Ithaca, N.Y.: Cornell University Press, 1983), 149; and Paul Volcker and Toyoo Gyohten, *Changing Fortunes: The World's Money and the Threat to American Leadership* (New York: Times Books, 1992).

22. For details of changes in Nixon's controls and the effect on cattlemen, see Rockoff, *Drastic Measures,* 207, 212. For end of controls, see Matusow, *Nixon's Economy,* 231–33.

23. Comptroller General of the United States, *The Voluntary Pay and Price Standards Have Had No Discernible Effect on Inflation: Report to the Congress* (Washington, D.C.: General Accounting Office, 1980), 104–6.

24. Quotes from Edward Nelson, "The Great Inflation of the Seventies: What Really Happened?" (Working Paper 2004-001, Federal Reserve Bank of St. Louis), 26, 28.

25. For bank failures, see Carter et al., *Historical Statistics of the United States,* vol. 2, 1019. For background on the gold standard and the Depression, see Barry Eichengreen, *Golden Fetters: The Gold Standard and The Great Depression, 1919–1939* (New York: Oxford University Press, 1992).

26. Personal interview, Allan Meltzer, March 20, 2005. See also Allan Meltzer, *A History of the Federal Reserve,* vol. 1, *1913–1951* (Chicago: University of Chicago Press, 2003).

27. For Johnson quotes, see Bremmer, *Chairman of the Fed,* 209. For Nixon quote, see Burton A. Abrams, "How Richard Nixon Pressured

Arthur Burns: Evidence from the Nixon Tapes," *Journal of Economic Perspectives* 20, no. 4 (Fall 2006): 177–88.

4: A COMPACT OF CONVICTION

1. For interest rates, see table B-71, *Economic Report of the President, 1997.*

2. For interest rates, see ibid.; "Interest Rate Anguish," *Time,* March 8, 1982, 74–83. For drop in industrial production, see table B-44 in the *Economic Report of the President* for both 1983 and 1984. For business failures and drops in housing starts see tables B-91 and B-47 in *Economic Report of the President, 1984.*

3. For details of teamsters contract and breakdown of pattern bargaining, see Agis Salpukas, "Regional Truckers Debate Labor Costs," *New York Times,* February 25, 1982; and William Serrin, "Nonunion Rivals and Dissent Are Troubling the Teamsters," *New York Times,* May 16, 1982.

4. For wholesale prices, see tables B-59 and B-60, *Economic Report of the President, 1984.* For labor costs, see table B-41.

5. Baker quote, *Time,* March 8, 1982, 76.

6. Accessed at http://www.reagan.utexas.edu/archives/speeches/1982/40382b.htm. Ronald Reagan, "Exchange with Reporters Following the Radio Address to the Nation on the Program for Economic Recovery," April 3, 1982. For a more detailed account of Reagan-Volcker meetings, see Greider, *Secrets of the Temple,* 378–81.

7. All inflation figures from table B-61, *Economic Report of the President, 1997.*

8. Volcker quote, personal interview, March 16, 2005.

9. LBJ quote from Allan Meltzer, "Origins of the Great Inflation," in "Reflections on Monetary Policy 25 Years After October 1979," special issue, *Federal Reserve Bank of St. Louis Review* 87, no. 2, part 2 (March–April 2005): 158. For Gonzales quote, see *Congressional Record* (September 21, 1981): H 21462.

10. For Byrd proposal, see Greider, *Secrets of the Temple,* 512. For Kemp view, see Allan Meltzer, *A History of the Federal Reserve,* vol. 2, chap. 8 (Chicago: University of Chicago Press, forthcoming).

11. Approval ratings from George C. Edwards with Alec Gallup, *Presidential Approval: A Sourcebook* (Baltimore: Johns Hopkins University Press, 1990).

12. For background on the Moyers documentary and Reagan's comment, see Lou Cannon, *President Reagan: The Role of a Lifetime* (New York: Simon & Schuster, 1991), 264–66. The *Newsweek* cover story was dated April 5, 1982.

13. Anderson quote from Cannon, *Role of a Lifetime,* 269. Volcker quote from Volcker and Gyohten, *Changing Fortunes,* 175.

14. Volcker quote from Volcker and Gyohten, *Changing Fortunes,* 175. Niskanen quote from personal interview, March 16, 2005. Anderson quote from Cannon, *The Role of a Lifetime,* 272.

15. Jordon quote from Meltzer, *A History of the Federal Reserve,* vol. 2.

16. For background on "bellyache," see Robert Novak and Roland Evans, *The Reagan Revolution* (New York: E. P. Dutton, 1981), 69. I am indebted to Bob Novak for pointing this out. For "hell of a mess," see United Press International story, November 20, 1982.

17. Quote on Volcker's obscurity from Greider, *Secrets of the Temple,* 181. Volcker quote on inflation from Fredric Smoler, "A View from the Fed," *Audacity* magazine, Fall 1994, 9. Barbara Volcker comment from *Time* magazine, March 8, 1982, 81.

18. Biographical details from *Time* magazine, March 8, 1982, 80–81; and personal interview.

19. Personal interview with Volcker, October 13, 2004; and Greider, *Secrets of the Temple,* 17–22, 45–47.

20. Eizenstat quote from Greider, *Secrets of the Temple,* 19. For recession forecasts, see David Lindsey, Robert Rasche and Athanasios Orphanides, "The Reform of October 1979: How It Happened and Why," in *Reflections on Monetary Policy 25 Years After October 1979,* 5.

21. For commodity prices, see Lindsey, Rasche and Orphanides, "Reform of October 1979," 197.

22. Interest rates from http://www.federalreserve.gov/releases/h15/data/m/fredfunds.txt.

23. For quote on checking balances, see Greider, *Secrets of the Temple,* 479.

24. Schultze quote from ibid., 183. This and the following paragraph draw heavily on Greider's account, pages 182–86.

25. For spending and unemployment figures, see *Economic Report of the President, 1981,* 139 and table B-31. Kahn quote from Biven, *Jimmy Carter's Economy,* 248–49.

26. For December 1981 unemployment rate, see table B-33 of the *Economic Report of the President, 1983.* Reuss quote from Lindsey, Rasche and Orphanides, "Reform of October 1979," 221.

27. Greider, *Secrets of the Temple,* 150.

28. Volcker, personal interview, March 16, 2005. See also Marvin Good-friend and Robert King, "The Incredible Volcker Disinflation" (paper prepared for the Carnegie-Rochester Conference on Public Policy, November 2004).

29. For Tennessee builders, see Cannon, *Role of a Lifetime,* 268. For Schultz quote, see Greider, *Secrets of the Temple,* 460.

30. For Gramley quote and personal hostility, see Greider, *Secrets of the Temple,* 460. For Yardeni quote, see ibid., 472.

31. For Braniff and Lionel, see ibid., 490. For International Harvester, see ibid., 478–79. For Gramley quote, see ibid., 503.

32. Transcript of Federal Open Market Committee (FOMC) meeting (Washington, D.C., June 30–July 1, 1982), 2, 7, 46.

33. For Volcker comments at FOMC meeting, see FOMC meeting transcript, 66; for Volcker comment on easing, see Perry Mehrling, "An Interview with Paul A. Volcker" in *Inside the Economist's Mind: Conversations with Eminent Economists,* ed. Paul A. Samuelson and William A. Barnett (Malden, Mass.: Blackwell Publishing, 2007), 183.

34. For discount rate cuts, Kaufman and stock market, see Greider, *Secrets of the Temple,* 510–11. On the sequence of events in the summer and fall of 1982, I am indebted to David Lindsey, former deputy director of the Fed's Division of Monetary Affairs, for an detailed analysis of the shifts in policy in 1982 and early 1983.

35. Greider and Schultz quotes from Greider, *Secrets of the Temple,* 463. Volcker's quote at October FOMC meeting is cited in Meltzer, *History of the Federal Reserve,* vol. 2, chaper 8 (forthcoming).

36. Bankruptcy statistics from table B-94, *Economic Report of the President, 1997.* Farm income figures from table B-95. Wilk quote from "Jobs: How to Get America Back to Work," *Newsweek,* October 18, 1983, 79.

5: CAPITALISM RESTORED

1. Calculations of government's share of national income from table 1.3, "Historic Tables," *Budget of the U.S. Government, Fiscal Year 2006* (Washington, D.C.: U.S. Government Printing Office, 2005). The 3 percent of GDP is for 1929; in the 1950s, federal spending averaged 18 percent of GDP.

2. For competition statistic, see Diego Comin and Thomas Philippon, "The Rise in Firm-Level Volatility: Causes and Consequences" (Working Paper 11388, National Bureau of Economic Research, Cambridge, Mass., May 2005). The Comin and Philippon study concerns only large firms. Other research focusing on all companies suggests a decline in volatility, accounted for exclusively by less volatility among smaller firms. But volatility for small firms still exceeds that of large firms; it has probably declined because the overall economy has been more stable. Psychological insecurity, in my view, has gotten worse. Workers in small firms still face greater uncertainties than those at large firms, and those at large firms face more uncertainties than in earlier postwar periods. See Steven J. Davis, John Haltiwanger, Ron Jarmin and Javier Miranda, "Volatility and Dispersion in Business Growth Rates: Publicly Traded Versus Privately Held Firms" (Working Paper 12354, National Bureau of Economic Research, Cambridge, Mass., June 2006).

3. Individual stock declines from Malkiel, *Random Walk Down Wall Street,* 86. Loss of stocks from personal communication with Kim Sheppard of Wilshire Associates, August 2007.

4. Quote from Sanford Jacoby, *Employing Bureaucracy: Managers, Unions, and the Transformation of Work in the 20th Century* (Mahwah, N.J.: Lawrence Erlbaum, 2004), 152. Although Jacoby's fine book provides background for this discussion, the quote of his is from Louis Uchitelle, *The Disposable American: Layoffs and Their Consequences* (New York: Knopf, 2006), 27.

5. Union membership from table Ba4783–91 in Carter et al., *Historical Statistics of the United States,* vol. 2. Calculation of nonfarm labor force share from ibid., table Ba478–86.

6. See Frank Levy and Peter Temin, *Inequality and Institutions in 20th Century America* (Working Paper 07-17, Massachusetts Institute of Technology, Department of Economics, Cambridge, Mass., 2007). See page 23 for *Fortune* quote.

7. Health insurance figures from table 103, *Statistical Abstract of the United States, 1974.*

8. Ernie Englander and Allen Kaufman, "The End of Managerial Ideology: From Corporate Social Responsibility to Corporate Social Indifference," *Enterprise and Society* 5, no. 3 (September 2004). This article cites opinion differences between small business owners and corporate managers. For a parallel—but more skeptical—treatment, see "The Myth of Management" in Samuelson, *Good Life and Its Discontents,* chap. 7.

9. See John Kenneth Galbraith, *The New Industrial State* (New York: Signet Books, 1967), 21, 18.

10. For the Coke episode, see Robert J. Samuelson, "The Sovereign Consumer," in *Untruth: Why the Conventional Wisdom Is (Almost Always) Wrong* (New York: AtRandom.com Books, 2001). The column is reprinted from *Newsweek,* July 29, 1985.

11. For London quote, see Paul London, *The Competition Solution: The Bipartisan Secret Behind American Prosperity* (Washington, D.C.: American Enterprise Press, 2005), 4. This and the following paragraph rely heavily on London.

12. Study cited in Roger Alcaly, *The New Economy* (New York: Farrar, Straus and Giroux, 2004), 210. See pages 209–34 for a lengthy discussion of these trends. The quote is on page 210.

13. See Doron P. Levin, "Stempel Quits Job as Top G.M. Officer in Rift with Board," *New York Times,* October 27, 1992; and Jonathan Weber, "IBM to Replace Chief Executive, Slash Dividend," *Los Angeles Times,* January 27, 1993.

14. For IBM secretaries, see Laurie Hays, "IBM Plans to Slash Secretaries' Salaries in Sweeping Review," *Wall Street Journal,* May 18, 1995. For union figures, see table 645, *Statistical Abstract of the United States, 2007,* available at http://www.census.gov.

15. "Foreign Stocks Get New Push," *Wall Street Journal,* November 8, 2005.

16. Trade figures from table A1, World Trade Organization annual reports, available at the WTO website, http://www.wto.org. Tariff figures from Douglas A. Irwin, *Free Trade Under Fire,* 2nd ed. (Princeton, N.J.: Princeton University Press, 2005), 20.

17. See Paul Kennedy, *The Rise and Fall of the Great Powers* (New York: Vintage Books, 1987). For quote, see Clyde V. Prestowitz, Jr., *Trading*

Places: How We Allowed Japan to Take the Lead (New York: Basic Books, 1988), 2.

18. GDP figures from Annex, table 1 in *Economic Outlook* (Paris: Organization for Economic Cooperation and Development, 2005).

19. Data on currency use from table 2 in Linda S. Goldberg and Cedric Tille, "Vehicle Currency Use in International Trade" (Working Paper 11172, National Bureau of Economic Research, Cambridge, Mass., February 2005). The figures are generally for 2002. Gold supply numbers in the late 1940s are from Robert Triffin, *Gold and the Dollar Crisis,* rev. ed. (New Haven, Conn.: Yale University Press, 1961), 72–73, table 14.

20. Trade percentages from table B-1, *Economic Report of the President, 2007,* based on national income and product accounts.

21. Trade figures calculated on a volume—not dollar—basis from table A1 on World Trade Organization website, http://www.wto.org.

22. Figure for the Marshall Plan from Robert J. Samuelson, *The Good Life and Its Discontents,* 42. In current dollars, today's economy is about fifty times larger than in 1950. Multiplying the $13.3 billion times fifty equals $665 billion. For the Eurodollar market, see Martin Mayer, *The Fate of the Dollar* (New York: Times Books, 1980), 130.

23. Figures on internationally held financial assets from the International Monetary Fund, provided by Sergei Antonshin and Rajan Raghuran, August 28, 2005.

24. See John Williamson and Molly Mahar, "A Survey of Financial Liberalization," *Essays in International Finance* 211 (November 1998), Department of Economics, Princeton University. On Europe, see Graciela Kaminsky and Sergio Schmukler, "Short-Run Pain, Long-Run Gain:

The Effects of Financial Liberalization" (Working Paper 9787, National Bureau of Economic Research, Cambridge, Mass., June 2003). Also see table 4.1 in John Williamson, *Curbing the Boom-Bust Cycle: Stabilizing Capital Flows to Emerging Markets* (Washington, D.C.: Peterson Institute of International Economics, 2005).

25. Eichengreen quote from personal interview, August 2005.

26. On economic conditions in the 1930s, see Harold James, *The End of Globalization: Lessons from the Great Depression* (Cambridge, Mass.: Harvard University Press, 2001), chap. 3, 125, 142.

27. Herbert Stein, "The Triumph of the Adaptive Society," in *On the Other Hand . . . Essays on Economics, Economists, and Politics* (Washington, D.C.: American Enterprise Institute, 1995), 27–28.

28. Roger Lowenstein, *Origins of the Crash: The Great Bubble and Its Undoing* (New York: Penguin Press, 2004), 2.

29. Joseph A. Schumpeter, *Capitalism, Socialism and Democracy* (New York: Harper Torchbooks, 1975), 84.

30. Alfred P. Sloan, Jr., *My Years with General Motors* (New York: Doubleday, 1972), xv.

31. Andrew S. Grove, *Only the Paranoid Survive* (New York: Currency, 1999), 3–4, 61, 77.

32. Sloan, *My Years With General Motors,* xv; and Grove, *Only the Paranoid Survive,* 6.

33. Quote about central bankers from Alan Greenspan, *The Age of Turbulence: Adventures in a New World* (New York: Penguin, 2007), 389–90. Longer quote from personal interview, March 4, 2005.

34. For an account of the July 1996 FOMC meeting, see Laurence H. Meyer, *A Term at the Fed: An Insider's View* (New York: Harper Business, 2004), 4–43. For the Greenspan quote, see Anthanasios Orphanides, "The Road to Price Stability" (speech given to the American Economic Association, January 2006). The original quote is from Alan Greenspan, "Risk and Uncertainty in Monetary Policy," *American Economic Review* 94, no. 2 (May 2004): 33–40.

35. Alan S. Blinder and Janet L. Yellen, *The Fabulous Decade: Macroeconomic Lessons from the 1990s* (New York: Century Foundation Press, 2001), 49.

6: PRECARIOUS PROSPERITY

1. See Uchitelle, *The Disposable American,* chap. 1, 9–11. A useful summary of Uchitelle's argument is found in James Lardner, "The Specter Haunting Your Office," *New York Review of Books,* June 14, 2007, 62–65.

2. Lardner, "Specter Haunting Your Office," 62.

3. See Robert G. Valetta, "Anxious Workers" (Economic Letter no. 2007-13, Federal Reserve Bank of San Francisco, June 1, 2007). See also Roger G. Valletta, "Rising Unemployment Duration in the United States: Causes and Consequences" (mimeo, Federal Reserve Bank of San Francisco), figure 2; and Henry S. Farber, "What Do We Know About Job Loss in the United States? Evidence from the Displaced Workers Survey, 1984–2004" (Working Paper no. 498, Princeton University Industrial Relations Section, June 2005), figure 2. The sources are the same for the following paragraph.

4. See *Income, Poverty and Health Insurance Coverage in the United States: 2005* (Washington, D.C.: U.S. Department of the Census, 2006), tables

A-1 for income and B-1 for poverty. For the college–high school wage gap, see Sheldon Danziger and Peter Gottschalk, *The American People, Census 2000: Changing Fortunes, Trends in Poverty and Inequality* (New York: Russell Sage Foundation; and Washington, D.C.: Population Reference Bureau, 2005), 20.

5. For the ratios of male earnings, see table IE-2 at http://www.census .gov/hhes/www/income/histinc/ie2html. Economists Robert Frank and Philip Cook coined the term "winner-take-all" society.

6. See Diego Comin and Thomas Philippon, "The Rise of Firm-Level Volatility: Causes and Consequences" in *NBER Macroeconomics Annual 2005* (Cambridge, Mass.: MIT Press, 2005).

7. See Hewitt press release, "Hewitt Study Shows Base Pay Increases Flat for 2006 with Variable Pay Plans Picking Up the Slack," August 31, 2005. Also see Thomas Lemieux, W. Bentley MacLeod and Daniel Parent, "Performance Pay and Wage Inequality" (Working Paper 13128, National Bureau of Economic Research, May 2007).

8. CEO pay from Carola Frydman and Raven E. Saks, "Executive Compensation: A New View from a Long-Term Perspective, 1936–2005" (Finance and Economic Discussion Series 2007–35, Federal Reserve Board, Washington, D.C.), table 3.

9. Poll done by the Conference Board, a business advisory group, and cited in Peter Gosselin, *High Wire: The Precarious Financial Lives of American Families* (New York: Basic Books, 2008), 56, 57 (bound galleys). Thanks to Gosselin for providing me with the galleys. Job tenure figures calculated from Bureau of Labor Statistics press release, "Employee Tenure in 2006," September 8, 2006, table 3. The data are for January 2006.

10. Edward Lazear, "Why Is There Mandatory Retirement?" *Journal of Political Economy* 87 (1979): 1261–84. Pension data from "Facts from EBRI: Retirement Trends in the United States over the Past Quarter Century," Employee Benefit Research Institute, June 2007. Employer-sponsored health insurance plans covered 62.1 percent of Americans in 1987, 64.2 percent in the peak year of 2000 and 59.7 percent in 2006. See *Income, Poverty, and Health Insurance Coverage in the United States: 2006* (Washington, D.C.: U.S. Census Bureau, August 2007), table C-1.

11. Jacob S. Hacker, *The Great Risk Shift: The Assault on American Jobs, Families, Health Care and Retirement . . . and How You Can Fight Back* (New York: Oxford University Press, 2006), 15–16.

12. For pension data, see "Facts from EBRI," 3. For health insurance, see Exhibits D and E, "Employer Health Benefits 2006: Summary of Findings," Kaiser Family Foundation. In 2006, workers' premiums covered 27 percent of the cost of a typical family policy, the same share as in 1998. Companies paid the rest. For single policies, workers' share rose from 14 percent to 16 percent over the same period.

13. See Gosselin, *High Wire,* 87, 90 (bound galleys).

14. Melissa Bjelland, Bruce Fallick, John Haltiwanger and Erika McEntarfer, "Employer-to-Employer Flows in the United States: Estimates Using Linked Employer-Employer Data" (Finance and Economic Discussion Series, Divisions of Research and Statistics and Monetary Affairs, Federal Reserve Board, Washington, D.C., June 2007).

15. Saez and Piketty data available at Emmanuel Saez's home page, http://elsa.berkley.edu/~saez/.

16. For household incomes over $100,000, *Income, Poverty, and Health Insurance Coverage, 2006,* table A-1. Household incomes by size available at www.census.gov under "detailed income statistics."

17. See Chulhee Lee, "Rising Family Income Inequality in the United States, 1968–2000: Impact of Changing Labor Supply, Wages and Family Structure" (Working Paper 11836, National Bureau of Economic Research, December 2005). In 1970, about 78 percent of family heads in the poorest fifth of families had jobs. By 2000, only 66 percent did. In 1970, 69 percent of the poorest families were couples; by 2000, only 39 percent were. By contrast, more than 90 percent of the wealthiest fifth of families were married couples in both periods; but in 2000, 89 percent had two earners, up from 62 percent in 1970. Note that the Lee study concerns families, not households. See also Gary Burtless, "Globalization and Income Polarization in Rich Countries," *Issues in Economic Policy* (2007), Brookings Institution. The estimate for health insurance also comes from economist Burtless. See Senate Finance Committee testimony, "Income Progress Across the American Income Distribution, 2000–2005," May 10, 2007, chart 3.

18. Percentages calculated from *Income, Poverty and Health Insurance Coverage, 2006,* table A-1.

19. Pew Research Center, *Inside the Middle Class: Bad Times Hit the Good Life* (Washington, D.C., 2008).

20. For stock market volumes, see *Securities Industry Fact Book,* 2007 ed. (New York: Securities Industry and Financial Markets Association, 2007). Personal communication, Martin Mayer, March 2008.

21. Personal interview, Josh Lerner, March 2008.

7: THE FUTURE OF AFFLUENCE

1. See Gary Gorton, "Slapped in the Face by the Invisible Hand: Banking and the Panic of 2007" (conference paper read at the Federal Reserve Bank of Atlanta, May 2009).

2. "Board of Trustees, Federal Old-Age and Survival Insurance and Federal Disability Insurance Funds," *The 2007 Annual Report* (Washington, D.C.: Government Printing Office, 2007), 83–95.

3. For population figures, see "U.S. Population Projections, 2005–2050," Pew Hispanic Center, Feb. 11, 2008, http://pewhispanic.org. For assimilation of Mexican Americans, see Edward E. Tellez and Vilma Ortiz, *Generations of Exclusion: Mexican Americans, Assimilation, and Race* (New York: Russell Sage Foundation, 2008), 140–42. The reference is in the following paragraph.

4. Data on home prices from the National Association of Realtors.

5. See Fabio Panetta, Paolo Angelini, et al, "The Recent Behaviour of Financial Market Volatility" (BIS Papers No. 29, Bank for International Settlements, August 2006).

6. Quoted in Mark Zandi, *Financial Shock: Global Panic and Government Bailouts—How We Got Here and What Must Be Done to Fix It,* updated ed. (Upper Saddle River, N.J.: FT Press, 2009), p. 75.

7. See Zandi, p. 156.

8. John Kenneth Galbraith, *The Affluent Society* (New York: New American Library, 1995), 13.

9. Robert H. Frank, *Falling Behind: How Rising Inequality Harms the Middle Class* (Berkeley: University of California Press, 2007).

10. Richard Easterlin, "Does Economic Growth Improve the Human Lot?" in *Nations and Households in Economic Growth: Essays in Honor of Moses Abramovitz,* ed. Paul David and Melvin Reder (New York: Academic Press, 1974). Data on happiness supplied by Tom Smith, National Opinion Research Center, September 14, 2005. Some recent research by economists Betsey Stevenson and Justin Wolfers claims to modify Easterlin's view slightly, though not for the United States. For a skeptical view of the new research, see John Cassidy, "Happiness Is . . . ," *Portfolio* (July 2008): 36.

11. For Bell, see Daniel Bell, *The Cultural Contradictions of Capitalism* (New York: Basic Books, 1978), 237–39. An earlier version of the essay appeared in the Fall 1974 edition of *The Public Interest.*

12. Benjamin M. Friedman, *The Moral Consequences of Economic Growth* (New York: Alfred A. Knopf, 2005), 4.

13. The assertion that about half of U.S. families receive some sort of benefit can be found in Samuelson, *Good Life and Its Discontents,* 158, and is based on a 1994 study by the Congressional Research Service, *Recipiency of Federal and State Government Benefits Among Families in 1992.* Although I was not able to locate later data, it's doubtful that the situation has changed much. For budget projections, see *The Long-Term Budget Outlook* (Washington, D.C.: Congressional Budget Office, 2005), table 1.1. The population projections are from the Census Bureau.

14. The estimate of $1 trillion in new annual taxes is derived as follows. Government spending is now about 20 percent of GDP. The Congressional Budget Office projects it to reach 27 percent of GDP under plausible assumptions about Social Security and health-care spending by 2030. My estimate assumes that spending on other programs, including interest on the debt, stays at their present shares of GDP. With taxes at about 18 percent of GDP, a tax increase of 9 percent of GDP would be needed to balance the budget. In 2007, U.S. GDP was almost $14 tril-

lion. One percent of GDP was nearly $140 billion. Nine times $140 billion is $1.26 trillion.

15. For health spending projections of 20 percent of GDP, see *National Health Care Projections, 2005–2015,* Centers for Medicare and Medicare Services, at www.cms.hhs.gov/NationalHealthExpendData, accessed September 11, 2006. For the 30 percent projection, see Robert E. Hall and Charles I. Jones, "The Value of Life and the Rise of Health Spending," *Quarterly Journal of Economics,* forthcoming. For the results of this Weinberg study and others, see the website for the Dartmouth Medical Atlas at http://www.dartmouthatlas.org.

16. Message to Congress, June 8, 1934, as reprinted in National Council on Social Welfare, *Fiftieth Anniversary Edition: The Report of the Committee on Economic Security of 1935* (Washington, D.C.: Project on the Federal Social Role, 1985).

17. Calculations of household indebtedness as a share of income from the Flow of Funds tables of the Federal Reserve, table B100, "Balance Sheet of Households and Non-profit Organizations," available at http://www.federalreserve.gov.

18. This paragraph and the next rely heavily on Martha Olney, *Buy Now, Pay Later: Advertising, Credit, and Consumer Durables in the 1920s* (Chapel Hill: University of North Carolina Press, 1991), as well as personal communication with Olney. Also see Lendol Calder, *Financing the American Dream: A Cultural History of Consumer Credit* (Princeton, N.J.: Princeton University Press, 1999). For terms of car loans, see 192–94; for pawnbrokers, see 42–49. On the history of home mortgages, see Richard K. Green and Susan M. Wachter, "The American Mortgage in Historical and International Context," *Journal of Economic Perspectives* 19, no. 4 (Fall 2005): 92–114.

19. Calder, *Financing the American Dream,* 30–31.

20. Data on debt by age from table 11B of Brian K. Bucks, Arthur B. Kennickell and Kevin B. Moore, "Recent Changes in U.S. Family Finances: Evidence from the 2001 and 2004 Survey of Consumer Finances," *Federal Reserve Bulletin, 2006* (March): A1–A38.

21. Trade figures since 1980 from World Trade Organization. Total exports from appendix, table 1, *World Trade Report 2006*. Growth in trade since 1980 from table A1, accessed from WTO website, http://wto.org. The estimate of the boost to U.S. incomes is a rough average of four separate studies from the late 1940s and early 1950s to the turn of the century. They are cited in Scott C. Bradford, Paul L. E. Grieco and Gary Clyde Hufbauer, "The Payoff to America from Global Integration," in *The United States and the World Economy* (Washington, D.C.: C. Fred Bergsten and the Institute for International Economics, 2005). Figures on income gains in Japan, South Korea and Spain from table C1-c and C3-ce in Angus Maddison, *The World Economy: A Millennial Perspective* (Paris: Organisation for Economic Cooperation and Development, 2006).

22. Global population figures from table 1356, *Statistical Abstract of the United States, 1974.*

23. Sylvester J. Schieber, "The End of the Golden Years," *The Milken Institute Review* (second quarter 2008): 54.

24. See Paul London, *The Competition Solution.*

25. For the 30 percent to 50 percent of elderly dependent in the 1930s, see National Conference on Social Welfare, *Fiftieth Anniversary Edition: The Report of the Committee on Economic Security of 1935* (Washington, D.C.: Project on the Federal Social Role, 1985), 24. For 75 percent without health insurance, see Amy Finkelstein, "The Aggregate Effects of Health Insurance: Evidence from the Introduction of Medicare" (Work-

ing Paper 11619, National Bureau of Economic Research, Cambridge, Mass., August 2005), 3.

26. For life expectancy in 1935, see Carter et al., *Historical Statistics of the United States,* vol. 1, 440, table Ab644–55.

27. For manufacturing jobs, see table B-46, *Economic Report of the President, 2008.* For total employment, see table B-45. For study of job loss, see Robert Lawrence, *Blue Collar Blues: Is Trade to Blame for Rising U.S. Income Inequality?* (Washington, D.C.: Peterson Institute for International Economics, 2008).

28. See Lawrence, *Blue-Collar Blues,* 37, 51.

29. For the 2007 estimate of Persian Gulf financial assets, see the Institute of International Finance, press release, January 16, 2008. For the 2020 projection, see "The Coming Oil Windfall in the Gulf," McKinsey Global Institute, January 2008.

30. This and the following paragraph rely on the International Energy Agency (IEA), *World Energy Outlook 2007* (Paris: International Energy Agency, 2007). See table 1.1 for both current use and projections to 2030. See page 59 for population projections. See Annex A for detailed projections. For 2030 projections of greenhouse gas emissions, see page 97. For projection of Chinese vehicles, see page 299.

31. For coal's share of electricity, see IEA, *World Energy Outlook 2007,* 593.

32. For 1938 unemployment—Hansen gave his original talk at the end of the year—see Carter et al., *Historical Statistics of the United States,* vol. 2, table Ba478–86. For Hansen's views, see Alvin Hansen, "Economic Progress and Declining Population Growth" in *The American Economic Review* (March 1939): 1–15.

33. Peter Lindert, *Growing Public: Social Spending and Economic Growth Since the Eighteenth Century* (New York: Cambridge University Press, 2004). See also Lindert, "Why the Welfare State Looks Like a Free Lunch" (working paper, Harvard University, November 2002 draft).

34. The arguments and language in the preceding four paragraphs draw heavily on Robert J. Samuelson, "What Caused the Financial Meltdown?" *Claremont Review of Books* 9, no. 2 (Spring 2009): 18–24.

35. See Alexis de Tocqueville, *Democracy in America,* vol. 2 (New York: Schocken Books, 1961), chap. 8.

INDEX

ROBERT J. SAMUELSON has written a column for *The Washington Post* since 1977 and for *Newsweek* since 1984. He has received numerous journalism awards and is the author of *The Good Life and Its Discontents: The American Dream in the Age of Entitlement, 1945–1995*. A collection of his columns, *Untruth: Why the Conventional Wisdom Is (Almost Always) Wrong,* was published in 2001. He and his wife, Judy Herr, have three children and live in Bethesda, Maryland.